A Feast
of Words

To Marian Hobson

A Feast of Words

Banquets and Table Talk in the Renaissance

Michel Jeanneret

Translated by Jeremy Whiteley
and Emma Hughes

University of Chicago Press

Originally published as *Des mets et des mots. Banquets et propos de table à la Renaissance* © Librairie José Corti, 1987

The University of Chicago Press, Chicago 60637
Polity Press, Cambridge
© 1991 by Polity Press
All rights reserved. Published 1991
Printed in Great Britain
00 99 98 97 96 95 94 93 92 91   5 4 3 2 1

Library of Congress Cataloging-in-Publication Data
Jeanneret, Michel.
    [Mets et des mots. English]
    A feast of words: banquets and table talk in the Renaissance/
Michel Jeanneret: translated by Jeremy Whiteley and Emma Hughes.
        p. cm.
    Translation of: Des mets et des mots.
    Includes bibliographical references and index.
    ISBN 0-226-39575-8 (cloth). — ISBN 0-226-39576-6 (pbk.)
    1. Dinners and dining—History.   2. Table talk—History.
I. Title.
GT2850.J4313   1991
394.1'2'09409024—dc20   91-16871
                                CIP

Contents

Translators' notes

We have generally translated the French 'banquet' as 'banquet', but the word has slightly different connotations in the two languages. In French it carries an allusion to Plato, whose *Symposium* is translated as *Le Banquet*: 'le banquet eucharistique' is the equivalent of 'the Eucharistic Feast' in devotional English – 'feast', with its overtones of 'love-feast' and 'feasting with friends', might be a closer English alternative, but we have used 'feast' throughout to translate various other terms.

Introduction

Our gastronomy is ill at ease: it oscillates between fast food and *nouvelle cuisine*, we compute the time it takes to eat a good meal and anxiously count calories. For the Victorians have passed on to us an austere morality and an instinctive mistrust of physical over-indulgence. This is not helped by the contemporary ethic which demands that we be both productive and healthy, which allocates a time for serious things, a time for worthy causes, and another special and carefully controlled time for celebration and good living. Thin people triumph over fat ones or give them a guilty conscience.

We live in a divided world, a world in which physical and mental pleasures are compartmentalized and ordered into a hierarchy: they either conflict with each other or are mutually exclusive. All sorts of ideological barriers exist between sense and the senses, between intellectual activity and the consumption of natural produce. The head and the stomach are at odds. Thought degenerates into abstraction and works to combat the influence of the body. We have to choose whether to speak or to eat: we must not speak with our mouth full.

However the banquet is the one thing that overcomes this division and allows for the reconciliation of opposites. It recognizes physical laws, reinstates the legitimate role of instinctive behaviour, but at the same time provides a place for conversation and a setting for good manners. The combination of words and food in a convivial scene gives rise to a special moment when thought and the senses enhance rather than just tolerate each other. The symposiac ideal reconciles the angel and the beast in the human, and it renews the interdependence between the mouth that eats and the mouth that speaks. It tries to revive the savour that pale knowledge no longer has and the knowledge that dulled taste no longer communicates. The banquet, throughout history, has provided special inspiration for the imagination precisely because it restores to us a no doubt mythic fulfilment which we think we have lost. After the divisions of the Fall, at table we rediscover, in the imagination, elements of original happiness and unity.

Since I cannot invite my readers to a practical demonstration of this, I shall have to rely on the evidence found in some texts. Worse still, these texts will be doubly distanced by being seen in the light not only of my commentary but also of translation. Paradise certainly seems to elude us when mediated to such an extent. If to narrate the symposium is to run the risk of falling short of the total experience of the feast, this is even more the case with secondary discourse, because it accentuates the disjunction between experience and narration. Neither the writer's words nor the critic's elucubrations will fill the stomach.

But perhaps the relation between the feast and narration of the feast is the other way around. Might not this complete pleasure, relegated to the dreams of the imagination, find some kind of realization through the words which express it, in the substantial and vigorous language of the feast? It is possible that the fable, far from being a debased reflection of the joys of the table, actually creates these in the telling and is the best approximation to them we have. It would therefore be up to literature to forge indirectly the link between those pleasures which ideologies have compromised. When banquets become textual objects and verbal creations, they can be appreciated through images and style. Words related to the stomach awaken in language all sorts of dormant powers, as if convivial talk, acquiring mimetic qualities, takes on the sensuality of a good meal. So reading, which touches and tastes verbal matter, itself becomes a feast. It is after all the same organ, the tongue, which savours words and delights in foods.

But this is not only an essay on the meal as a product of the imagination or as a narrative artefact. It also deals with the Renaissance and is an enquiry into some aspects of sixteenth-century anthropology and aesthetics. The relationship works both ways: if the paradigm of the banquet can serve as a special guide to highlight significant tendencies in Humanist culture, this culture in turn illustrates the problems and reveals the tensions alluded to above.

In the Renaissance educated and cultured people, concerned about elegance and civility, establish a vast network of precepts to oversee table manners: lessons on conduct, advice on the menu, rules about the service. At the same time, they regulate the conversation of diners and define the tone appropriate to convivial intercourse. A whole normative programme is instituted; the domestication of appetites and the controlling of nature by art pave the way for a more polite and cultured society.

Compensatory fantasies are therefore all the more powerful. As if to conserve the splendour and the freedom of good eating, a whole range of texts invents grandiose feasts and fantastic scenarios which overturn the principles of moderation. At the same time they adopt an exuberant style which subverts normal usage and pushes to the limit the innovative potential of language. They defy the rules and, in order to express the power of desire, they imitate, in and through words, the abundance of banquets freed from censure. Imagination takes over.

Both parts of this book are organized around the opposition between the definition of a code and its transgression. The first part deals with the representation of meals and of table manners: we will see abstemiousness and excess, models of seemly behaviour along with fantasies of over-indulgence. The second part concentrates on the diner's speech and the language of food; here too, I shall show how convivial discourse fluctuates between sobriety and drunkenness, between notions of self-control and the invention of eccentric idioms.

I want to show that in the wide space between these two extremes lie some of the major themes of the Renaissance; the banquet is a model through which society, symbolically, fixes both its priorities and its contradictions. Some of the myths of the time – the great debate about nature and culture, the realization of the individual's full potential through the simultaneous development of both body and mind – are crystallized in the ordering of the ceremony or the invention of fabulous feasts. Through the diners'

speech and their verbal concoctions some of the major characteristics of sixteenth-century language and style can be discerned;
the taste for abundance and diversity, the practice of polyphony,
the free manipulation of narrative forms and the unfettered
creation of new languages. In short, my aim is to capture, through
the banquet, the festive and playful side of the Renaissance, its
motley culture and the inventiveness of its literature before the
arrival of Classicism which, in one fell swoop, repressed and
marginalized all this exuberance.

The historical period covered by this study is not strictly defined.
The Renaissance reached its height in France in the sixteenth
century, and most of the texts referred to date from this time. But
the Renaissance started earlier in Italy and this means that I have to
go back further. In addition the distinction between the Renaissance
and the Middle Ages, which is so clear elsewhere, is made
problematic here by the perpetuation of eating rituals or burlesque
practices whose continuity I shall show. Above all, the predominance
of antiquity in the memory of the Humanists inevitably leads to a
continual toing and froing in time. The identification with Greek
and Latin models was so strong and their relevance was felt to be
so great that it is not possible to treat them in isolation. A chapter
is devoted to them, but they are referred to throughout the study.
Moreover, I have not tried to follow a chronological order nor to
carry out an exhaustive study.

Because ideas and texts circulated internationally among educated
people, I have also ignored linguistic and geographical frontiers.
French authors, particularly Rabelais, were the starting point of
my research. But it is not possible, in a bilingual culture like that
which existed in France at that time, to separate French from Latin,
or to forget that Italy, for learned people and artists, was always on
the horizon. I have tried to capture the multitude of resonances
which is lent to Humanist discourse by this intermingling of
languages and traditions and this combination of different voices.

I have crossed not only the boundaries of language but also those
of genre, and I refer to texts of very different kinds. I examine
didactic treatises and poetic works, fiction and learned compilations;
I juxtapose the serious with the comic, and popular tradition with
erudite philology. The theme of conviviality has ramifications in
many areas of life, thought and writing. I have tried to indicate the

extent of its polymorphous and composite quality. But there is another reason for the eclecticism of my study, a reason which determined my methodology and needs some explanation.

What today we speak of or see as 'literature' was not, in the Renaissance, a notion which differentiated one kind of writing from another: or at least this notion did not correspond to the category defined by this word today. The opposition between the literary and the non-literary was not relevant then, except as regards poetry, which sometimes had a special status. The idea that a literary critic such as myself can limit his research to a clearly defined field of study and that the historian, philosopher or art historian can each examine separate areas is anachronistic as far as the sixteenth century is concerned and is completely alien to the way it organizes knowledge.

It is only since about the end of the eighteenth century that some relatively precise criteria have defined what literature is. It is primarily defined through a series of negatives. In our terminology, literature is something which has no utilitarian function, is outside the jurisdiction of institutions, and is free from accepted morality and order. Since Romanticism, social commitment, the transmission of knowledge or the demonstration of technical expertise have been replaced by an absolute value: the affirmation of the subject and individual self-expression. At the same time we have the notion of the autonomous work of art which contains its own justification; it is governed solely by the principle of internal cohesion or it produces sense through structure, like an independent, self-signifying system. So, in general terms, modern literature is defined as being exceptional and free from the constraints of instrumental discourse.[1]

This sketchy definition is no doubt simplistic, but it is relevant here in so far as none of these principles applies to what we today call sixteenth-century 'literature'. Neither the criterion of 'literarity' nor the subdivisions of the field of discourse currently in force provides a useful classification of Renaissance texts. It is true that certain poetic forms – for example the love sonnet, the lyrical ode and the epic – are of a specific nature and correspond to recognizable generic categories. But elsewhere the field is less well

---

[1] See T. Todorov, 'La notion de littérature'.

marked out, and objectives are not clearly differentiated. The
litterae, in Humanist terms, engage in both philology and history,
both the field of knowledge and the field of thought; they also
include high literature, without feeling the need to distinguish one
from the other. In Montaigne's *Essays*, for example, how can one
dissociate the moral philosophy from the encyclopaedic and the
literary? In the work of other authors, how can one separate the
poetic impulse from the political, the theological or the scientific
imperative? A historian of the sixteenth century such as Natalie
Zemon Davis finds it natural, in her *Fiction in the Archives*,[2] to
examine narratives and literary performance, although she does not
neglect her usual source material. Conversely, literary critics
constantly come up against historical questions in the works which
are academically accepted to be in their field. The combination of
themes and forms is so diverse that they defy any one-dimensional
methodology. Who can claim to have the breadth of vision to
comprehend the enormous variety and infinite modulations of
Rabelais's work? Many specialists find material in it, but none can
exhaust the multiplicity of possible readings. Extreme literarity is
combined in Rabelais with extreme referentiality. It is certain that
any attempt to distinguish what is literature from what is not
would mutilate these works, which remain untouched by the
mania for taxonomy current among the theorists of the classical age.

The twin concepts of intertextuality and polyphony, elaborated
by Mikhail Bakhtin, provide a very appropriate theoretical model
for approaching this situation.[3] According to Bakhtin, any
utterance is always part of a network of other utterances, which it
assimilates and transforms and with which, implicitly, there is
some exchange. A lone voice cannot be heard except in concert
with the other voices which resonate within social space. Therefore
no text, however refined, is ever isolated or autonomous. It
absorbs and combines with snatches of many kinds of discourse,
written or oral, learned or popular, parochial or exotic, etc.
Whether or not it is literary, an utterance is always a collection of

---

[2] Natalie Zemon Davis, *Fiction in the Archives. Pardon Tales and their Tellers
in Sixteenth Century France*.

[3] See Mikhaïl Bakhtin, *Problems of Dostoevsky's Poetics, Rabelais and his
World* and *Esthétique et théorie du roman*. See also T. Todorov, *Mikhail Bakhtin,
le principe dialogique*.

composite elements; it stands at the crossroads of other languages, it affects them and is affected by them.

The centrifugal and polyphonic tendency of discourse varies, Bakhtin continues, according to genre – the novel is particularly prone to this – and according to the political situation: a society, at any one moment, is more or less centralized and more or less homogeneous. Now, the sixteenth century is a time of enormous diversity, which greatly favours this interplay and *bricolage*. Within complex works, whether they be erudite compositions or fictional texts, elements from many sources are grouped together: echoes of everyday conversation, parts of familiar stories, borrowings from particular specialized jargon or from some professional or social sphere. Rabelais's tales[4] give Bakhtin the best possible illustration of this: there, the voices of the people meet those of the Church and those of the learned; the vocabulary of celebration overlays that of war, fear exists alongside laughter and farce accompanies moral reflections.

The value of this theory is that it enables us to understand better that so-called literary texts have no distinctive profile. They participate in the ideological debates of the time; they form part of a vast and continuing dialogue, through all sorts of interactions and migrations, between the languages of different sectors of society. They are no doubt more elaborate, more ambiguous or more playful than other texts, they transcend their basic documentary value and may challenge or refute received ideas, but they none the less belong to this vast transtextual network in which all elements are interdependent.

These premises, I hope, give a better idea of the way in which very diverse discourses may be examined together, as they are in this book. This approach will also explain why the book contains few monographic analyses but many comparative perspectives and frequently moves from one document to another. Following Bakhtin, I have postulated that Renaissance culture was a vast system which is certainly disparate and full of tensions and contradictions, but which can be read as a single text.

The fact that I study questions bordering on anthropology and cultural history does not therefore imply that I renounce the

---

[4] See François Rabelais, *The Histories of Gargantua and Pantagruel.*

methodology of literary analysis. My training is as a literary critic and I have worked on the texts as texts. People account for their perception of things or create the world of their desires by elaborating discourses or constructing representations. The means we use to express ourselves is a collection of signs or a system of configurations through which the elemental reality is mediated. Therefore, *a posteriori*, we only receive messages which are secondary and already encoded; we reach our object through structures, models and stereotypes whose mechanisms we need to understand.

My interest is precisely in such a problem of representation and expression: not the table itself, but the discourse about the table and the discourse at table. My aim is not to reconstruct a speculative 'historical reality'; I will not provide exhaustive documentation of rituals and customs associated with eating, nor study the actual practice of cooks and diners. Instead of showing the Humanists as they cook or as they eat, I examine them as writers on conviviality, seeing how they reproduced – or produced – feasts through words. Rather than concentrating on the referents for their own sake, I analyse signs and myths and reconstruct one of the models through which people represent the world.

Whatever the extent of the discursive elements I study, whether they are limited to a single book or derive from the interplay of intertextual echoes, I always have in mind that building up information about things is the product of the internal operations of a system of signs and that the illusion of reality is the result of verbal manipulations. There is no reason to ignore the contributions of structuralism in a study of discourse provided that this does not imprison us in the concept of the text as an end in itself.

The kind of literary analysis which pays attention to variations in words and to the significance of narrative forms is relevant for another reason. The scene of the feast and discourse on food lead writers to extraordinary linguistic discoveries. In order to express the taste and savour of dishes, descriptions of banquets serve up to the reader words which charm the ear and excite the palate. The language of greed digs deep into the dictionary, it creates a profusion of metaphors and farcical expressions; there is doubtless no other semantic field which has such a euphoric and creatively energetic vocabulary and grammar as that of cookery, apart, perhaps, from sex. Rabelais is famous for his wordplay and his stylistic exuberance. We shall see that the theme of food excites him in a unique way; and we will also discover that he is far from being alone in this among the chorus of those who eulogize good food.

The laughter, farce and invention which characterize the language of food are not gratuitous: they free words from their instrumentality, they create a festive atmosphere and they contribute towards the imaginative creation of a happier, more spontaneous world. The tricks of parody and comic reversals of serious discourse and official formulae also play an important role here: they challenge the established hierarchy, they reassert the legitimacy of natural instincts and the dignity of the supposedly vulgar. It is as if stylistic invention and the subversive power of comedy defy censure and liberate repressed desire. Through the magic of language, the rights of the body and its impulses are restored, abundance replaces austerity, and pleasures which are normally covert or repressed can be indulged. Although in certain cases fiction does contribute to the maintenance of order and the regulation of social and moral forces, elsewhere it also promotes the dream element and the creation of freedom or pleasure. I hope to show in this book the effectiveness of the theme of food and the comic vision which often goes with it in the symbolic construction of an alternative world.

The importance of these symbolic practices and these imaginary mediations cannot be overstressed. Contemporary anthropologists and historians assess them for they know that any given community expresses itself as much through its representations as through its actions. It follows that 'literary' texts, for their part, merit the greatest attention. Desires made substantial by fiction and transformations which are reflected by a language without inhibitions are part of the culture that contains them; but even more they actually form the mentality and determine the sensitivity of a community. Although some texts flout established values and substitute a different world, they should not be marginalized. They reproduce the tensions in society, they reveal the hidden face of the system and, in order either to reinforce, displace or subvert them, interact with all the other mediations, be they intellectual or affective, which model representations of 'reality'.

In the verbal concoctions and the textual outpourings generated by the theme of food, I therefore try to show, underneath all the comedy, the ideological element. The narrative tricks and the flights of language are not always innocent; once they are situated in their socio-cultural environment, interpreted according to the conditions of their production and reception, and re-established in the intertextual network in which they operate, they are revealed as the impulses of an overall programme which it is valuable to reconstruct.

A good conversation at table, as we will see later, must be diverse and open, it must put all the guests at ease. With this in mind, I wanted this book to be varied and welcoming; I have tried to encourage a dialogue between the different texts, problems and methods. We need to break down artificial categories and to combat the baleful effects of academic specializations. The study of representations is part anthropology, part linguistic analysis and part cultural history. Above all, I wanted to combine here, in a single work on a single theme, the related approaches of literature and history: if all goes well, this book will be received like the banquets it studies, as a symposium, with a conversation and a menu adapted to everyone's taste. It may be that, for scholars like ourselves, the table and the pleasures it affords are not such a bad example!

I should like to thank the friends who have helped me: Lucien Dällenbach, Guglielmo Gorni, André Hurst and Carlo Ossola. Terence Cave read the whole of the manuscript, with great perspicacity. This book is dedicated to my wife, Marian Hobson. She certainly has an extensive knowledge of both feasts and words!

PART I

Pleasure and the norm

1

Humanism on holiday

In its search for a new anthropology, the Renaissance gives the banquet a special role. Festive scenes and convivial rites provide Humanists with some of the signs which express their vision of the world and in which their desires can be realized. A mythology of food is elaborated which expresses both a morality of pleasure and the demands of a refined culture, both a popular archetype and an erudite tradition. The joys of the table symbolize the intellectual development of the period and its immense thirst for knowledge, but they also assert the role of the physical and liberate the language of instinct. An integrated approach to life is instituted, ranging from literary reflections on the glory of food to the drawing up of rules for good conduct at meals.

It is true that the imaginary world of banquets is timeless. From time immemorial and in more than one culture, the feast celebrates a triple alliance. It links men to the gods, it shows their place in the natural world and it reinforces social interdependence. People at table realize their full potential; they attain a perfect balance and completeness. The Renaissance adds new vigour to these constant factors. The ideal of the meal as the location of a totalizing experience is charged with particular significance. It brings together disparate strands of an ideology and it inspires the precepts and fables which will be analysed in the following chapters.

The feast of the gods

In a short allegorical tale, *Fabula de homine* (1518), the Spanish philosopher Vivès, taking up a favourite theme of the Italian Humanists, praises the dignity of man. A setting has to be provided, and so Vivès seats his hero at the table of the gods.

To celebrate her birthday, Juno has given a sumptuous meal for the gods of Olympus. But the happy atmosphere would not be complete without a spectacle. A stage appears – it is the theatre of the world. One actor in particular charms the merry throng: the man, who possesses the features and powers of his creator, Jupiter. He is an ingenious mimic who is capable of playing all the roles. First he represents a plant, then various animals, then he appears as himself, a social creature who is fair, wise and courteous. But he has not finished his ascent through the different forms of life. (Here one is reminded of another symbol of the spirit of the Renaissance, Hugo's Satyr in *La Légende des siècles*, pp. 445–64.) Soon he shakes off his mortal form and takes on, before the very eyes of the captivated gods, their own form. After a final metamorphosis, he appears on stage looking as splendid and powerful as Jupiter himself. He looks so like this god that the Olympians hesitate for a moment and ask: is this just an illusion or is it really the master of the universe?

By putting on a divine face, man has shown how great he is. Now he can get down off the stage, mingle with the gods and satisfy their curiosity. In his mortal form, he is admired on account of his ingenious and well-proportioned limbs. He is further praised since he is seen as an intelligent being, a master of wisdom and of knowledge. He has held up a mirror to the gods and they saw that they were beautiful. To make his triumph complete, all that remains is to invite him to the gods' table: 'Jupiter ordered that he be served ambrosia and nectar from what was left of the banquet. Turning their backs on the spectacle, many of the gods shared the refreshment with him' (Vivès, *Fabula de homine*, p. 8). He puts on divine trappings and, sitting with the elite of the pantheon, watches the rest of the spectacle. Supper time comes and another splendid banquet is served at which Juno offers the man a seat of honour. He puts his mask (*persona*, i.e. his body) back on,

> for it had received much praise. Since he was so well adapted to the needs of man, he was judged worthy of the gods' table and of the most sumptuous feast. He received the gift of sensation and enjoyed the everlasting pleasure of the banquet. (Ibid.)

Vivès exploits the polyvalence of this symbol. To sit down to a feast is primarily to liberate the senses and to be introduced to pleasure by consuming the fruits of the earth. The gods also derive sensuous enjoyment as they contemplate the drama of life from their table. We shall return to this theme whereby the person who eats communes with the world about him and, figuratively, appropriates natural resources.[1] But if Vivès's banquet can serve as a symbol of Humanist thought, it is above all as a sign of perfect fulfilment. The man in the fable is admitted to the celestial meal because he has proved that he can be all things at once – a true microcosm of the entire gamut of beings, from the most natural to the most spiritual – and has shown the whole range of his attributes, from physical beauty to outstanding intellectual faculties. Even then, God's creature aspires to other kinds of satisfaction besides the fleeting consumption of the earth's bounty. The banquet also foreshadows the communion of the bread of the angels and celestial beatitude at the table of the blessed. This makes us appreciate that the feast as a locus of pleasure and plenitude has a multitude of resonances in Renaissance symbolism. Through the feast is expressed the confidence of an age when it was believed that, with God's grace, people could grow in harmony with nature while living in the heart of society.

The appeal of the feast of the gods does not only lie in the Humanist theme of the dignity of man: there is an element of hedonism in it too. When the gods are shown feasting, we are given a summary of all desirable pleasure. The table with abundant food but where bodies and matter are weightless is a refined variation on the popular fair or a more formalized version of the legend of the

[1] See The al fresco meal, below.

Land of Cockaigne where dishes throw themselves on the insatiable appetites of the diners. While heavenly draughts confer immortality, the luxuriant foods of the earth prolong life. In either case, the accumulation of victuals gives the consumer the promise of eternal happiness.

The mythological banquet has a special place in Mannerist painting,[2] in Italy, first of all, then in the Fontainebleau School and then in northern Europe. A table laden with fruits and flowers, with a string of gods arranged around it and some musical instruments to accompany the dancing would comprise, in a heightened perspective, the archetypal festive scene, in an atmosphere of beauty, luxury and joy. Everything is there in abundance – Hebe pours out ambrosia and nectar, Bacchus or Fauns fill goblets. Love is in the air: Venus or the Nymphs show how graceful they are, couples are intertwined and the guests are often there to celebrate a wedding, for example the marriage of Thetis and Peleas or of Psyche and Eros. Quarrels are temporarily forgotten and the warring factions of Olympus are in agreement for once. Sensual and spiritual pleasures come together when, against a background of eroticism and good food, Apollo plays his lyre, Pan his pipes, the Muses sing, the Graces dance, Minerva meditates and Diana stays sober.

Such scenes are not original: the painters are following learned models which they find in myths and poems, such as those by Jean Lemaire des Belges, the most famous of the 'Grands Rhétoriqueurs' school of poets. In *Les Illustrations de Gaule et singularitez de Troye* – a long mythological and allegorical tale designed to show that the line of the kings of France has its origins in the heroic epoch of the Trojan princes – he provides a paradigm (in the vulgar tongue) of an Olympian wedding feast (I, 29). Everything is described in detail: the setting – a lawn strewn with fragrant plants, both gods and heroes being waited on and all intent on gastronomic pleasure, the splendour of the tables and the crockery, 'ambrosian foods preserved in manna from heaven' (ibid., p. 218), and charming musical entertainment. This work was circulated from the beginning of the French Renaissance and helped to fix this scene in people's minds.

[2] See H. Bardon, *Le Festin des dieux. Essai sur l'humanisme dans les arts plastiques.*

So, for the mannered elite, there is the spectacle of a complete feast, more worthy than peasant revels and more restrained than the excesses of the carnival. Furthermore, it is part of a written culture which gives it more authority.[3] I will return to this later:[4] in the same way that princes in their games and amorous pursuits dress up as gods and act out scenes from mythology, they will remember, as they decide how their banquets are to be laid out, the divine splendour depicted on the walls of their palaces.

The spiritual value of these depictions is negligible. Religion reduces itself to a human scale and nourishes a discourse which is resolutely Humanist. However, in many cultures, the meal is a traditional rite of participation in the sacred, one of the ceremonies where human beings are in contact with the hereafter and glimpse the heavenly bliss of immortality.[5] Although the pagan splendour of Olympus perhaps obscures this initiatory aspect, the Last Supper fully illustrates it. Christ's sacrifice is celebrated through bread and wine, and the gathering around a table symbolizes the communion of the saints. Apart from this central scene, scripture uses the semiotics of food freely elsewhere: from the laws of the Ancient Alliance governing diet to their modification according to the spirit of the Gospels, from manna to the loaves and the fishes, from the Passover meal to those where Christ appears to the Apostles, food is laden with values that theology and ecclesiastical practice will reflect and impress upon the Christian mind.

It is therefore surprising that in many artistic disciplines the Renaissance, despite being full of religious debate, prefers the profane, anthropocentric version of the meal. This can be seen firstly in its iconography: the Last Supper and the introduction of the Eucharist, which were favoured subjects up to the fifteenth century and later in Baroque painting, are rarely represented in the Renaissance. The Mannerist ethos prefers images of human sensual pleasure to the action of transforming earthly food into spiritual nourishment. This is also true of literature, as this book will prove:

[3] The passages most often used in the iconography of the feast of the gods seem to have been Ovid, *Fasti*, I, 391ff and VI, 319ff and Apuleius, *Metamorphoses*, VI, 24. See also Homer, *The Iliad*, I, 573–611.

[4] See chapter 2, The pomp of princes.

[5] See G. Dumézil, *Le Festin d'immortalité. Etude de mythologie comparée indo-européenne.*

stories of banquets, the theme of conviviality and the treatment of
table manners are all full of references to paradigms from antiquity
and to popular traditions (which are just as influential), while
biblical references remain in the background. Normally Humanism
is more successful in fusing the Christian tradition with the Greco-
Latin heritage.

There is a reason for this: it is precisely the relevance of the
religious themes and their importance in contemporary ecclesiastical
disputes which keep them out of literary or artistic practice. The
two registers are of a different order and they scarcely communicate.
This is particularly true of the debate about the Last Supper. The
contentious question of the real presence and the spiritual
manducation of the Eucharist raise problems that are too complex
and explosive to inspire anything but erudite commentaries,
spiritual meditations or pamphlets. Fiction remains cautious. As a
general rule, the respect shown by Protestant and Evangelist
milieux for holy writ limits the way in which it is used creatively.
One cannot rewrite the Marriage at Cana with the same freedom as
one can a Horatian ode. Theologians protect their territory, and
the more acute doctrinal dissent becomes, the more it forces
authors to be extremely prudent.

Although the controversy over the true interpretation of the
Last Supper barely strays into the realm of symposiac literature,
other Christian or moral themes do sometimes overlay it. One
example is the debate on abstinence and the observance of dietary
rules. In the spirit of the Gospels, the calendar which describes
days of abstinence is largely discredited – as Rabelais's satires
demonstrate.[6] Erasmus is not alone in criticizing the narrow
strictures of the Church on the subject of fasting. Marot is not
alone in being worried about having saved his bacon for Lent.[7]
Elsewhere, loving one's neighbour is particularly well expressed in
the altruistic practice of conviviality. Respect for a sober diet,

---

[6] Except where otherwise stated, all references to Rabelais are to *The Histories
of Gargantua and Pantagruel*, which contains *Gargantua, Pantagruel, The Third
Book, The Fourth Book* and *The Fifth Book*. Here, see the references to Lent and
the Carnival and to days of fasting and feasting in *The Fourth Book*.

[7] See the ballad 'Contre celle qui fut s'amye' (*Oeuvres diverses*, pp. 162–4) and
passim in Marot's work. Whether the expression 'to save one's bacon' should be
understood as an idiom or literally is not relevant here. Like most Evangelists,
Marot was mistrustful of the practice of fasting.

according to some edifying fables, is thought to favour the intellectual and spiritual appetites.[8] Or, as in Vivès, the meal can even be an allegory of human destiny. Guided by their syncretic instincts, the Humanists enjoy discovering affinities and continuity between different traditions: Eros in Plato's *Symposium* prefigures Caritas in the Gospels and the agapes of the developing Church. Christ's teachings at table continue the Greek practice of the philosophical symposium. However, as we will repeatedly see, the characteristics and tone of the narrative, and the majority of the ideological references and stylistic techniques, remain profane and refer either to classical models or to those of popular festivals. Dante's *Convivio* revolves around a network of food metaphors directly inspired by biblical and patristic symbols: but two centuries later the cultural horizon has changed. A new range of *topoi* has replaced the old and these mainly go back to classical sources.

A short treatise by Marsilius Ficino on the institution of the banquet[9] confirms the themes of Vivès and the tendencies of the period as described above. Ficino too celebrates the convivial ceremony as one of the most complete and balanced forms of human experience. Faithful to the Humanist ethos, he too combines metaphysical demands with a need for pragmatism, according to a formula in which different principles of classical thought compete, classical thought being the most likely to promote the development of the individual in all areas of activity. Ficino too, in a typical final twist, looks for a guarantee in the Bible. He puts forward as proof the use of food in Christ's miracles, he invokes the sacrament of the Eucharist, and he repeats that the feast is a symbol of a different kind of hunger and celebration and that God alone ultimately fills men's hearts. But these final assurances come too late to give the banquet a truly Christian significance. The important matters, for Ficino, lie elsewhere.

[8] See Erasmus's *Convivia*, particularly the *Convivium christianum*. Moreover this dialogue is one of the few texts which attempts to give a literary account of the Evangelical version of the Last Supper. References to the *Convivia* are either to those contained in *Colloquies*, tr. C. R. Thompson, or, when they are not included in this translation, to French translations. See chapter 7, Erasmus: feasting on words.

[9] *De sufficientia, fine, forma, materia, modo, condimento, authoritate convivii*, a letter to Bernhardus Bembo of Venice.

The main argument, in his view, lies in the way in which certain
parameters come together. The defence of the banquet is purely a
syncretic one; it mixes up a variety of heterogeneous sources and
theses which allow him to represent it as a totalizing experience.
For here too the feast is seen as the actualization of all humanity's
powers. It is at the intersection of two vital axes in so far as it
causes opposites to coincide. The Christian tradition and the way
the feast conforms to classical models only determine one of the
co-ordinates of the system. The other elements of the synthesis are
built up on different levels and make up a model outline definition
of the symposiac ideal of the Renaissance. Each of the levels will be
explored, with reference to particular texts, in the rest of this
chapter. Ficino's treatise gives us our plan.

A human being is composed of body and spirit: the banquet,
more than any other activity, unifies these elements. It reinforces
the individual's intermediate position between the world of ideas
and the world of matter, as that pivotal microcosm where opposite
poles meet. Recognizing that physiology and the intellect have
equal importance, Ficino the Florentine makes the convivial scene
the place where both reach their maximum potential:

> Only the meal [*convivium*] embraces all parts of man, for . . . it restores
> the limbs, renews the humours, revives the mind, refreshes the senses
> and sustains and sharpens reason. (Ficino, *De sufficientia*, p. 739)

According to the principles of ancient medicine, physical functions
and psychological states are interdependent, so that food does not
only affect the body but also influences the workings of the mind.
Thus the banquet regenerates all the vital functions and achieves
the integration of human faculties in a harmony without hierarchy.
Obviously the Greek ideal of fulfilment in moderation provides a
strong underpinning.

The same classical model also advocates a musical accompaniment
to the banquet, an echo of the celestial harmony which appeals to
and moves the mind while the body is being renewed. The banquet
with music provides its own sort of *concordia discors*, giving
pleasure to the senses while reviving the traces of supernatural
beauty which can be found in an inspired melody. The role of
conversation during meals is similar; alternating between serious

subjects and entertaining remarks, between the utilitarian and the mellow (as it should with gentlemen who are neither pedantic nor ignorant), it brings into play several different levels of the personality. This too, on account of its diversity, is at the intersection of opposite poles which it reconciles. At the same time, says Ficino, another link is forged: the individual in company, sharing his pleasure and knowledge, is incorporated in the group. The table is a microcosm of society, the ideal place for communication, the nexus where ideas are exchanged, where social relationships are formed and where people learn how to respect each other. But while becoming a man amongst men, the dinner guest establishes one more link along another axis. Through food and wine he communes with nature and is integrated into the working of the land and seasonal changes. Recalling Pythagoras, Ficino recommends simple and pure food which respects the character of natural produce.

Ficino's analysis is to a large extent conditioned by idealization and literary tradition. It would be wrong, however, to assimilate the model he provides to a mere storehouse of abstract ideas. We will see later[10] that although the Humanists, when they sit down to a meal, remember what they have read, they do not, for all that, sacrifice their pleasure. A famous episode from the history of the neo-Platonist circle of Lorenzo di Medici shows that theory can also have a practical side. At the beginning of his commentary on Plato's *Symposium* (*Commentarium in Convivium Platonis*, p. 136), Ficino tells how the Careggio Academy held a meal to celebrate the anniversary of Plato's birth and death on 7 November.[11] During the meal, the guests, copying the feast at Agathon's in the *Symposium*, read and then acted out each part of the classical text. But they do more than merely provide a gloss on the archetypal classical banquet. The ceremony (which is described very succinctly) is like the application of the theoretical model: the aim is philosophical, the speeches reach a high level of metaphysical speculation, but the setting is the feast, the meal creates a convivial atmosphere, pleasant company is assured and the rustic decor is discreetly outlined. Whatever the historical accuracy of the story,

[10] See chapters 2 and 3.
[11] The meal is supposed to have taken place on 7 November 1468.

the aim of bringing together at table both pleasure and thought, feast and words, remains intact. This is the Humanist situation *par excellence*: the power of a text like the *Symposium* is not limited to its philological or ideological value: it also dictates how to live. The Careggio celebration too postulates the oneness of the person.

The al fresco meal

According to Suetonius, Nero had a dining room built in his Golden House, which 'was circular and constantly revolved day and night, like the heavens' (*The Lives of the Caesars*, VI, 31). This is a fine symbol of the communion of the diner with the cosmos: the feast shows how humans belong to the world of matter and to the cycle of production. Nature comes into the house in the form of the foodstuffs on the table and the symbiotic relationship between the person who eats and the physical world becomes tighter. When the Romans strewed flowers in their dining rooms or paved them with mosaics representing plants and animals, when people at table put on crowns of leaves and when nowadays we put vases of flowers on our tables, the same interrelation of food and nature's bounty is at play. The meal establishes a close continuity between the microcosm and the macrocosm, the eater and the eaten. The appetite (from the Latin *petere*, to seek to attain or to seek to obtain) is that which allows man to come close to the world, to swallow it, to capture its energy and convert it into his own substance.

The Renaissance paid great attention to this aspect of the banquet: it was led to do this not only by classical examples, but also by folklore, agricultural rituals and seasonal celebrations. The scenario of the rustic festival has many variants in the texts. Whether it be seen through the conventions of idyllic or pastoral literature, whether it adopts the hedonistic aspect of Horace's odes with their rural festivities,[12] or whether as in Ronsard it takes the form of Dionysian rejoicing,[13] it is always a celebration (in the

[12] Horace, *The Odes and Epodes*.
[13] See *Les Bacchanales ou le folastrissime voyage d'Hercueil*, in *Oeuvres complètes*, vol. III, pp. 184ff, and *Dithyrambes à la pompe du bouc de Jodelle*, vol. V, pp. 53ff. There are further versions of this episode by other poets of the Pléiade.

noble language of poetry) of natural produce and the regenerative activity of eating, steeped in its original rural setting. There is also a popular version of this theme, all the more expressive for not having been affected by erudite tradition. Here we must pause to consider the example of Rabelais, for whom the voluptuousness of food only reaches its full potential if it is integrated in the fecundity of the world about us. Two opening passages – one from the beginning of *Gargantua*, the other from the beginning of *Pantagruel* – will serve to illustrate this point.[14]

In each of the stories the origin of the hero and his entry into the tale is marked by a great blow-out. Gargantua comes into the world in the middle of a country fair in the fields (Rabelais, *Gargantua*, chs. 4–5). Gargamelle has eaten too much and gives birth at the feast surrounded by the exuberant debauchery of the crowd which is stuffing itself with meats and getting as drunk *ad libitum*. Everything is there in abundance – 367,014 oxen have been killed, and so

> the tripes were plentiful, as you will understand, and so appetizing that everyone licked his fingers. But . . . they could not possibly be kept any longer, for they were tainted, which seemed most improper. So it was resolved that they should be consumed without more ado. (Ibid., p. 48)

The appetites are gigantic and irrepressible: nature lavishes its produce on humankind which effortlessly and remorselessly swallows it from 'full ladles' (ibid.) in order to maintain as much vital energy as possible. Neither the death of the animals that are eaten nor the bad weather are unlucky, since they allow strength to be renewed and the fruitful season to return. To revel when there is such profusion is not just an individual experience, it is also to be part of the cycle of all living things. The child being born in the middle of revelry while bodies are being renewed, and the lack of distinction between feeding and breeding, show the richness of the theme. Moreover, Gargantua comes very close to being expelled during an attack of diarrhoea, as if giving birth were part and parcel

---

[14] Almost everything about food, the body and feasts in Rabelais has been said by Bakhtin in *Rabelais and his World*. What follows does not reiterate but inevitably overlaps with what is said in this major work.

of the food cycle and renewing the body and perpetuating the species were one and the same thing.

The copious menu of the giants reads like a symbol of a happy communion between humankind and the earth – the physical body and the heavenly body. Eating and drinking, in Rabelais's version of the symbolism of revellers, are part of the great cycle of fertility. In the same way that meals for monks take place in a refectory – a place where one is 'remade', so, in Rabelais, absorbing food regenerates and restores.[15] There has rarely been a better metaphor of 'Mother Nature': the earth, which harbours all wealth and protects life, covers the giants' table with food and links eating to the development of the universe. But the collective significance of food does not exclude its role in the individual destiny. If we follow Gargantua's development, it seems that, for the individual, eating one's fill also means becoming oneself. The baby becomes himself and takes his place in the world as soon as he starts to drink:

> For if by chance he was vexed, angry, displeased, or peeved, if he stamped, if he wept or if he screamed, they always brought him drink to restore his temper, and immediately he became quiet and happy. (Ibid., p. 54)

The child is in fact only repeating the original gesture of his tribe: his relation to the world, his language, even his name – everything which, in the first stages of life, shapes his identity – seems to relate to some phase in the digestive cycle between oral and anal satisfaction, in the absorption and sensuous transformation of what goes into the mouth.

The feast at the beginning of *Gargantua* has a precise date: it takes place on 3 February in the middle of the Carnival, a time of profusion and triumph over shortage. It is also a time which heralds the return of spring and germination. Soon plants will start to grow again and new life will triumph over the season of death. But the banquet is part of another symbolic chronology beyond the calendar of seasonal festivities. Behind the image of the baby and the peasants deriving pleasure from all quarters lies the

---

[15] On the symbolism of food, see F. Lange, *Manger ou les jeux et les creux du plat*.

paradigm of original happiness. The start of the story and of life have the atmosphere of the beginning of the world, in a popular version of the Golden Age. The fecundity and abundance, the participation of the one in the whole and the universal well-being can be read as relics of the Garden of Eden, of Arcadia or of the Land of Cockaigne; signs of some paradise regained through the gift of inexhaustible food.

The most reliable indicator is that, just as before the Fall, in this era there is no evil nor threat of punishment. In his innocence and purity, the natural human being is aware of neither good nor evil. All desires – an insatiable appetitie for good food, an unquenchable thirst and great sex drive – seem permissible here. There is no immodesty and no debasement in the mouth which devours or the sex organs which procreate; they are rather the signs of unfettered and overpowering strength. What original sin has repressed and condemned is recycled into the positive process of nature. Hedonistic drives, neither good nor bad, exist in their own right. There is no moral censure and no social taboo to limit the way in which appetites are expressed or satisfied. The attraction of the rustic festival is so overwhelming and the legitimacy of food so powerful that they cancel out the teachings of morality and religion. Authority (be it father, God or the law) which judges people and makes them guilty, does not yet hold sway. Greed places them firmly in nature; it is therefore good.

The first chapter of *Pantagruel* also contains a birth – that of the race of giants – and it too starts the story with a lavish celebration of the stomach. The scenario is broadly speaking the same as in *Gargantua* but at the level of a myth, dealing with the history of the universe. The primitive act, the originating gesture which creates the tribe, is that of eating. The story goes back to the first days of humanity and rewrites the myth of the Creation in its own way. The fruits of the earth then were so copious and flavoursome, and the first men were so greedy, that their sated bodies soon swelled and became deformed. So the dynasty of giants was born from the combined effects of natural abundance and enormous appetite. In the beginning was overeating and indigestion.

This bulimia could have turned out badly, as the desire for the forbidden fruit did in Genesis. The emergence of grotesque bodies, distended and disfigured by excess food, could have been the

sanction for this excess. For the punishment to fit the crime, lumps
and swellings would have been the body's penalty for abusing
good food, and gluttons would have paid the price for their
debauchery by becoming deformed. But natural morality is
different. The mouth and the stomach, far from putting human
destiny in jeopardy, initiate the conquest of the future; they store
up the energy which ensures that the species is continued and that
the book grows. Although intemperance is blatant, disgrace is
eliminated and the classical norm of moderation is disqualified.
Spontaneous appetites and the atmosphere of euphoria eradicate
the latent connotations of ugliness and punishment. As at the dawn
of Gargantua's life, we are in the innocent world before the Fall.

For Rabelais is rewriting the book of Genesis and completely
overturning the fable of Paradise Lost. As in the Garden of Eden,
everything starts with the desire for a fruit – except that in Rabelais
the fruit is not forbidden. Whereas God commands that the fruit of
the tree of knowledge shall not be eaten – 'for in the day that thou
eatest thereof thou shalt surely die' (Genesis 2: 17) – there is no
prohibition or punishment here; knowledge may be eaten. While
Adam and Eve, in the traditional version, are guilty and ashamed
and hide their nakedness, the grotesque bodies in Rabelais show
themselves with carefree immodesty: they have not yet become
aware of good and evil. Adam is finally expelled from paradise and
condemned to cultivate the cursed soil in the sweat of his brow
(Genesis 3: 17–19): but Rabelais eradicates this rift beween man
and nature as well. He readily accepts that greed dictates man's
primary actions, but he rejects any connection between greed and
crime or suffering.

The murder committed by Cain also undergoes a significant
transformation:

> A little after Abel was killed by his brother Cain, the earth, being
> soaked in the blood of the righteous, was that day so fertile in all
> those fruits that from her loins she bears for us, and especially in
> medlars, that from time immemorial it has been called the year of the
> great medlars. (*Pantagruel*, p. 171)

Instead of a curse and sterility – God says to Cain: 'When thou
tillest the ground, it shall not henceforth yield unto thee her

strength' (Genesis 4: 12) – we have a glut of material produce and of the forces of regeneration. Blood fertilizes the earth and produces a large quantity of medlar fruits 'pleasant to the eyes and a delight to taste' (*Pantagruel*, p. 171). Evil does not give rise to evil, but is transformed into part of the beneficial cycle of fecundity.

Another reversal completes the picture in Rabelais's pre-moral and guiltless version of Genesis. From the drunkenness of Noah Rabelais retains little more than its joyful and familiar aspect, the invention of 'that ambrosial, delicious, precious, celestial, joyous, and deific liquor which is called *drink*'. (ibid.). Once more, intemperance shifts from the negative to the positive and, far from bringing shame, brings credit to 'Noah, that holy man' (ibid.). As for the garment with which Noah's sons prudishly cover his nakedness (Genesis 9: 23), Rabelais's story, which celebrates the body in all its forms and rejects hypocritical notions of decency, is of course quick to forget it.

We will see later what energy these parodies – which transform traditional genealogy through humour and give the accepted version of the Creation the slip – give to Rabelais's writing.[16] The representation of the eating scenes is charged with a further imaginative dynamism. If everything starts with a feast in *Gargantua* and *Pantagruel*, this is because by consuming the fruits of the earth people realize their full potential in certain respects. The body has a feeling of sensual expansion, the human being is in control of natural resources and ascribes to a naturalist ethos which removes inhibition and defies censure. Whether, as in Rabelais, they take on the proportions of a cosmic orgy or, as in the poetic tradition, they adopt more disciplined forms, the al fresco meal and the relation between the eater and the eaten surely crystallize one of the attractions which the symposiac paradigm held in the Renaissance.

Conviviality

'One should not so much consider what one eats as with whom one eats it . . . There is no dish so sweet to me, and no sauce so

<hr />

16 See chapter 4, A mouth full of words.

appetizing, as those derived from the company' (Montaigne, *Essays*, III, 13; p. 391).[17] Here Montaigne defines another constant: the act of eating does not only belong to the world of instinct, it also helps to build social relations. It is therefore not just a matter of giving in to appetite, but of reconciling spontaneity and experience, of moderating hedonistic impulses by learning a code of behaviour. The disciplined relationship with others acts as a corrective to unfettered natural forces. The mouth that speaks controls the mouth that eats; the body which is subject to the constraints of social life imposes rules on the natural body.

We will see that the way in which meals establish a confraternity of speech, manners and thoughts is an aspect which always fires the imagination and helps to form customs. The banquet is a collective ceremony, the time above all others when an individual learns to share pleasure and to heighten it by talking with others. The Humanists like to remind us of the etymology of the Latin word *convivium*: from *convivere*, to live together. They stress the prefix *con* and, following Isidore of Seville,[18] list meaningful synonyms; *convivium* is like *convictus* (communal life), *conlocutio* (conversation), *convescor* (to eat together), *communio* (community), *conciliatio* (association), and so on. They sometimes quote a passage from Cicero which criticizes Greek sensuality but also celebrates the collective aspect of the meal:

> Our fathers did well in calling the reclining of friends at feasts a *convivium*, because it implies a communion of life [*vitae coniunctio*], which is a better designation than that of the Greeks, who call it sometimes a 'drinking together' [*compotatio*] and sometimes an 'eating together' [*concenatio*], thereby apparently exalting what is of least value in these associations above that which gives them their greatest charm. (*Cato Maior: De senectute*, XIII, 45)[19]

---

[17] References to Montaigne are either to *Les Essais*, ed. P. Villey, or, where the quotation is included in the abridged English translation, to *Essays*, tr. J. M. Cohen.

[18] Isidore of Seville, *Etymologiarum sive Originum libri XX*, XX, 1, 3. Most of book XX is about the vocabulary of food.

[19] See also *The Letters to his Friends*, IX, 24, 3. For other definitions and etymological studies, see J. G. Stuckius, *Antiquitatum convivialium libri III*, I, 1–2.

Whether they be reflections of social structures or imaginative projections, anthropological documents or fictive elaborations, these texts do not necessarily have a single impulse. They may celebrate pleasure and plenty, but there are also many descriptions of conviviality as a collective act and a sphere where groups are formed. There are references from all cultures and all eras, a sign of the eclectic curiosity of the Renaissance. Homer for example is quoted, showing that the banquet, since the dawn of antiquity, has had a central role in the feudal society of princes and warriors, while Hesiod describes peasants gathering around a shared meal. As for Latin writers, they celebrate the intimate meal with friends – Cicero describing the pleasure of informal conversation and Horace the joy of rustic festivities. This is a model that the Humanists claimed as their own and frequently imitated. References abound too to the first Christians and their love-feasts, to medieval guilds and their fraternal banquets and to the learned circles of the Italian Renaissance with their meetings over meals. Even sailors' tales of ritual eating among American cannibals fire the imagination and in a weird way confirm that communal life is frequently ordered around a feast. Historians, cosmographers and compilers provide a mass of examples which had an influence on manners[20] and fiction. We only need to go back to Rabelais to see that the al fresco meal incorporates or adumbrates the complementary experience of conviviality.

Pantagruel and *Gargantua* are slightly reminiscent of the *Bildungsroman*: their heroes develop from the impulsive phase of childhood, when desires are not bound by rules, to the appreciation of order, discipline and the laws which govern life in society. The splendour of the feast is destined to be transcended and its place taken by reason.

The two phases of Gargantua's education are significant.[21] The child learns nothing from the old-fashioned sophistry of his tutors and allows his greed free rein: he does nothing but eat, drink and sleep, he lurks in the kitchen and he vegetates and stagnates like an animal (albeit enjoying himself). But there is a time for everything: Gargantua reaches school age without modifying his behaviour; he

[20] See chapter 2.
[21] A more detailed analysis of this can be found in M. Jeanneret, '*Gargantua* 4–24: l'uniforme et le discontinu'.

continues to stuff himself and has no manners, and so is in the wrong. However when the good Humanist teacher, Ponocrates, comes along, the young man's lifestyle changes completely. He observes meal times, has a diet of good, wholesome food, eats in company and is careful to balance gastronomic delights with reading and discussion of erudite works. The meal has become a civilized activity, a cultural rite, and there is no doubt that this evolution is positively marked by Rabelais.[22]

It is easy to trace this introduction to conviviality, this realization that another person is essential to the enjoyment of meals. A few examples from *Gargantua* and *Pantagruel* will suffice. Gargantua has only just been born when he establishes contact with others through the wine he offers around. He drinks his fill but at the same time turns outward to the assembled company: 'he cried out . . . "Drink! Drink! Drink!", as if inviting the whole world to drink, so loud that he was heard through all the lands of Booze and Bibulous' (*Gargantua*, p. 52). Individual satisfaction and public rejoicing are combined. His innate propensity for drink gives rise in Gargantua both to his tendency to vegetate and to his liking for company. According to a poetic etymology, to quench one's thirst (*se désaltérer*) would therefore be to suppress one's otherness (*altérité*), to stop being other and to break down through wine the barriers separating one from the rest of society. From then on, Gargantua progresses from childish pleasure and solitary pursuits to the benefits of education and to knowing how to live well, to the duties of civil life and the exercise of power. At each stage of this apprenticeship, his access to new activities and new groups of people is marked by a banquet or a drink of wine. This is the ideal focal point around which people can gather to enjoy themselves, the pivot around which society is organized; it is also a theme which recurs throughout the book and which gives cohesion to the narrative despite its digressions.

The civilizing quality of food and its role in building a happy society are evident in both of the wars described by Rabelais: the one against the Dipsodes in *Pantagruel* and the one against Picrochole in *Gargantua*.

---

[22] On the way in which things alimentary are taken over by table manners and diet, see chapters 2 and 3.

The enemies are brutes who do not know how to live or eat. Twice Picrochole and his men, after refusing cakes and ruining the harvest, turn down an invitation to share a meal as a peace offering (*Gargantua*, chs. 32 and 34). Eating, for these ruffians, does not provide an opportunity for conciliation, but rather arouses hostility and leads to pillage: ruining neighbourly relations, declaring war and showing contempt for fine food are one and the same. Picrochole the usurper replies to his lieutenant who is worried about the state of their supplies: ' "We shall have only too many provisions . . . Are we here to eat or to fight?" ' (ibid., p. 109).

On the other side, Grandgousier and his friends try to lessen the fury of the battle and provide a corrective to it by indulging in banquets. They do not run away from the battle, but, because they are amenable, civil and good-natured, they celebrate more than they kill. Much of the account of the Picrocholine war takes place at Grandgousier's table, whether it be the description of a skirmish, the decision to plan a particular tactic or, better still, to have a good time. Ponocrates is in a hurry to confront the enemy, but the good king has other ideas: ' "But this is certainly not the time," said Grandgousier. "I want to give you a feast this evening and to offer you a good welcome." This said, they made supper ready' (p. 120). They put pleasure first and prepare themselves for action by having a feast: thus they stoke up their vital energy and already fulfil the conditions for victory.

The process is similar in the war against the Dipsodes in *Pantagruel*. Pantagruel's army has chosen 'hand on pot and glass in fist' (p. 261) as its slogan. But a good bottle should be shared, and the victors freely let their enemies join their rejoicings. As soon as they have their first success Pantagruel 'had refreshment brought and a feast spread for them on the shore with great jollity; and he made them drink too, with their bellies to the ground, and their prisoner as well' (p. 250). From then on, military prowess alternates with picnics and libations; strategy is planned over a bottle of wine, then carried out in the field, except where the two things happen at once, as for example when they get the enemy drunk in order to deceive them (ch. 28). Elsewhere Panurge suggests a truce so that they can eat; the armies will fraternize over a banquet, while the two leaders engage in single combat:

'It's not we who make war. Give us something to eat with you while
our masters fight.' Which the king and the giants readily agreed to
do, inviting them to share their feast. (Ibid., p. 261)

Food therefore moderates violence, and the war, interspersed as it
is with gastronomic episodes, acquires human proportions. In that
it brings men together in a communal ritual, conviviality has a
pacifying and civilizing role. It is the basis for the art of good living
and it posits a society where the individual, without ignoring the
stomach, none the less recognizes the need for communal living.
This shows how complex the theme is: it echoes the traditions of
the popular festival and gives form to collective ideals of freedom,
of satiation and unbridled pleasure, but it is also a plea for the
refinement and restrictions of life in society. We therefore find two
sets of values, two phases in the history of the individual or of
humanity as a whole side by side in Rabelais's work. These are also
two vital components of the symposiac ideal.

The head and the stomach

When Gargantua sits at the table of his teacher Ponocrates he does
more than perfect his social graces; he learns to complement
sensual pleasure with intellectual stimulation. He looks after his
stomach but does not stop cultivating his mind: he listens to
readings, comments on his lessons and enters into 'good, learned
and profitable conversation' (Rabelais, *Gargantua*, p. 91). For
man, who is composed of both mind and body, to talk at meal
times is to express the complete self. He shares his pleasure
equitably between sense and the senses: he brings into balance
desires which are normally disjoined. This is the third strength of
the banquet: not only does it celebrate the union of man and nature
and of man and society, it also symbolizes the integration of body
and spirit. For the Humanists, who strive to realize the full human
potential, the meal, during which one eats one's fill while thinking
out loud, is an ideal model.

Montaigne contrasts eating with the sexual act:

We eat well and drink like fish, but these are not activities which
prevent intellectual processes. We remain in control throughout.

However, copulation puts all other thoughts in abeyance, it degrades
and debases, by its imperious nature, all the theology and philosophy
of a Plato. (*Essais*, III, 5; p. 877)

Reason is clouded by sex, whereas food does not threaten lucidity.
Making love reduces us to the level of animals, while a meal allows us
to reconcile the angel and the beast in us. Renaissance treatises and
fiction contain many variations on this theme. It is of course
conversation which promotes the mind and means that the wise man
can go from his library to his dining room without giving up the
demands of thought. The Ancients wanted both Bacchus and the
Muses to preside at banquets, for 'learned and entertaining words . . .
delight the body and mind as much as wine does, or more (G.
Bouchet, *Les Sérées*, vol. I, p. ix). If Montaigne praises the Greeks
and Romans for setting aside 'for eating, which is an important
action in life, several hours and the better part of the night' (*Essays*,
III, 13; p. 388), this is because the meal is an opportunity for total
pleasure thanks to 'such good talk and agreeable entertainment as
men of intelligence are able to provide for one another' (ibid., p. 394).
The psychosomatic bases of classical medicine provide a lesson
here: since the body and spirit seem to be interdependent and
human behaviour proceeds from their interaction, a special
importance is attached to opportunities for showing the properties
of both at the same time. The dual aspect of the banquet provides a
good opportunity to prove the hypothesis that man is a single
being, neither sensual nor spiritual, but a combination of the two.

The mouth as an organ of both eating and speaking serves to
illustrate this thesis. Ingestion and expression, care for the body
and manifestation of the spirit, all take place through the mouth, a
symbol of the close links between these functions. In his treatise on
tongues, Erasmus stresses this duality: the same organ serves to
'take in food and drink, to emit sound and to articulate speech'
(*Lingua*, pp. 242–3). Such a contiguous relationship emphasizes
the physical dimension of utterance; speaking while one eats, one
becomes aware that words are material substance and physiological
phenomena. Words bring to the senses, already sharpened by food,
further sensuous pleasure. In the second part of this book I will
investigate the occurrences of this theme in literature.

Different writers emphasize the synthesis of the intellectual and the physical in different ways: some promote conversation and strive to moderate sensual desire, whereas others exploit the combination to protest against wisdom which is too austere. Erasmus seems to be one of the former. He is concerned with the balanced human being and frequently discusses food and writes about table manners and questions of diet.[23] In his search for a complete ethical code, he recognizes the central role of the meal but never fails, in the interests of good taste, to recommend sobriety; it is precisely because spirit and body are interdependent that a frugal diet is necessary. The entire Hippocratic tradition corroborates this thesis.[24] On the other hand Montaigne, who is often irritated by morality which insists on edification, which is hostile to nature and which wants to exploit symposiac activity for its own ends, counters in the name of natural principles. In his last essay, *On experience*, he goes into his eating habits in some detail and claims, contrary to doctors and moralists, that pleasure is a legitimate impulse. His close scrutiny of his diet and his indulgence of his 'appetite' are part of a polemic. He exploits the traditional opposition of mind and body to discredit unilateral emphases on the mind. Ethereal ideas and fine words are not as good as the taste of roast meat:

> Ask some ordinary man to tell you one day the ideas and fancies with which he fills his head, and for which he diverts his thoughts from a good meal, even grudging the time he spends in eating it. You will find that not one of all the dishes on your table has so little flavour as the fine things with which he is entertaining his mind . . . and you will find that all his talk and aspirations are worth less than your warmed up stew. (*Essays*, III, 13; pp. 404–5)

Removing thought and speech altogether from meals would be to plunge into sensualism and would also lead the meal to atrophy. Over and above the controversy and the personal details, Montaigne has in common with the Humanists a search for a unifying, balanced view of man. The same essay in which he defends the body against the hegemony of the head finishes by promoting 'temperament', an ideal balance which strives to

---

[23] See chapters 2 and 3.
[24] See chapter 3, Diet, and Medicine v. cookery.

encompass all possibilities and to attain, by the middle road, the 'immediate pleasures . . . that are perceived by the mind, and conveyed to it by the senses' (ibid., p. 395). Montaigne's apposite formula here ('intellectuellement sensibles, sensiblement intellectuels', *Essais*, III, 13; p. 1107), with its chiasmus and double oxymoron, reflects the meeting of opposites. Now the meal provides just such a synthesis: it unites that which sectarian systems had separated and gives the mind its rightful place in relation to the body:

> I hate to be told that my spirit should be in the clouds while my body is at table. I would not have the mind pinned or sprawling there, but I would have it attentive; it should sit, not recline. Aristippus spoke for the body only, as if we had no soul; Zeno dealt only with the soul, as if we had no body; and both were mistaken. Pythagoras . . . followed a philosophy that was all contemplation, while that of Socrates was all deeds and conduct; Plato found a mean between the two. (*Essays*, III, 13; p. 396)

In sixteenth-century French, the verb 'to feed' (*nourrir*) has, apart from its literal meaning, the sense of 'to educate', and Montaigne, among others, likes to play with this ambiguity.[25] He uses other alimentary metaphors for intellectual activity: the thirst for knowledge, spicing up food with conversation, consuming knowledge as one consumes a fruit, and so on. Even though banal, these analogies are not insignificant. They point to a common ground where food for the mind and food for the body are expressed in the same terminology. Eating and learning are the same: they are two ways of absorbing the world, two levels of human activity which can be confused in a single word.

The attempt to integrate the two elements also imposes on conversation certain constraints upon which theoreticians readily agree.[26] The thinking and speaking head must be prevented from monopolizing the conversation with laborious speeches, which would vitiate the stomach's pleasure. Philosophy expounded at meals must be watered down. It can contribute to the festive

---

[25] On food metaphors, see chapter 5, Metaphors of bibliophagy. On the theme of food in *On experience*, see C. Dickson, 'L'invitation de Montaigne au banquet de la vie: *De l'Expérience*'.

[26] For a fuller discussion, see chapter 4, Convivial speech.

atmosphere by touching on all subjects, laughing when others laugh and digressing readily when others change the subject. It comes out of its ivory tower to deal with problems of everyday life, coming within the grasp of all the guests and facing up to interrogation by the profane. Can it maintain its validity when wine is loosening tongues and the stomach digesting? The feast is a testing ground, where philosophy is challenged by the juxtaposition of food and jokes and emerges from these with renewed vigour. For Montaigne, who is hostile to pointless speculation and keen to give wisdom a practical application, table talk is a good way of bringing philosophy down to earth. Thus he belongs to the tradition, which goes back to Socrates, in which thought is grounded in the reality of time and place and adapts itself to the person one is talking to, and in which moral philosophy takes the place of metaphysics. Plutarch himself, the great theoretician of conviviality, recalls, when discussing symposiac discourse, that 'the height of sagacity is to talk philosophy without seeming to do so' (*Table Talk*, vol. VIII, p. 15).[27]

A recipe for success, if one wants to involve all table companions and use all one's faculties, is to let the conversation wander and to talk of everything and nothing. A variety of themes and registers[28] stops any one person dominating and prevents the balance being upset. There must be something for everyone: seriousness should alternate with entertainment, learned people should allow nonsense to creep in and classical erudition should rub shoulders with popular comedy. No one can take over the conversation, for the ideal of totality excludes any kind of totalitarianism from the table. Good guests are spontaneously eclectic; obeying no rule other than that of controlled improvisation, without any over-rigid system or method, they chat *de omni re scibili et quibusdam aliis*. The banquet gives an outstanding opportunity to those who want to take the dogma out of philosophy.

If table talk touches on all subjects and welcomes all voices, the meal itself, as an institution at the heart of everyday life, also fires the imagination because of the number of activities it brings together and gives rise to. It is the pivotal point of domestic life,

---

[27] On Plutarch, see chapter 4 and chapter 6, Greedy grammarians.
[28] See chapters 6 and 7.

the activity around which family life is organized. To remove the table is tantamount to ruining the whole house, writes Plutarch; it is to condemn everyone to solitude, to deny offerings to the gods, to close the door on strangers, in short, to jeopardize 'the most humane and the first acts of communion between man and man' (*The Dinner of the Seven Wise Men*, p. 417). It is also, continues Plutarch (echoing Persius),[29] to violate the very workings of economic life: to ruin agriculture, to lay the land fallow, to make redundant arts and crafts connected with food – 'the overturning and confusion of our highest concerns' (ibid., pp. 417–19). Rabelais expounds the same commonplace in his panegyric on Messer Gaster (*The Fourth Book*, chs. 61–2), who is pompously acclaimed for his mastery of the arts and for his technical innovations. Rabelais endlessly highlights the universal influence of the stomach in all areas, a fundamental and motivating agent that uses all the resources of the body and the spirit and all the powers of nature and culture to keep the wolf from the door. Gradually everything comes back to the incontrovertible law of the stomach, as in the Latin fable of the members and the belly.[30] Rabelais is not alone in hyperbolic exploitation of this theme. A Humanist theoretician, Stuckius, also repeats that the meal has a universal influence:

> Meals have ramifications in all sectors of human life, they spread into all activities, to the point where there is scarcely an occupation that they do not precede, accompany or follow . . . Formerly, and today too, nothing happens in public or in private, on the domestic or the military front, in religious or profane life, without a meal. (*Antiquitatum convivialium*, p. 12v.)

The banquet therefore imposes itself on people's minds as a protean and omnipresent institution. The guests, as they talk, connect it to a whole variety of phenomena and, conversely, it spreads into all walks of life. Like Rabelais in his catalogue of the prodigious achievements of Gaster, Giordano Bruno, at the start of a description of a meal, suggests in a litany the protean heterogeneity of the paradigm and the infinite number of its manifestations. *His*

---

[29] Juvenal and Persius, *Satires*, Prologue 8ff.
[30] See *Livy* [Ab urbe condita], vol. I, tr B. O. Foster, II, 32; p. 325.

banquet, he says, will not be that of nectar for Jove, nor that of Adam, that of Ahasuerus,[31] or Lucullus, of Lycaon,[32] of Thyestes, of Tantalus, of Plato, of Diogenes,[33] or the banquet of leeches . . . (Bruno, *The Ash Wednesday Supper*, p. 67).[34] But these models remain on the horizon and provide the writer interested in the subject with an almost endless supply of material. Stuckius opens his vast encyclopaedia of banquets without false modesty:

> Since meals embrace almost all aspects of human life, the person who writes about them cannot help in doing so but write about most of the functions of human life. (Preface to *Antiquitatum convivialium*)

The present book does not seek to embrace all aspects of human life. But the meal as a representation of a special kind of totality is important to the rest of my study: it is intimately linked to the expansive, composite and voluble nature of the stories of banquets which we will come across further on.

[31] See Esther, 1 and 7.
[32] See Ovid, *The Metamorphoses*, I, 216–31: Lycaon offers Jupiter a meal of human flesh.
[33] Diogenes the cynic (413–327 BC), who lived in complete poverty.
[34] On this text, see chapter 7, Giordano Bruno: the failed banquet.

2

Ceremonies and manners

The meal as an institution gives rise to two kinds of discourse which rival yet complement each other. On the one hand, as we saw in the previous chapter, philosophers and storytellers examine the symbolic value of banquets and construct imaginary scenarios. On the other hand, practical treatises adopt a normative perspective and, being more sensitive to the demands of social life, define goals and rules for everyday use. The spontaneous symbiosis of the eater and the world is paralleled by a desire to transform matter and to constrain natural impulses. The fraternity of the feast is contrasted with signs of difference between people: the display of wealth and manners, and respect for the constraints imposed by the ritual, which reveal the social standing of the guests. A historical analysis of the actual development of manners is beyond the scope of this book,[1] but I will, in the next two chapters, examine one important aspect of the Humanist theory: good table manners. The sources consulted here are didactic and documentary; they are outside literature, but nevertheless show how topical the theme was and what a hold it had on ways of thinking.

---

[1] On manners in the sixteenth century, see A. Franklin, *La Vie privée d'autrefois. La Cuisine*; N. Elias, *La Civilisation des mœurs*; C. Ossola, 'L'Homme accompli. La Civilisation des cours comme art de la conversation'; and J. Garrisson, 'D'où viennent nos manières de table?'

Civility

Rabelais, in his all-embracing vision of the world, was able to combine the freedom of feasts – country festivals and carnival carousals – with apprenticeship in *savoir-vivre*. At the same time, but on another level, polite society – concerned with refinement and influenced by courtly and scholarly circles – produced a series of treatises which are uncompromising in condemning greed, which show how a guest at a meal can distinguish himself from the masses and which aim to stifle instinct in favour of elegant manners. The code of folk traditions and popular rejoicing plays no part here, except as something which is forbidden and which is the one thing that should be repressed. A whole system of rules and techniques for well-educated people exercises tight control over the facts and gestures of eating. Meals become a matter of style.

The sixteenth century did not, of course, invent table manners. Complex protocol has always directed the behaviour of the diners and procedure at meals. Rules, for example, saying that guests should have due regard for others, and should be clean and restrained, and rules about how the meal should be served are doubtless as old as society itself. From the Middle Ages onwards, tutors became aware that teaching elementary rules about how to behave at meals provided an effective means of educating children.[2] Collections of precepts on politeness, hygiene and decency circulated, often in Latin, and were still being printed in the sixteenth century. At the same time, some refined circles of the aristocracy were elaborating a demanding code of *savoir-vivre*, the code of courtesy, in which good table manners naturally had a place.

So the oral and written tradition of rules for behaviour and compendia of good manners already existed. But when Erasmus comes on to the scene, he gives this tradition a strength and pertinence which it never had before. He revitalizes the old

---

[2] See for example Hugues de Saint-Victor, *De institutione novitiorum* (twelfth century), translated in the fifteenth century by J. de Vignay and J. Sulpice as *La Civilité* (1483), and imitated in French by G. Durand (1545).

maxims, lends his authority to them and integrates them into Humanist culture. When, in 1530, he published his *De civilitate morum puerilium*, a collection of rules about politeness and manners, it did not seem at first sight new. The precepts of discretion, tact and cleanliness are more or less the same as those found in the Middle Ages and the ritual of meals is again seen as an excellent opportunity for putting to the test and improving one's behaviour. Of the seven chapters in *De civilitate*, the fourth, *De conviviis*, is however not only by far the longest: compared to the static maxims of the medieval tradition, the scope and scale of Erasmus's work is completely different. For the Humanist, learning how to control animal instincts and how to live with others is an essential part of being human. *Civilitas* moderates the free drive of instinct and distinguishes the man of society and culture from peasants and beasts, whose appetites go unchecked. Observance of etiquette is the outward and visible sign of inner distinction; it reveals the individual's good nature and generous tendencies. For Erasmus, writing about politeness and gentlemanliness is not a digression nor is it demeaning, for *civilitas morum* is part of philosophy; its status may be low – 'a very crude part of philosophy' (*De civilitate*, p. 273) – but good manners form the basis of moral rectitude and there is no wisdom and no fulfilment of life without self-control, respect for others and contribution to the maintenance of disciplined society.

If civility in general and table manners in particular are part of practical philosophy, then it follows that they play a prominent part in education. For Erasmus, a good education includes learning how to behave in society:

> The task of fashioning the young is made up of many parts, the first and consequently the most important of which consists of planting the seeds of piety in the tender heart; second in instilling a love for, and thorough knowledge of, the liberal arts; the third in giving instruction in the duties of life; the fourth in training in good manners [*civilitas morum*] right from the very earliest years. (Ibid., p. 273)

This volume, aimed at children, soon became a school textbook. This is a significant development: from now on, learning to be polite is not only a matter for the family, but also forms part of the

Humanist pedagogical programme. Several studies[3] have shown that *De civilitate* was enormously successful. Through the number of editions and of translations into the vulgar language, the number of adaptations and imitations and through the kind of typography used,[4] Erasmus's short treatise became a classic school text for about three centuries: it formed the basis of discipline and was the standard work of reference in the teaching of good manners. It was rewritten in various ways (in verse, as memorable axioms, as questions and answers) up till the eighteenth century and it spread and popularized throughout literate Europe the necessity of good manners. Generations of schoolchildren acquired a knowledge of basic Latin and even learnt to read from it.[5]

Such success is proof that drawing up rules for politeness met a considerable need in contemporary society. In the model of behaviour described by Erasmus, a whole class, much bigger than the court class of the Middle Ages, seems to have found the communal ideal it was looking for. Even the notion of 'courtesy' is replaced in Erasmus by *civilitas* ('being a citizen') in the same way that other words he uses, for example *urbanitas* and *honestas*, show how his work goes beyond aristocratic circles. Knowing how to behave is no longer the preserve of noblemen: the moralist provides the code for everyone who goes to school, and henceforth it affects the majority. Clearly Erasmus wants to democratize things so that everyone has the right to learn the laws of good behaviour and, doubtless aware that this is an innovation, he stresses it frequently. Through the young prince, Henri de Bourgogne, to whom the book is dedicated, he addresses 'the entire fellowship of boys' (*universo puerorum sodalitatio*) (ibid., p. 289), for whom basic politeness is even more necessary. If they follow the educated nobility or imitate 'children of illustrious descent' (p. 273), they will rectify the chance circumstances of birth; for although one does not choose one's parents, and may belong to the disadvantaged class of 'those for whom destiny has

[3] In addition to Elias, *La Civilisation des moeurs*, and the introductions to the French edition, *La Civilité puérile*, by A. Bonneau and P. Ariès, see F. Bierlaire, 'Erasmus at School: the *De Civilitate morum puerilium libellus*' and Erasme, la table et les manières de table'.

[4] The so-called 'civility' type was introduced in textbooks on civility from 1559 and owes its popularity to them.

[5] See chapter 4, Philologists or logophiles?

decreed an ordinary, humble, or even rustic lot', one can nevertheless through education acquire 'the elegance of good manners' (p. 289). In this way a new, more authentic nobility can emerge – not defined by blood, but by heart and mind: 'everyone who cultivates the mind in liberal studies must be taken to be noble' (p. 274). While Castiglione, in his famous treatise,[6] still gives courtiers exclusive rights to *savoir-vivre*, Erasmus extends to others the privilege of manners and gives it a new authenticity.

Whatever the scale of the project, the aim is essentially pragmatic and the level of instruction limited: the well-educated diner will take off his hat, will not put his fingers in the sauce and will not wipe them on his clothes, he will not throw leftovers under the tablecloth, nor on to it, nor back into the dish, he will not lick his plate, and so on. And Erasmus's contribution was not enough to make refined and clean habits at table universal. For a long time afterwards, people would continue to eat without a spoon or a fork. To judge by the prescriptive texts which were still being circulated in the eighteenth century, table manners must have remained very coarse; and even later, people were still being told not to blow their nose on their napkin, not to stuff themselves, nor to scratch or spit. But the fact remains that Erasmus and his followers were clearly intent on using the ritual of meals to change manners and to make society more disciplined. Moreover some of his *Colloquia* (dialogues) complement the lessons of the *De civilitate*, illustrating and reinforcing the practical side of Erasmus's project: of these, six conversations take place during a meal or are about the art of the symposium.[7] Friends who eat and talk together in a playful and courteous atmosphere give a pleasing demonstration of the rules of restraint, sobriety and urbanity. Reading these conversations was to familiarize oneself with the serene tone and the atmosphere of human sympathy which the treatise also sought to bring to the table.

The relevance of the question of civility is confirmed by another classic work on the subject, Giovanni Della Casa's *Galateo* (1558),

[6] Castiglione's *The Book of the Courtier* does not go into detail about table manners, and it did not have a direct influence on matters concerning food. It is therefore not discussed here.

[7] *Convivium profanum, C. fabulosum, C. sobrium, C. religiosum, C. poeticum, Dispar c.* For a study of these texts from the point of view of what is said at table, see chapter 7, Erasmus: feasting on words.

which was also destined for immediate success, running into many
Italian editions and being translated into several languages.[8] It is no
doubt an imitation of *De civilitate*, but differs from it in two ways:
it is addressed to gentlemen and, unlike Erasmus, uses the art of
living as an indication of social distinction; and it deals less with
table manners, which barely take up two chapters out of thirty.
Despite these differences, the project is the same. In both cases, the
aim is to control the body and to restrain sensuality in order not to
disgust others; the diner does not derive pleasure from physical
enjoyment, but rather from the satisfaction of putting other people
at their ease and receiving from them a sign of acceptance amongst
well-educated people. The two works have in common an
instinctive knowledge of the rules of good behaviour and the
recognition of that pleasant constraint which Erasmus calls *decor*:
decorum, that which is appropriate, elegant and charming. In
discourse on civility, verbs are rarely used in the indicative form.
They are usually modalized, either being dependent on an
impersonal structure – variations on 'it is necessary' or 'it is
becoming' – or being put into the imperative or subjunctive.
Erasmus and Della Casa both use the language of order and
restraint: do this and do not do that. In other words, tame your
natural instincts and be totally in control of your behaviour.

There is a clear contradiction between these prescriptions and
the poet's tendency to follow the call of desire. There is an
enormous gulf between the euphoric dreams I described in the first
chapter and the censorious basis of the system of good manners,
showing both the range of themes linked to conviviality and the
friction that existed in cultivated society. The discipline required
by *savoir-vivre* challenges the licence of literary fables and
morality. Thus *De civilitate* and *Galateo* both denounce one of the
great myths of symposiac fiction: that wine should be praised as a
source of inspiration. Della Casa strenuously attacks the sophistry
of authors who invoke the suspect model of the Greeks,
advocating drunkenness and claiming to free themselves from the
constraints of reason:

> We often find that learned men, by their grandiose talk, can prove
> that right is wrong and wrong is right . . . Whatever the ancient

[8] See M. Richter, *Giovanni Della Casa in Francia nel secolo XVI*.

chronicles may say about it, for my part I thank God that for all the many other plagues which have come to us from beyond the Alps, this most pernicious custom of making game of drunkenness, and even admiring it, has not yet reached as far as this. (*Galateo*, pp. 100–1)

These words are banal, but their lesson is clear. Whereas Rabelais and Ronsard, celebrating the joys of drink, are writing literature, decent people, concerned with their image in society, make their conduct conform to the precepts of Erasmus or Della Casa. But fortunately there are no such watertight distinctions; the art of life can also be a life in art. We will see that the dream of an additional level of pleasure or beauty even finds its way into discourse on manners.

Manners and Mannerism

In Erasmus's definition, civility, which is guaranteed by moral commitment and natural politeness, implies an authentic and integrated way of living. The aesthetic of manners therefore has an ethical basis; elegance is not just a show put on for others, it also corresponds to an inherent necessity. But such a system, once it begins to be propagated, contains the seeds of its own destruction. It is designed to be seen and admired, and so risks overdoing things. Whatever the pedagogues say, politeness and good conduct always presuppose an element of pretence and role-playing. Knowing how to live, once dissociated from knowing how to be, becomes nothing more than knowing how to seem. Good conduct risks becoming ostentation or deception – a series of automatic gestures and masks imposed by social intercourse.

This phenomenon is universal: manners are always potentially mannered. The code of politeness is an inherently inauthentic system which is bound to be duplicitous because it can never eradicate passion. Moralists of all eras have revealed its tricks: simulation and affectation have always been an intrinsic part of civilization. Such accepted values are always going to be dramatized or caricatured as they are in the likes of Molière's *petits marquis*, *précieuses* and Tartuffe. This duplicity has a particular effect on the rules of conviviality in the sixteenth century: the symposiac ethic is narrowed down to a matter of etiquette and the ideal of the meal among friends, which regenerates the whole person, is threatened by ceremonial, exhibitionism and technique.

It is not surprising to find this same kind of ambivalence in the age of Mannerism. The social side of civility, in the courts and the salons, takes on the aspect of a search for a formal elegance and refinement which conforms to current fashions. It is not necessary, in order to put this into context, to examine Mannerism in any great depth here.[9] *Maniera*, in the vocabulary of the Renaissance, does not only refer to a tendency in art towards stylization; it is also something that promotes a stylish life, affectation in one's relations with others and sophistication of conduct. While the plastic arts cultivate a beauty which is affected, ornamental, geometric and hostile to natural profusion, and deal in artificial forms and rare, even extravagant, discoveries, the elite, for their part, adopt manners and create a decor which themselves look like works of art. Painters, musicians and poets collaborate to give to the feasts which punctuate life at court an extraordinary glamour; the splendour of palaces and gardens, the extravagance and harmony of dress and decoration all reveal a collective tendency to make the real world an aesthetic object. Table manners are also subject to this tendency. Under the dual influence of their inherent ambiguity and of fashion, they part company with Erasmus's ideal and find their way into the ever more subtle search for beautiful manners in general. Humanist ethics are being overtaken by Mannerist aesthetics, but the two tendencies are far from being mutually exclusive, and are both present throughout the sixteenth century, to varying extents according to the social milieu and its aims. Noble circles, intent on emulating the court, rely among other things on symposiac ceremonial to show off their distinguished behaviour. The rest of this chapter is devoted to the experiments they undertook in this field.

After those of Erasmus and Della Casa, the next on the list of classic works about civility marks a significant evolution. Like its precursors, Stefano Guazzo's semi-theoretical, semi-practical manual *La civil Conversazione* (1574) had a vast readership throughout

[9] See J. Shearman, *Mannerism*, for a full account.

Europe.[10] But here the rules for the art of good living reach hitherto unknown heights of refinement. For the most part, they refer to the art of making conversation, the most telling expression of a society absorbed in contemplating its own urbanity. The first three books of the treatise set out a general system of conversation as the melting pot of social life, and the fourth shows how this can be actually applied: it is the description of a banquet, the occasion *par excellence* when words are revealed in all their graces. I shall concentrate on this latter text, which is a prime example of the extreme mannerization of manners.

A small circle of provincial nobility, six noblemen and four ladies, gathers in Casale for a feast in honour of Duke Vespasien Gonzago. The story tells us nothing of the menu or the quality of the food, for pleasure derived from food is vulgar and excluded as a subject from the dialogue. The meal is so sanitized that it does not nourish, but rather provides the guests with a suitable setting and pretext to show off the elegance of their manners and the distinguished nature of their language. As a whole the ceremony is reduced to an exercise in tact, finesse and discretion: an opportunity to illustrate the refined gestures, the casual tone and the supreme ease of people who know how to live. Rather than make themselves heavy by eating, they prefer to play: they set each other riddles, act out declarations of love and listen to music and poetry. They drink out of hand-blown glasses artistically shaped like boats, which inspire sly remarks. Everything seems so gracious and so easy that the final comparison between the banquet and a dream does not seem out of place. The diners, having attained a degree of refinement where the greatest artifice seems natural, do derive some pleasure, but a kind of pleasure which has been worked hard for, attained through the will and perceived by the mind.

Everything about the banquet and the entertainment is filtered through the choice words of the diners. Description gives way almost entirely to dialogue: most of the book consists of direct or indirect speech. For conversation is the real food: it changes the language of the body into anodyne formulae and, by sublimating appetites, culture systematically neutralizes nature. Words make

[10] Apart from numerous Italian editions, there are many translations, into French, English, German, Spanish and Latin. See Ossola, 'L'Homme accompli'.

the feast disappear: the guests satisfy their hunger complaisantly through the spectacle of the art of living and the art of conversation. Taste deserts the domain of the senses, it now only exists as *good* taste, a psychological aptitude free from material constraints. To feed the conversation, the most commonplace and inoffensive subjects are the best; they provide an opportunity for wordplay and wit, and no one asks for more. Neither the cares of the outside world nor sustained thought have any place in the banqueting hall. What is at stake in the conversation is serious though: attacks of melancholy must be fended off, and this is precisely why the banter never stops. Over-serious themes are wrapped up in frivolous language and defused by fatuous remarks. The speakers are happy to chat about love, they excel in the casuistry of feelings, but only on condition that they never have to act on their words; they mime passion and feign emotion, merely for effect.

The tongue, which now has a social rather than an alimentary role, thus speaks for the sake of speaking. So great is the preoccupation with style that the dialogue has no content, only form; it does not convey information, but rather offers an opportunity for the accumulation of ingenious turns of phrase. The slighter the content, the higher the manners – although too much affectation would be in bad taste. The speakers, through much wit, paradox and hyperbole, reach a level of artifice where style has a value in itself on account of its grace and subtlety. The conversation is peppered with literary references and quotations from Petrarch, Boccaccio and Bembo, which also contribute to this rarified atmosphere. Guazzo's message is clear: life must be made into a work of art and become so refined that the meal is no more than an abstract and almost imperceptible setting for manners which have acquired all the dignity of an absolute.

The society described in *La civil Conversazione*, organized according to a strict hierarchical and ethical code, thus views the banquet as a collection of rigorously ordered signs. The choice and placing of the guests, the order in which the courses are served, the quantity and presentation of the food and the distribution of the conversation – everything has a meaning and invites interpretation. In these conditions, every variation from the norm is immediately noticed and every deviation from the ritual is seen as significant. A table at which everyone is equal, like at the Last Supper, a frugal table, as during Lent, or a table from which etiquette is absent, like that of the ordinary people, are understood by the literate public in terms of the model they are transgressing. To ignore the system is to be unaware of the relevance of the variations.

In *Macbeth*, for example, the famous banquet at which Banquo's ghost appears (III, iv) only acquires real significance because of the rules it breaks. The banquet has all the appearance of a ceremony in the normal form: Macbeth is giving a feast for his vassals to celebrate his royalty and to show his authority. Everyone knows that to symbolize the pact between master and subject the event must follow the rules of etiquette. ' "You know your own degrees; sit down" ', says Macbeth to his guests, and his wife, later on, says that ' "the sauce to meat is ceremony;/ Meeting were bare without it".' But the host, by his incongruous behaviour, upsets the smooth running of the feast; one of the most forceful aspects of this scene lies in the way in which the principles of conviviality are subverted. Macbeth's conduct becomes progressively more scandalous. Instead of taking his place at the head of the table as befits his status, Macbeth begins by mingling with the guests. Soon after, he forgets them and goes off to one side to talk to the murderer. Finally, and most importantly, he alone sees the bloody ghost of Banquo and, terrified and mad, causes great anxiety in everyone around the table; he describes appalling visions and says absurd things. ' "You have displac'd the mirth, broke the good meeting,/ With most admir'd disorder" ', says Lady Macbeth reproachfully; then, amid confusion, she sends the guests away. Banquo's apparition makes a splendid banquet into an anti-banquet sullied by death and horror. The violence of the scene is intensified by the reference to the ritual of table manners in the society of the time. Perhaps it needed someone with Shakespeare's power to dare to overthrow the rules in such a way.[11]

The pomp of princes

As a system of signs for the cultured classes, the meal does not only provide models of what it is to be well educated and to know how

[11] There is another scandalous meal in *Timon of Athens* (III, vi).

to behave. It also serves political ambition, is a mark of economic power and, in its symbolic language, can help stabilize a social hierarchy, the interdependence of the group or various kinds of contract. The discourse of manners and the discourse of power are not, of course, mutually exclusive. It is well known that manners have long been a means of exercising authority and that displays of politeness, under the *ancien régime*, went hand in hand with successful career progression. There are many documents to prove that during the Renaissance the banquet was a political tool. Stress is laid on affluence and ceremonial, on the role of spectacle and the quality of the arrangements. The aim is to make an impression through the 'pomp and magnificence' and through the 'rules, costumes and ceremonies of the meal, the many courses and the different, disguised foods' (Antoine Du Verdier, *Les diverses Leçons*, ch. 23, p. 218). The prince reinforces his own image and publicizes himself through the splendour of his feasts. I shall examine a few examples here, first from Italian, then from French sources.

A short treatise, *De conviventia*, by the Humanist Giovanni Pontano sets the tone. At first it seems to adopt the edifying clichés of the moralists, proclaiming its disapproval of gluttony and recommending sober and intimate meals to counter the abuses of overeating. Like so many others, it upholds the Latin ideal of *familiaritas*: the pleasure of modest meals and impromptu chatting among friends. It sets this domestic version of conviviality against the sumptuous public feasts, with their overladen tables which are designed to impress, and most of the book is devoted to the organization of these great events. One might expect the latter to be righteously criticized, but, on the contrary, Pontano admits that he is fascinated by them. Above all he recognizes the legitimacy of feasts in the social and political apparatus. Whether it is a family celebrating a birthday, or a ceremonial banquet given for the people by a powerful man, Pontano enjoys describing pomp, magnanimity and luxury. There is nothing like the display of wealth and an opulent menu for gaining the favour of the mob. Pleasure derives from the abundance (*copia*) and the splendour (*splendor*) of the service as performance. The host must open all his drawers:

You have to display everything in the house, cover the coffers and the panels with gold and silver, decorate the dining rooms, scatter flowers on the floor, arrange everything so that, as Horace says, the house itself is laughing. (*De conviventia*, 144r.)

Since the aim is to impress, nothing must be spared. Pontano heaps on the hyperbole: one must celebrate 'sumptuously, abundantly, elegantly and splendidly' (ibid., 143v.). The feasts must not only provide food, it must make a visual impression and satisfy the eye. The wise master will not be content to be generous with the food, but will flatter his guests by the scope of the spectacle: floral decorations, a succession of dishes, trophies, game from the hunt, music and, thanks to sugar, sideboards laden with confectionery. Then Pontano describes in detail some public feasts held in Naples. These were important events in the history of the court and the town. The position the Humanist Pontano finds himself in is interesting: he sets out to promote the quiet joys of moderation and, right up to the end, remains concerned about decency. But he steadily comes round to the political importance of the ceremonial meal and ends up by giving his backing to the grandiose and self-publicizing festivities which are part of the life of a city. In a significant collaboration the erudite man outlines, for the princes, a theory of the banquet as a tool of public life and, for their part, the princes will not fail to request the help of the learned to guarantee the sophistication of their ceremonies.

Now let us examine the work of someone with practical experience of the feast. Cristoforo di Messisbugo worked as *maître d'hôtel*[12] at the court of the Dukes of Este in Ferrara during the first decades of the sixteenth century. He was a gentleman in his own right, related to illustrious families, and, through his skill as chief steward of the pleasures of the table, he earned such esteem that Charles V conferred on him in 1533 the title of Count Palatine. His functions ranged from seeing to the smallest details of the cooking to the organization of the court's most splendid celebrations. Such was his authority that he brought together the fruits of his experience in a textbook (*Banchetti, compositioni di*

---

[12] The word *scalco* denotes either, in the narrow sense, the carver, or, in the wider sense, the steward in charge of catering in a large household.

vivande et apparecchio generale, 1549), written in three parts and destined for others in his profession. The first part deals with the domestic apparatus necessary for holding princely banquets: there is an inventory of indispensable kitchen utensils and household gadgets and lists of jobs to be performed by the staff and of foodstuffs to be preserved. The second part describes fourteen real feasts, chosen to illustrate different types of celebration. The third part contains 315 recipes. The precise nature of the information provided gives the book an especial value.

It is the second part which is of interest here: the list of banquets, some more sumptuous and complex than others, which Messisbugo witnessed, whether he presided over them himself or whether they were given for his masters. For each, the information is systematically provided: the occasion, the guests, the setting (the way the table was laid and the entertainment), the detail of the menu, with the number of dishes served in each course. I shall examine here the first meal he describes, a model of supreme magnificence, but which is characteristic of the trouble taken in the Renaissance over the arrangement of the symposiac ceremony.

The first refinement is that the meal consisted solely of fish and fresh vegetables (with no meat). It was given by Cardinal Hippolyte of Este (who was to build a little later the famous villa at Tivoli) for his brother, Hercules, Duke of Ferrara, his wife, Renée of France, and other lords in their retinue – a total of fifty-four guests. The feast begins in the evening with hoop-la, a performance of a farce[13] and a concert. During all this, a table is put up in the garden covered with

> three tablecloths one on top of the other, with napkins variously placed and folded, in a divine way. This table was marvellously decorated with different flowers and arms, with salt cellars and knives. Above it was beautiful foliage with festoons and various finely crafted trophies. (*Banchetti*, p. 31)

Then bread rolls, titbits and salads are laid out and, among these, figures of Venus, Bacchus and Cupid in sugar: a trinity of pleasure which will later be replaced by other voluptuous statuettes, in

[13] At another feast given by the Dukes of Este and described by Messisbugo, a comedy by Ariosto was performed.

candied sesame and honey paste, of naked Moors with crowns of leaves and 'hiding the parts which are naturally hidden' (p. 38). On one side of the table are sideboards and on the other, in a copse, are the musicians who will play and sing throughout the meal.

At ten o'clock, writes Messisbugo, the guests, duly entertained by the game, the play and the concert, process towards the banqueting table accompanied by dancers and musicians playing the cithara, lute, harp and flute. Each of the courses will be accompanied by different music, by ballets or by impromptu clowning, all of which takes place around the guests and gives the ceremony a playful character somewhere between the erotic and the grotesque.

As for the menu, it is enormous: eighteen courses with eight dishes in each. The cooks' inventiveness has risen to the occasion. So for the first course there is:

- trout patties;

- a hundred halved and spiced hard-boiled eggs;

- sturgeon roe, pike spleens and other fish offal, fried with orange, cinnamon and sugar;

- boiled sturgeon with a garlic sauce, representing His Lordship's motto;

- sixty fried bream;

- cornflour soup;

- pizza with flaky pastry, Catalan style;

- small fried fish from the River Po. (pp. 32–4)

Most of the dishes are served on large platters spaced at intervals along the table, but some are presented on individual plates. The guests eat for seven hours, according to a pattern which is carefully calculated by the steward, with the entertainments providing breaks. Surprise and increasing extravagance are part of the plan. After the ninth course – oysters, oranges and pears – the guests think the meal is over: but the first tablecloth is removed, the table is decorated again and the feast goes on. The same happens before the dessert: fruit, sweets, nougat and ices are arranged on the bottom cloth which appears just as unexpectedly. Finally a silver nacelle is brought on laden with presents for everyone. It is five in the morning. There is one more dance by torchlight and then everyone goes home.

It was not unknown in France to combine pleasure with the display of power. The court of the Dukes of Burgundy was already renowned throughout Europe for its splendid festivities and luxurious banquets. Francis I, besotted with things Italian and sensitive to pomp and good manners, was conscious of the importance of the meal in his political and diplomatic machinations. Nevertheless, it seems that the arrival of Catherine de Medici, bringing the customs of the Italian princes, gave new splendour to the ceremonial meal. Contrary to the view that was held for a long time, the Italian influence affected not so much cooking (which throughout the sixteenth century was still based on medieval recipes) as the staging of meals.[14] The court of the last of the Valois, dominated by Catherine, the widow of Henri II, used and abused festivities such as royal entries with processions and public rejoicing, chivalrous tournaments and parades, ballets and masquerades to try to bolster its waning authority. The dramatic celebration of power, the reinforcement of hierarchy by ceremonial rules and the display of wealth all compensated for or concealed the atmosphere of disorder. At such entertainments, the leaders of rival factions would find themselves at the same table, and, subject to the laws of etiquette, would feign submission to the authority of the crown: this was a precarious conviviality, set against a background of civil war.

In sixteenth-century France, princely festivities (however complex and varied they were) invariably included a banquet or a more modest meal. For the decor (which normally involved allegorical and mythic representations) the services of painters were engaged, tapestries were hung and chandeliers and flaming torches were used. In the banqueting hall, the scent of floral ornaments, fragrant herbs and spices filled the air and helped conceal, as far as possible,

[14] See B. Ketcham Wheaton, *Savouring the Past. The French Kitchen and Table from 1300 to 1789*, and, on feasts, R. Strong, *Splendour at Court: Renaissance Spectacle and Illusion*.

the smell of sweat and smoke. Silver and gold ware and ceramic or other finely worked vessels were there to be looked at as well as used. The dishes were brought in by a procession of valets in special livery reflecting their individual rank. The food itself also appealed more to the eyes than to the palate. The favourite dishes were set pieces: as in the Middle Ages, poultry and pheasants were preferred, as well as swans served whole with their plumage. Tarts, pies, fruit and confectionery were often arranged and shaped to look like emblems, often referring to the escutcheon or the colours of the family being feted or alluding cleverly to contemporary events. The network of coded messages could also extend to the action of the play, the characters in the ballet or to the words of poems or songs which were sometimes composed specially for the occasion.

Various documents – for example the records of the stewards or brotherhoods responsible for organizing festivities or lists in the accounts of particular towns – demonstrate the quantity, diversity and rarity of the ingredients of this kind of celebration. But the money was not spent in vain. Whether such extravagant festivities were given as a spectacle for the ordinary people (for example during royal journeys), or whether they were private but heard of through rumour, they appealed to the popular imagination and contributed to the mythology with which those in power surrounded themselves.

The *Description de l'Isle des Hermaphrodites* by Thomas Artus (1605), a satire on behaviour at the court of Henri III, shows how much importance was attached to the ceremonial of meals in the royal entourage (pp. 60–1, 98–111).[15] Although it may not provide actual evidence, the fact that the pamphlet dwells on the courtiers' extravagant food at least points to the tendency and the legend that grew up around it. But the satire does have the ring of truth because the menus chime with the sophisticated and bizarre atmosphere predominant at court. They obtained the rarest foods – extraordinary fish, unheard of seasonings and snow and ice to keep drinks cold – for show as well as for gastronomic purposes. The cooking was elaborate, using complicated recipes and subtle mixtures which were designed to disguise the ingredients as much as

---

[15] See also the commentary by Wheaton, *Savouring the Past*, pp. 52–6.

possible. This subversion of nature and display of culinary
virtuosity are a recognizable expression of Mannerist culture. Here
again the pleasure lies more in the form than the content, more in
surprise than in flavour, which is also true of the calculated effects
of lavish expense and spectacle. The ways in which the foodstuffs
were transformed and the table decorated had at all costs to be
innovative; likewise pastries, confectionery, preserves and luxurious
table settings. Ornate dishes and gold objects were presented.
Tablecloths were artfully folded, again to look pleasing; huge
numbers of napkins were used and, for the sake of hygiene, were
changed at every course. To criticize the affectation of the
effeminate favourites, Thomas Artus points to something which, at
the end of the sixteenth century, was still a rarity: giving everyone a
knife, spoon and fork, which they even use, he observes ironically,
for artichokes, asparagus and peas. It is an astonishing spectacle:
the diners are so refined that they no longer touch their food with
their hands!

As we know, the court was often a catalyst in the development of
manners and fashions, so much so that when there was no shortage
of food the bourgeoisie also tended to transform meals into
prestigious ceremonies. Under the influence of social emulation,
menus get longer and household equipment gets more complex. In
1555, Pierre Belon, out of nostalgia for the sobriety of times past,
notes in his *L'Histoire de la nature des oyseaux*[16] that the taste for
luxury has spread not only to the food but also to the tableware:

> It is an astonishing fact that the French take so much pleasure in the
> variety of courses that at a simple bourgeois meal you will see two,
> three or four dozen dirty dishes, enough to occupy two men for a
> day in cleaning them. (Ibid., p. 62)

A similar account is provided by Jean Bodin in his *Discours sur les
causes de l'extrême cherté* of 1574.[17] Among the reasons he cites for
the general rise in the cost of living, he emphasizes the amount of
both food and utensils that are made and squandered, for

---

[16] *L'Histoire de la nature des oyseaux, avec leurs descriptions et naïfs portraicts
retirez du naturel.*

[17] *Discours sur les causes de l'extreme cherté qui est aujourd'huy en France, et sur
les moyens d'y remedier.*

today everyone makes it his business to arrange feasts, and a feast is no good unless there is an infinite variety of sophisticated dishes to whet the appetite and stimulate the constitution. (Ibid., pp. 438–9)

At the same time, caterers were becoming more numerous and restaurant owners richer.[18] And in their homes, French people lived equally well. Bodin discovers an increasing wealth 'of gold and silver dishes' (p. 441) in people's homes. Above all, he condemns the lengthening of menus and the elaborate cooking to be found even in everyday meals:

At an ordinary dinner, one is not content to have three ordinary courses, the first of boiled meat, the second of roast meat and the third fruit; moreover, each course has to be done in five or six different ways, with many sauces or chopped meats, or in pastry, with all sorts of minced meats and other motley arrangements, which is highly wasteful; whereas if the old frugality was still in place, and one just had at a feast five or six sorts of food, one course of each kind, cooked in natural juices without the addition of all these new delicacies, there would not be such a waste and food would be cheaper. (Ibid., p. 438)

As we have seen, princes covered up political crises by splendid and elaborate feasts. In a similar desire to compensate for hardship, it seems that the less privileged classes alleviated the suffering of the civil war and chronic fear of food shortages by having extravagant meals.

Officers of the mouth

It was not only the diners who were affected by the increasing complication of the convivial occasion and the ritualization of

[18] This is corroborated by the Venetian ambassador in Paris, Jérôme Lippomano, in 1577: 'The French spend money more readily on food and on what they call eating well than on anything else. That is why there are so many butchers, meat wholesalers, grill owners, food merchants, pastry cooks, restaurant and inn owners that it is truly confusing' (quoted by J.-F. Revel, *Un Festin en paroles. Histoire littéraire de la sensibilité gastronomique de l'Antiquité à nos jours*, p. 151).

meals. The whole activity in the wings was also involved. The range of manners concerning food and the tendency towards codification extended into every part of the system, from production to consumption. The cooking, the service and everything else involved in the ceremony became so specialized as to be technically astounding. The effect of the princes' investment, which soon, as we have seen, passed on to the rich middle classes, served to diversify and professionalize the various functions associated with feasts. Cooks, now more than ever, deserve to be called artists;[19] in the next chapter, we will see the care and skill they bring to the construction of menus according to rules of healthy eating. But the concern for method involves other areas, both human and material: the technicians and their tools.

This tendency is most marked in Italy, and is revealed in two types of textbook, both of which attest to the extraordinary care taken over the organization of meals. The first kind are general surveys, which list all that you must know and have, from A to Z, for a feast to be successful. The second kind are works which specialize in a particular aspect of the banquet programme – the wines, the management of the kitchen, how to carve meat and so on.[20] Such treatises again show the involvement of the wealthy classes, presupposing as they do considerable household expenditure.

The general works are usually written by a *scalco*, a chief steward or major-domo like Messisbugo, whose instructions are written for professionals – and there must have been many of these in order to justify the printing of such impressive books. One by Bartolomeo Scappi (*Opera*, 1570) contains 900 pages and is a veritable encyclopaedia of cookery and serving, crammed full of details, from the right way to manage staff to special recipes for the convalescent or the sick. Domenico Romoli's logistical work of 1560 (*La singolare Dottrina dell'ufficio dello scalco*) is no less elaborate: this gentleman, familiar with life at court and passionately keen on literature, wrote 800 pages on the running of the alimentary sector in a great house. I can only list the main points here from his table of contents. On the one hand there is the

---

[19] On the metaphor of the cook as artist, see chapter 6, Greedy grammarians.
[20] On this whole question, see E. Faccioli, *Arte della cucina. Libri de ricette, testi sopra lo scalco, il trinciante e i vini, dal 14 al 19 secolo*, and L. Firpo, *Gastronomia del Rinascimento*, which both quote extensively from such works.

hierarchy of the staff and the relationships within the house, from the lord, through the *scalco* – the kingpin of the workforce – to the lowest valet; the different tasks are reviewed and shared between kitchen staff, the buyer, the 'yeoman for the mouth', the wine waiter, the bread man, the carver, the waiters, and so on. On the other hand are all the details about the food itself: a list of recipes, advice on choosing and storing food, lessons in natural history, and above all rules of diet: the effects of a particular food on health, the quantity of food desirable, physical exercises, etc. It is all documented, classified and backed up by learned quotations. It is an enormous work which doubtless raises the study of food to the status of a serious science, gives discipline to the activity of eating and protects it from complicity with natural instincts.

The project is even clearer in a treatise of the second kind, which is remarkable because of its degree of specialization. *Il Trinciante* by Vincenzo Cervio (1581)[21] is a technical composition and a plea by a carver in defence of the fine points of his profession. The carving of meat is perhaps only a detail in the symposiac spectacle, but it is elevated here, on account of the competence and skill needed, to a great art. For it is one thing crudely to hack up a chicken to satisfy one's hunger, but quite another to carve it elegantly and precisely so as to present each guest with a fine, aesthetically pleasing piece. The author grudgingly consents to share his status with two other officers of equal importance, the *scalco* and the wine waiter.

All foods which can be cut up in public are duly dissected in the book, even eggs, melons and artichokes. For in this field nothing is left to chance. The value and the interest of the carver's work lie in its difficulty. Although the author, in order to be exhaustive, devotes a chapter to pies and tarts, he dismisses them scornfully as child's play. It is meat, poultry and fish which interest him and he expounds on these in one section after another.

A carver's first concern, Cervio explains, is his instruments. He describes the shape, proportions and measurements of different knives and forks, how to hold them, their precise use and the right movements to make with them. Just as, he says, if you want to ride

---

[21] There are key extracts from this in Faccioli, *Arte della cucina*, and Firpo, *Gastronomia del Rinascimento*.

a horse, you must patiently get to know all the secrets of horse-riding,

> in the same way, whoever wants to learn to carve must first know how forks and knives are made, how they are tempered, how to clean them, how to sharpen them, how to hold them, how to use them, what position to take with your body when you use them, and many other things. (Quoted in Faccioli, *Arte della cucina*, vol. II, p. 70)

Like the knight, the carver must have perfect control over his bearing and movements, so that a deliberately planned stroke gradually takes on the ease and elegance of a reflex action. For the aim, as in art, is to overcome naturally the greatest difficulties. The exercise is in fact rather like acrobatics: the carver holds the meat in the air with only the fork holding it up, and he takes pride in the fact that he does not accidentally drop it or let it drip. He carefully skewers the food, sticking his fork in at the centre of gravity, then proceeds to carve using meticulously calculated strokes. But one must keep this in proportion: if a piece appears too crumbly, too moist or too heavy, variations are allowed.

Such precise control of gesture and posture and such demanding physical training are only paralleled at the time in treatises on fencing and riding. The fact that the art of carving food bears comparison with knightly activities says much about the respectability it commands. To appreciate the meticulous movements and the serious intention behind the work, it will suffice to quote one of the shortest chapters here – the one about the quail:

> To carve it, you take the small fork and the small knife, you stick the end of the knife under the neck and you turn the bird so that the breast faces downwards; you skewer it in the back with the fork, lift it up gracefully and, turning the feet down, you make two cuts in the right leg, then turning the feet up, make two cuts in the left leg, then turn the feet down again. Next you place the quail with its breast facing you and make two cuts where the wings join; then, inserting the knife, you cut across the breastbone. If you put the point of the knife under the neck, you can lift the quail off the fork. Thus dismembered, but not distributed, you arrange it on the dish which will be at hand and, having added the required quantity of salt, you gracefully present it to your lord, or, as I have frequently said, you have it taken to him. (Ibid., p. 85)

'You gracefully present it to your lord' – this says it all. The quality of the display and the precision of the operation are intended for the master of the house, the holder of power, and they contribute to the glory of his court. Moreover the carver arranges to be constantly in his lord's field of vision, and he offers his art up to him. Grace is a leitmotiv in Cervio's work. The master craftsman has such a perfect grasp of his profession that effort and planning are carefully hidden and do not mar the pure beauty of the spectacle. The height of affectation appears natural. The carver is agile and graceful like a dancer, he defies gravity and is in control of every movement: he gives back to the bird he is dismembering a featherlight touch.

The carving scene is only a short moment in the ceremony, but its appeal is obvious. Concentrating on this is like stopping half-way through the alimentary sequence, after the phase of production in the kitchen and before the phase of ingestion at table, at a point where art triumphs unreservedly over nature. Here the food is divorced from any gastronomic intentions: it serves as an illustration of technical dexterity and of a science which is both anatomical and botanical; it offers above all a refined pleasure, where good taste entirely replaces the sense of taste. The stomach and the mouth are temporarily out of the picture; everything here happens between the head, the eyes and the hands. In his book, Cervio often uses the verb *ragionare* to situate his craft firmly in the realm of reason and to confirm the role of calculation and will. The celebration of manual dexterity also scotches any over-indulgence of the instincts. The hand is the agent of the handiwork, it fashions raw materials and gives objects a beautiful shape. Through the hand and the handiwork, the head establishes its control over matter. Once the project becomes exclusive and specialized, as in Cervio, once the style becomes an end in itself, this is Mannerism, simply displaced from the *savoir-vivre* of the diners to the *savoir-faire* of the officers of the mouth.

Whatever their role, all the actors in this great play must obey a ritual in which every gesture and every phase is predetermined. Subject to the laws of civility, the banquet seems like a great machine which sublimates natural desires and produces pleasure at one remove – the pleasure of parade and protocol, the joy of the festival disciplined by the mind, the satisfaction of orchestrating a ceremony which is so strict that it neutralizes the vulgarity of the senses.

3

Rules for the appetite

The two tendencies in the Humanist code of the table – manners and ceremonial – were already present in the classical theory of conviviality. This chapter attempts to reconstruct the dialogue that the Renaissance conducted with its Greek and Roman models both about the customs described in the previous chapter and about another recurrent aspect of rules governing meals – dietary principles, and the control of diet for health purposes. Such an analysis is indispensable here, since the attraction exercised by antiquity affected even modes of behaviour at table and menus. The Humanists' symposiac vision and, by extension, their organization of eating rituals are imbued with archaeological reverie and shot through with philological science. There is a whole network of interreferences, but I shall limit myself to a few significant relationships between classical and Humanist literature.[1]

An archaeology of the table

From the beginning of Greek history, the meal played a major symbolic role in society. In the houses of Homer's princes, the banqueting table is the centre of communal life: a place to meet and welcome others, a place where warriors make alliances. A little later, the Athenian *symposion* became an important nexus of pleasure to which Dionysos, the Muses, wine, dance, music and

---

[1] See also chapter 6, Greedy grammarians.

poetry all contributed their charms. The banquet had many functions – political, social or cultural, and often all three at the same time – but it was always the end product of a high degree of organization. For the Greeks, the table was a place where enjoyment and the law overlapped, where sensuality and constraint acted as mutual correctives.[2] For evidence of this ambivalence, which is part and parcel of the theme of conviviality throughout its whole history (and is marked in the Renaissance, as we have seen, by the themes of festivity and civility), I shall turn first to that great authority of the Humanists, Plato.[3]

The first two books of the *Laws* deal with the good use that is to be made of the banquet (*symposion*) in the education of the citizen. An Athenian is in conversation with a Spartan. Through fear of sensuality and intoxication, Sparta rigorously forbids banquets. Military virtues are incompatible with pleasure: any compromise with excessive celebration threatens the life of the city. The Athenian, who is against such austerity, takes a more subtle position. A rounded education is not only a matter of acquiring military values. To ban games and to prohibit the joys of the table is arbitrarily to condemn an aspect of life which Athens is not prepared to sacrifice. The well-informed legislator, instead of ignoring pleasure, will rather try to accommodate it and will teach the citizenry how to devote themselves to it without submitting to it. Wisdom does not consist in shying away from enjoyment, but in getting used to it in order to control it. The banquet is good, and educationally useful, because it exposes the drinker to the dangers of drunkenness and teaches him to resist them. The control of pleasure is part of the practice of pleasure and temperance is the result of disciplined intemperance.

For one must not, says Plato, simply give pleasure full rein. It is necessary for a sober and wise head to be in charge of the banquet, to determine the quantity, mixture and regularity of the drinks served and to let the guests drift along under control – so that they flirt with, but do not succumb to, intoxication. This is the civilized 'Dionysism' of the Athenians: it allows for passion and acknowledges the spontaneous explosion of appetite, on condition that it can

---

[2] See F. Dupont, *Le Plaisir et la loi. Du 'Banquet' de Platon au 'Satiricon'*.
[3] On Plato's *Symposium*, see chapter 6, Philosophy at meal time.

contain them through moderation and harmony. At the banquet one experiences what is forbidden, but under the control of reason. We shall see that discourse at meals, and particularly philosophical discourse, is credited with the same regulatory role as the head of the banquet; it is part of the merry atmosphere, while also being proof of mental alertness.

So the Athenian contrasts a recognition of the ambiguity of the feast with the narrow morality which unilaterally rejects it as evil. The feast is neutral: it is only good or bad as a function of how it is used:

> If a State shall make use of the institution now mentioned [the controlled banquet] in a lawful and orderly manner, regarding it in a serious light and practising it with temperance . . . [such pleasures] must all be made use of in the manner described. But if, on the other hand, this institution is regarded in the light of play, and if anyone that likes is to be allowed to drink whenever he likes and with any companions he likes, and that in conjunction with all sorts of other institutions, – then I would refuse to vote for allowing such a State or such an individual ever to indulge in drink. (Plato, *Laws*, 673e–674a)

The intervention of the legislator suffices to turn evil into good. Pleasure and rules, moderation and immoderation: these are the paradoxes around which a dialectic is structured which determines the scope of the banquet:

> As to wine, the account given by other people apparently is that it was bestowed on us men as a punishment, to make us mad; but our own account, on the contrary, declares that it is a medicine [*pharmakon*] given for the purpose of securing modesty of soul and health and strength of the body. (Ibid., 672d)

So the banquet is a *pharmakon*, a term which Plato uses frequently: both poison and remedy, alternatively malevolent and benevolent, capable of making the drinker succumb to his instincts or, conversely, of inculcating self-control. Platonic homeopathy exposes the subject to two experiments which are opposite yet interdependent. Man at table is on the boundary between two extremes, error and the correction of error, delirium and reason, which are interlinked and can always turn into their opposite.[4]

Plato immediately elevates symposiac theory to the highest level. For the oscillation between one pole and the other allows the banquet to achieve a synthesis of opposite values: this is the ideal of totality discussed in the first chapter. To regiment the pleasures of the table is to work towards a greater sensuality. In the legislator's methodology, education aims to promote a freedom in which passion has no place; it protects the drinker from the bestiality of drunkenness and keeps him within a sphere where lucidity and pleasure enhance one another. The degrading domination of the wine which numbs the faculties is contrasted with the exaltation of the wine which loosens the tongue and stimulates the intellect. The pleasure of fine fare is therefore heightened by the refinements of culture, agile thought processes and the company of others. The Athenian elite seems to have actually achieved this totality in their *symposia* – after-dinner conversations and entertainments in a Dionysian atmosphere of gaiety which frees the spirit without weighing it down. The first lyrical poets (Alcaeus, Sappho, and later Anacreon) all meant their verses – which were often drinking songs – to be for after-dinner recreation, and even Plato's *Symposium* is proof of the affinity between Dionysian inspiration and philosophical sophistication. Because they know how to drink, Socrates' companions attain the most complete pleasure, the height of gaiety and eloquence, of sensual excitement and perceptiveness.

Throughout the literary history of the banquet, Plato's archetype will inevitably be borne in mind. But the balance of opposites will not be maintained. Pleasure and the norm will be dissociated and usually become antagonistic. In some, the table will stimulate moral precepts, in others, a hedonism hamstrung by its own excesses. The two great theorists of conviviality in late antiquity, Plutarch and Athenaeus, who were widely read in the Renaissance, illustrate this disjunction very well.

Plutarch's *Table Talk (Symposiaka)* and *The Dinner of the Seven Wise Men*[5] contain the most extensive documentation in antiquity

---

[4] On writing as *pharmakon* in *Phaedrus* and the notion of *pharmakon* in general in Plato, see Derrida, 'La Pharmacie de Platon'.

[5] On these texts, see also chapter 6, Greedy grammarians. Macrobius takes up in the *Saturnalia* some of Plutarch's precepts.

of table manners and their codification. But for Plutarch the description of convivial habits is not an end in itself; his aim is normative and tends to abstract the banquet from the sphere of eating and to purge it of Dionysian festivities in order to align it completely with the noblest joys of the intellect. The mind and the body are separated and hierarchized; primitive unity is shattered and symposiac activity is ordered according to the dualism which Plato had transcended.

In both of Plutarch's dialogues, people are sitting at table and talk, among other things, about good conduct at meals. The situation itself is significant: the convivial decor, the menu, the entertainment and the enjoyment are scarcely hinted at and more often skirted around, as if to banish the evils of sensuous pleasure. They do not really provide a setting; at one remove, they serve rather as objects of conversation. The guests at Plutarch's banquet derive no pleasure from eating, drinking or playing, but rather from chatting about serious things and especially from ordering the ceremony of eating and preventing abuses. They are wise people, removed from material impulses and opposed to luxury, who work to ensure that the banquet follows the principles of morality and *savoir-vivre*. They use reason to counter the excesses of the appetite; the military metaphor and the demand for order are explicit – it is

> the same man's duty to organize infantry divisions to be as terrifying and dinner-parties to be as agreeable as possible, for . . . both were the result of good organization. (*Table Talk*, vol. VIII, p. 27)

According to Plutarch, the banquet is a complex system which does require a strategy; its interest lies in logistics and ethics, and there must be no compromise with hedonistic tendencies. Not that the aspects of play and gaiety – inherent in the nature of the banquet – are repressed, but they are integrated into a normative perspective. The ceremony is not there to provide enjoyment for the eyes, taste or stomach: its pleasure lies in the rules it proposes.

To speak of meals, in *Table Talk*, is therefore necessarily to debate problems of etiquette. Plutarch's compilation is a list of ethical prescriptions and practical advice. The titles of some of the topics dealt with give an idea of the tone: 'Whether philosophy is a fitting topic for conversation at a drinking party' (I, 1) (yes, on condition that the conversation stays simple and is accessible to everyone); 'What sort of man the symposiarch should be' (I, 4) (someone who can gauge the quantity of wine needed, who can ensure that people get on well together, can vary the entertainments, etc.); 'Whether people of old did better with portions served to each, or people of today, who dine from a common supply' (II, 10) (the pros and cons of serving everyone together); 'Whether flower-garlands should be used at drinking-parties' (III, 1) (what is permissible and what is not concerning dress); 'What kinds of entertainment are most appropriate at dinner' (VII, 8) (a catalogue of forbidden entertainments such as improper dances and comedies, mime, farce, etc.; and approved entertainments such as country dancing, New Comedy, cithara or flute music, songs, etc.: on condition that no one forgets that 'philosophic discourse' (ibid., vol. IX, p. 89) should play the main role). It is true that the opinions expressed often vary and that some questions are left open, but only in limited areas. The rules of sobriety, moderation and affability, the defence of reasonable discourse against the voice of natural desires and the critique of hedonism are all constants. The banquet has become the privileged locus for the display of education and sublimation; it functions as a sign of moral qualities.

Apart from the authority of Plutarch himself, his use of quotation and the numerous regulatory precepts which he attributes to famous Greek authorities ensured the popularity of his convivial code. The Renaissance made extensive use of his *Moralia* in general and his *Table Talk* in particular,[6] and there is little doubt that the aim of policing the meal found a theoretical justification as well as a series of practical lessons in his work.

If Plutarch consolidates the normative side of conviviality, Athenaeus, who was equally familiar to the Humanists,[7] takes an interest in the ceremony and gives his backing to the hyperbolic representation of fantastic feasts. His *Deipnosophists*[8] is an immense encyclopaedia of the ins and outs of the question of food in the classical world. It is a collection of quotations from authors and from literary and ethnographical documents about cooking,

---

[6] See chapter 6 notes 30, 31 and 32.
[7] See chapter 6, notes 30, 31 and 33.
[8] On Athenaeus, see chapter 6, Greedy grammarians.

ingredients and techniques and about symposiac practice. But the aim is not didactic. Athenaeus is an archaeologist and a philologist, motivated by an insatiable curiosity about table manners and the texts that discuss them. He compiles an enormous anthology, quoting from 1500 works which are now lost and from 800 texts: he provides evidence not only of his own prowess but also of the vogue for food as a literary theme and a subject of study among Greek and Latin writers. All the available material on banquets from all historical and geographical settings seems to be gathered and roughly classified here, from Homer to the Roman Emperors, from the Gauls to the Indians. All kinds of food are reviewed, themselves as varied as the settings, the occasions, the national customs and the local resources which produce them.

In the fragments he quotes, Athenaeus pays enormous attention to detail. Whether because of a passion for documentary knowledge or for anthropology, he dwells on the most minute table objects, utensils, and decoration as well as on behaviour throughout the meal. Just as Plutarch, contemptuous of material things, was interested in manners and stressed the superiority of the word, so Athenaeus draws attention to the real world. He overlooks nothing on the concrete side of the banquet, from the ingredients of dishes to the history of the tableware, from costumes to music. He not only describes the rarest foods and lingers over how to serve them, he also scrutinizes the surroundings and the accessories: the dining room, lay-out of the tables and other furniture; the order of the dishes and the pace of the feast; the role of games; the number and rank of the guests, etc.

But he does not only satisfy a demand for information, he also provides food for the imagination. In Athenaeus the learned man's curiosity and the voyeur's fascination go hand in hand and, from time to time, gastronomy takes on fantastic proportions. Free from all kinds of inhibition, *The Deipnosophists* gives pride of place to extraordinary meals and stunning spectacles. Books IV and XII in particular abound with anecdotes about extravagant festivities which, whether historically accurate or legendary, vie with each other in splendour. The cooking, with its enormous menus, bizarre and rare dishes and strange exotic recipes itself whets the appetite. But in addition there are all the trappings of luxury and pomp: great spectacular machines, the display of jewels and rich clothing, and the distribution of gifts. Athenaeus records with delight the most desirable things that money and imagination can invent in the service of the stomach. *The Deipnosophists* is as much a monument for the defence and illustration of pleasure as a mere collection of documents. Not that his aim is philosophical; he relates, he describes, and the picturesque nature of his tales and their preposterous and licentious force provide their own justification.

He is not short of examples. A Persian despot serves whole, every day, a thousand dead animals – camels, oxen, donkeys, horses and ostriches (*Deipnosophists*, IV, 143a, 145e). Rich Romans add colour to their banquets with a gladiatorial contest including a fight to the death (ibid., IV, 153f–154a), while the Celts fence over the best portions (IV, 154b–c). In Athens, Antony is venerated as Dionysos and, from a stage, offers the crowd the spectacle of a Bacchic orgy (IV, 148b–d). Cleopatra changes crockery, furniture and wall hangings at each meal and gives them to her guests (IV, 147f–148a). A Celtic lord feeds entire peoples by building huge kitchens along the roadside where four hundred servants cook bulls, wild boar and mutton in vast cauldrons (IV, 150d–f).

The feasts of oriental monarchs – Persian, Mede, Lydian, Scythian, Egyptian, etc. – hold a particular fascination for Athenaeus. The enormous expenditure, the vast scale of the palaces and the dishes and the display of jewels and precious metals give them a mythical splendour. But elsewhere, the dining habits of entire populations are retold in wonderment: the Etruscans who, in their extravagant lust, were served by naked slave-girls (XII, 517d); the Sybarites who made horses dance at their banquets (XII, 520c) and who went to drinking sessions with their chamber-pots (XII, 519e), or the Capuans or Sicilian Greeks who were masters of decadent sensuality. Athenaeus's examples get more numerous and excessive. The alimentary excess in his accounts is all the more enticing as it is often spiced with erotic depravity. Here too, hyperbole keeps alive the fantasy: there are public couplings (XII, 517d–f), the effeminate manners of the greedy (XII, 526d–e), homosexuality encouraged by licentiousness at table, aphrodisiac foods and, almost everywhere, meals to which, against all the rules, women are invited and where lascivious female dancers and flute-players are brought to stimulate desire. There are whole volumes full of examples of extremes of pleasure, whether in sensuous intimacy

around Sardanapalus, Alexander the Great or Epicurus, or on the
scale of whole nations dedicated to hedonism. It can well be
imagined that the mass of information gathered by Athenaeus, and
his paradigm of the sumptuous banquet, had all the more impact
because they were accompanied by such mouth-watering material.
There is no doubt that, alongside more edifying models, visions of
antique orgies, whether or not they came from Athenaeus,[9]
exercised the imagination of the Humanists and stimulated their
research into the archaeology of the table.

For in the Renaissance there were learned men available to
compile this material, distribute it and encourage its circulation. In
the intellectuals' vast undertaking of going through the texts and
scrutinizing the classical world, a considerable amount of work was
done on Greek and Roman banquets. Their study is part philology
(understanding matters concerning meals through the proper texts
and through a rigorous examination of specialized vocabulary),[10] part
archaeology (building up a picture of how meals were organized)
and part anthropology (understanding the meaning of the symposiac
institution). Cooking and diet have no place here: they come from
a different area of study.[11] The material and social systems, the
signs of conviviality and their function formed the main interest:
not what, but how people ate; not gastronomy, but spectacle.

The four specific studies I will consider[12] are all similar. They are
written in Latin, and are the work of Humanists more preoccupied
with theoretical knowledge than with its application. They are the
product of astonishing literary erudition, crammed full of quotations
(from, amongst others, Plutarch and Athenaeus) and they are
mostly concerned with classifying the enormous corpus of existing
material on which they are based. In logical sequences of short
chapters, they give a large quantity of information on each of the

---

[9] The *Cena Trimalchionis* sequence in Petronius's *Satyricon* was unknown
before the seventeenth century. Suetonius, on the other hand, provides
memorable examples of imperial banquets.

[10] See chapter 4, Philologists or logophiles?

[11] See below, Diet, and Medicine v. cookery.

[12] Stuckius, *Antiquitatum convivialium*, J. C. Bulengerus, *De conviviis libri
quatuor*, and P. Ciacconius Toletanus, *De triclinio, sive de modo convivandi apud
priscos Romanos et de conviviorum apparatu*, with, as an appendix, a compilation
by Fulvius Ursinus. See also E. Puteanus, *Reliquiae convivii prisci, tum ritus alii*.
There are probably other collections of this kind.

parameters of the classical meal and record variations as a function of time and place. Precise definitions, clear taxonomy and exhaustiveness are constant features.

Let us look, for example, at the largest study in this group, the work by Stuckius of Zurich (1582). It has 838 pages of folio size, divided into ninety-nine chapters, a list of about 550 authors and a subject index with about 2500 entries. Although the author says that the convivial ritual at the heart of social life touches on everything, he keeps strictly to his subject matter: everything one needs to know, from A to Z, about the meals of all the nations of the antique world, to which, as a good Protestant, he adds the Hebrews and the first Christians. Apart from the lexical detail, Stuckius's aim is to put some order into the mass of his source material. His catalogue of symposiac science is divided into three books: the first on different kinds of meals, ordered according to menu, time of day, occasion, type of guests, whether it is public or private, religious or profane; the second on decor, equipment and service; the third on the items on the menu, the drinks, the conversation and the entertainment. Little space is devoted to cooking and physiological matters. The ceremonial procedure, ethical principles and all the cultural and social aspects of the meal dominate. Thus there are three chapters on how to invite people (II, 1–3); four chapters on tables (II, 16–19); four chapters on waiters (II, 20–3); four chapters on the guests' dress (II, 26–9), two chapters on greetings (II, 31–2), etc.

Such an investment on the part of authors, publishers and readers is understandable: the meal seems to be one of the best documented institutions of the classical world and it gives a rare insight into everyday life and times past. Writers try to reconstruct as much as possible what the customs of the people were and how behaviour varied according to social class. Inevitably, though, splendid feasts and subversive extravagance occupy centre stage. However austere the treatise, aesthetics often defies ethics and the attraction of the celebration leads beyond the merely descriptive. It will be recalled that Pontano abandoned his ideal of moderation and was seduced by scenes of pomp and abundance – *splendor, voluptas, copia* and *ornatus*.[13] Petrus Ciacconius, Raphael Maffeius

---

[13] See chapter 2, The pomp of princes.

and Justus Lipsius,[14] who were familiar with the chronicles of late antiquity, readily include tales of lascivious feasts to add colour to the greyness of their compilations. But Plutarch is looking over Athenaeus's shoulder: edifying warnings and calls for moderation follow to tone down excess and to ease the conscience; the introduction of references to the Christian symbolism of food often provides the same corrective. This is confirmation, in the very writing of the learned, of the ambivalence of the banquet with its festive and normative sides.

The archaeologists of the table carry out learned research and do not set themselves utilitarian goals. Their interest is normally confined to antiquity, they work on venerable texts and leave to teachers, stewards and other practitioners the job of elaborating empirical rules. Except for a few fleeting references, their treatises rarely deal with contemporary manners.[15] But the fact remains that there was an educated public who read their works, and all this knowledge, however bookish and historical, was available to readers to supplement their image of conviviality and its practice.[16] In Humanism, highbrow research and the ordering of everyday life were not separated; philology served a praxis. Whether in order to refine their own table manners (in the tradition of Plutarch),[17] or to give their meals something of the lustre of the banquets of antiquity (following Athenaeus), Renaissance men found in the works of classical compilers and their contemporary counterparts a theoretical framework, a sense of authority and a mass of examples which show through into their own books and influence their conduct.

[14] For Maffeius, see *Commentariorum urbanorum octo et triginta libri*, book XXXII, *De modestia*; Lipsius, *Antiquarum lectionum commentarius*. On the convivial manners of the Ancients, see also Ludovicus Caelius Rhodiginus, *Lectionum antiquarum libri triginta*, especially books XXVII and XXVIII.

[15] See however the comparative study by Ianus Cornarius, *De conviviorum veterum Graecorum et hoc tempore Germanorum ritibus, moribus ac sermonibus*, in which a short introductory treatise on ancient and modern banquets is followed by the Latin translation by the same author of Plato's and Xenophon's *Symposia*.

[16] An example of this kind of osmosis can be found in Bouchet's introductory *Discours* to *Les Sérées*.

[17] Many moralists set out rules of conviviality based on the classical examples. Some distil positive lessons from them (e.g. Ricciardus's entry on *convivium*, which mainly draws on Homer and Athenaeus, in *Commentaria symbolica*). Others quote the excesses of the Ancients as examples to be avoided (e.g. Du Verdier, *Les diverses Leçons*, chapter 23).

Diet

Another discipline, apart from the regulation of manners and ceremonies, contributed in the Renaissance to the normalization of the meal: dietetics. The medical science counters gluttony with the need for a sensible diet: it prescribes rational control over one's eating for those with undisciplined brute appetites. Science comes to the table, controls the menus and works with the moralists in converting the natural into the cultural. Just like the institution of civility, it seeks to control bodily instincts and subject them to a form of social censure. This process too is a matter for intellectuals: it is part of the Hippocratic tradition and really affects only the speech and food of the educated elite. The fact still remains that the concern for balance in what one ate was an important element in the convivial theme in the sixteenth century and (although it is not possible to go into the details of classical dietetics here) it requires some examination.

Medical science which lacks the biochemical means to cure ills relies largely on the appropriate use of food. Since Pythagoras and Hippocrates, food and drink have been part of personal hygiene, which was itself an important element of medical science. A whole range of remedies was based on the choice of foodstuffs and the proportion of these in each dish. For the composition and quantity of food were held to affect all of a person's functions, the bodily ones, of course, but also, in a system where physiology and psychology were seen as interdependent, the mental ones. Two fundamental doctrines, the system of humours and that of the spirits, account for the role of nutrition in health and the cure of diseases. The relevance of the categorization of humours and spirits, and their influence on the organization of meals, can be seen in scientific literature (as we shall see in the next section) and in fiction. They even crop up where they are least expected: in the middle of Rabelaisian frolics.[18] Amongst other principles,

---

[18] As a medical student in Montpellier, and then a practitioner, Rabelais was well aware of the theories of Hippocrates and Galen. In 1532, he published *Hippocratis et Galeni libri aliquot* and edited the *Epistolae medicinales* by the Italian doctor, Manardi.

Gargantua's education includes those of dietetics. Picking them out in the book will help to explain their mechanisms.[19]

In his relationship with food, the young Gargantua goes through three very different phases. As we may recall,[20] he is born during a lavish feast and, always hungry and thirsty, he initially sees the world as an inexhaustible source of pleasure; neither over-abundance, the liberation of the senses nor the development of organic life restrain the child's appetite. The second phase opens with the intervention of old-fashioned tutors. The way of life has not changed – the stomach still rules and Gargantua still develops organically – but this is now negatively marked. Suffering from the effects of poor hygiene, the young man stagnates; gluttony, until now joyous and legitimate, becomes reprehensible. Finally Ponocrates, the good tutor, arrives and Gargantua's menu changes from repletion to frugality; the stomach, subjected to a reasonable diet, no longer lays down the law; instincts are controlled, the body is trained, but the joys of eating are rediscovered: our hero can once again eat with a clear conscience.

There are many ways in which these modulations and the progressive distancing from primitive carousing can be understood; one of these involves the theory of dietetics.

From his earliest days to when he receives his first tuition, Gargantua's bulimia takes on alternately two contrasting values. Why? Gargantua as a baby can succumb to libidinous tendencies without punishment or scruple: but this must change once he starts receiving an education and is on the way to becoming a healthy, reasonable man. It is normal for the development of natural impulses to give way to the disciplining of the body and brute instinct. But Gargantua continues to give in to his appetites and obey his stomach and, full of food, he lets his mind lie idle. Eating anything at any time, undisciplined drinking, ignoring the pattern of meals followed by exercise: this is unhealthy, and typical of the incompetence of 'his Tutors, the Sophists' (*Gargantua*, p. 81), ignorant as they are of high literature. According to Ponocrates the Humanist, it is a 'bad habit' (ibid., p. 86 – 'mauvaise diète') that

[19] See also R. Antonioli, *Rabelais et la médecine*, and M. Jeanneret, 'Alimentation, digestion, réflexion dans Rabelais', and '*Gargantua* 4–24: l'uniforme et le discontinu'.

[20] See chapter 1, The al fresco meal.

medical orthodoxy will have to correct. An educated man should know how to order his eating according to the laws of natural philosophy. Therefore Gargantua – a symbol in this respect of the Renaissance man – learns to moderate his tendencies, now seen as morbid, in the light of classical medicine.

This is one of the thrusts of Ponocrates's teaching (chs. 23–4). The first theory to which he refers (by implication) is that of the spirits (*spiritus*).[21] Spirits, which are volatile, vaporous and mobile, free from the constraints of matter although not totally immaterial, are corpuscles which circulate throughout the body (even reaching the brain) and which affect many vital functions. The filtering and distillation during digestion passes food products into the blood-stream, and it is from the blood that, after successive refinements, the different spirits emanate. Galen distinguished three sorts of spirits, of varying degrees of subtlety: natural spirits, produced in the liver, are relatively heavy and crude and spread throughout the body to nourish it; vital spirits, which are lighter and send vital warmth from the heart to the limbs via the arteries; and animal spirits, extremely refined and fluid, which come from the brain and give movement to the limbs and turn impulses from the brain into actions through the nervous system (*De alimentorum facultatibus libri III*).

The dietary recommendations of Ponocrates follow from this theory. Since it is necessary to eat to renew the spirits as a whole, one must avoid the rigours of fasting: meals have a clearly defined place in Gargantua's day. Conversely, the level of intellectual work required demands that food should not be taken in excess, for an over-full stomach could inhibit thought processes. Immoderate eating vitiates the refinement of the spirits, for example, so that those which reach the brain are thick and heavy and so fulfil their functions badly. Too large a meal also threatens to unbalance the distribution of the spirits, which have a huge role to play in digestion: if the body is concentrating all its energies on digesting the contents of the stomach, no energy is available for thought. Ponocrates is well aware of this and not only reduces Gargantua's menus, but also suggests that he do some relaxing work after dinner which does not require too much mental effort:

[21] On this theory, see for example, Ficino, *De triplici vita* and J. Huarte, *L'Examen des esprits pour les sciences*.

And while they waited for his meal to be prepared and digested they
made a thousand pretty instruments and geometrical figures . . .
After this they amused themselves by singing music . . . his digestion
being complete, he got rid of his natural excrements, and then
returned to his principal study. (*Gargantua*, pp. 88–9)

For the same reason, there is a marked difference between his two
daily meals:

And notice here that Gargantua's dinner was sober and frugal, for he
only ate enough to stay the gnawings of his stomach. But his supper
was copious and large, for then he took all that he needed to stay and
nourish himself. This is the proper regimen prescribed by the art of
good, sound medicine. (Ibid., p. 91)

Eating too much at lunchtime would compromise the afternoon's
work: the evening meal, however, can be more abundant, since the
spirits can concentrate entirely on digestion at night when they
have no other function.

The other parameter that determines Gargantua's new diet is the
Hippocratic theory of humours, formalized by Galen and still
adhered to in the sixteenth century. On rainy days,

they ate more soberly than on other days, of more desiccative and
extenuating dishes, as a method of correcting the humid inclemency
of the air, communicated to the body by necessary proximity, and so
that they might receive no harm from not having taken their usual
exercise. (Ibid., p. 93)

The principle of counterbalancing the humidity of the climate with
the dryness of one's food comes from the science of the humours.
This assimilates the health of mind and body to the maintaining of
a constant balance in the organism between the four elementary
qualities of heat, cold, dryness and dampness. The harmonious
mixture of these is seen in the composition of the four fundamental
liquids: phlegm (cold and damp), blood (hot and damp), bile (hot
and dry) and black bile (cold and dry). The correct balance of these
ensures the regularity of physiological and psychological functions,
but can be threatened by various things. Internal causes, such as
the age of the patient, his activities or his habits, or external ones,

such as the seasons, the climate or the time of day, give rise to dysfunction in the humoral temperament: it is the diet which must compensate for all these destabilizing and pathogenic factors. Those who know what foods are made up of, i.e. to what extent they are hot, cold, dry or wet, can thus compensate for any excess or shortage which may alter the body's equilibrium.

Now Ponocrates knows that a sedentary life, without physical activity, produces an excess of humidity and phlegm, leading to a shortage of the body heat necessary for vital functions. He is also aware that a damp climate must be counterbalanced by dry food. As a good Humanist, he knows all the properties of food and drink and the effect of physical exercise. He carefully controls the use of these so as to correct dyscrasia or the excess or the shortage of humours, and thus to ensure the best possible functioning of the whole psychosomatic apparatus. He is not only keen to understand the principles of a good diet but also to make his pupil understand them. While they swallow their food, the master and pupil speak of

> the virtues, properties, efficacy, and nature of whatever was served to them at table . . . From this talk Gargantua learned in a very short time all the relevant passages in Pliny, Athenaeus, Dioscorides, Julius Pollux, Galen, Porphyrius, Oppian, Polybius, Heliodorus, Aristotle, Aelian, and others. As they held these conversations they often had the afore-mentioned books brought to table, to make sure of their quotations. (Ibid., p. 88)

This is characteristic: the Humanist likes to know the composition and effect of foods. The joy of eating is accompanied by the joy of learning; the meal provides the opportunity for a practical lesson in natural philosophy.[22] If one is to believe Rabelais, there is no shortage of treatises on eating to use when laying down the law on nutrition. We shall see in fact that such treatises, whether ancient or modern, were proliferating.

---

[22] To talk about food while eating: we shall see below (chapter 4, Convivial speech, and chapter 6, Greedy grammarians) that this is one of the most common tendencies of table talk, which Plutarch calls *Sympotika*.

Medicine v. cookery

No new cookery book seems to have been published in France in the sixteenth century.[23] Various collections of recipes were in circulation in the Middle Ages and, in the Renaissance, these were merely reprinted.[24] Between Taillevent's *Le Viandier de Guillaume Tirel*, the *Ménagier de Paris*[25] or other practical books of the fourteenth and fifteenth centuries, and La Varenne's *Le Cuisinier françois*[26] (which, in 1651, marked a clean break with medieval traditions), there is surprisingly little change in the corpus of recipe books.[27]

There are various reasons for this phenomenon. Culinary practice in the sixteenth century seems to have been very conservative: the gastronomic revolution once attributed to the arrival in France of the Medicis and to Italian influence only happened, at the very most, in some particular areas (for example pastry-making, confectionery and the preparation of luxurious collations). The real evolution in taste is difficult to evaluate, since, by definition, it largely eludes written accounts. Recipes are passed on by word of mouth; those who use them are not intellectuals, and changes are recorded only by chance or some time after they have happened. Herein lies the second cause for the phenomenon: cooks' practice is not widely known; only rarely is it given the privilege of publication.

[23] The situation was different in England, Germany and Italy. On this, see Franklin, *La Vie privée d'autrefois*, Revel, *Un Festin en paroles*, and especially Wheaton, *Savouring the Past*.

[24] See for example, Pierre Pidoux, *La Fleur de toute cuysine, contenant la manière d'habiller toutes viandes tant chair que poisson* (1540), *Le Livre fort excellent de cuysine tres-utille et proffitable contenant en soy la maniere dhabiller toutes viandes. Avec la maniere de servir es Bacquetz et festins* (Anon., 1542) and their various reprints under different titles. The abundance of references in Georges Vicaire's *Bibliographie gastronomique* disguises this stagnation by giving the impression of diversity.

[25] Anon., *Le Ménagier de Paris, traité de morale et d'économie domestique composé vers 1393, par un bourgeois parisien*.

[26] *Le Cuisinier françois enseignant la maniere de bien apprester et assaisonner toutes sortes de viandes grasses et maigres, legumes, patisseries, et autres mets qui se servent tant sur les tables des grands que des particuliers*.

[27] Wheaton however points to a new cookery book, written in French, but published in Liège in 1604: Lancelot de Casteau's *Ouverture de cuisine*.

One can therefore deduce that cultivated people did not take an active interest in culinary art; gastronomy as such was not, for Humanists, something to be studied and it did not deserve to be communicated through science. This too can be explained by various complementary factors.

The moral criticism of greed is not the least important of these. Condemnation of gluttony – one of the seven deadly sins – is present in edifying litanies across the centuries and no doubt contributed to the Humanists' reservations. The Bible's teaching, which was far and away the most respected, goes in this direction. Since the catastrophic 'first banquet . . . at which Adam and Eve ate of the forbidden fruit' (Fioravanti, *Miroir universel des arts et sciences*, I, 10, 'On the art of cookery and its effects'), sobriety is the order of the day; the Old Testament's prescriptions regarding food, frugal meals in the spirit of the Gospels and the Church's decrees on fasting and on the merits of abstinence all associate spirituality with austerity, discredit good food and foster a moralizing tradition to which intellectuals are not immune. Moreover classical literature is not outdone by the Bible. On this point as on many others, Plutarch marshals all sorts of exhortations to temperance and gives them a new currency. In one of his moral dialogues, sixteenth-century readers could find, for example, a savage attack on food attributed to Solon, where vegetarian arguments are used and where there is such an obsession with purity that even the organs of digestion are condemned:

> Would it not, then, be right and fair, my friend, in order to cut out injustice, to cut out also bowels and stomach and liver, which afford us no perception or craving for anything noble, but are like cooking utensils, such as choppers and kettles, and, in another respect, like a baker's outfit, ovens and dough-containers and kneading bowls? (*The Dinner of the Seven Wise Men*, pp. 421–3)[28]

Such mistrust of the stomach, inspired by Plato,[29] makes it necessary to repress base appetite. Food is a sign of the body's fall from grace and is at best a necessary evil; such disapproval is worthy of Anchorites and Cenobites.

[28] See also, elsewhere in the *Moralia*, the treatise *De tuenda sanitate*.
[29] See *Phaedrus*, 64a–67b, and the texts referred to below.

Secular wisdom and Christian ethics overlap here, and this feeds a rich tradition of commonplace wisdom about the stomach's imperiousness, the intellectual atrophy of gluttons and the scandal of banquets. Hunger defies reason, glutton dulls the spirit and leads to temptation, steam from the kitchen clouds the mind, etc.: similar adages and received ideas are present in the works of the most respected authors, such as Petrarch,[30] and Erasmus,[31] as well as in other documents which reflect popular morality most closely.[32] Refined cooking inspires particularly violent criticism: it leads to over-consumption and disease, it adulterates natural produce and epitomizes all the deceit of art which disguises nature. The following charge is representative:

> As for man, all the fruits of the earth . . . do not satisfy him, but to remove everything natural from them, he has to disguise, titivate or complicate them, changing the substantial into the contingent, changing nature into artifice, so that the fancy is tickled by such tempting morsels and the body is more or less forced to take more of them than is necessary: then when the vessel is overloaded and the stomach good and full, the senses are all so disturbed that none of them can function properly. (Boaistuau, *Le Théâtre du monde*, p. 76)[33]

The condemnation of cookery as the art of deceit goes back to Plato. In a famous passage in the *Gorgias*, Socrates attacks rhetoric, which he says is so powerful that it even convinces people of unjust things: it is but a caricature of justice and owes its power to flattery alone. At the physical level, he adds, two legitimate arts can also take on a shameful form: toiletry is the deceitful side of physical

[30] See the chapters 'De conviviis', 'De lauto victu', 'De tenui victu' and 'De gula' in *De remediis utriusque fortunae libri II*.

[31] There are an impressive number in *Adagiorum chiliades quatuor*. See for example the index entries under 'Fames' and 'Intemperantia'.

[32] For example Nicolas de La Chesnaye, *La Nef de santé avec le gouvernail du corps humain et la condannacion des bancquetz à la louenge de la diepte et sobriété* (1507).

[33] See also Du Verdier, *Les diverses Leçons*, chapter 23; Fioravanti, *Miroir universel des arts et sciences*, I, 10, and Puteanus, *Comus, ou Banquet dissolu des Cimmériens, songe où par une infinité de belles feintes . . . les mœurs dépravées de ce siècle . . . sont . . . décrites, reprises et condamnées . . .*

exercise, just as cookery, through its artifice, tries to supplant medicine:

> Cooking assumes the form of medicine, and pretends to know what foods are best for the body; so that if a cook or a doctor had to contend before boys, or before men as foolish as boys, as to which of the two, the doctor or the cook, understands the question of sound and noxious foods, the doctor would starve to death. Flattery, however, is what I call it, and I say that this sort of thing is a disgrace. (Plato, *Gorgias*, 464de)[34]

Cooking is doubly at fault: morally, because it 'cares nothing for what is the best' (ibid., 464d) and only seeks to please, and epistemologically, since (in contrast to medicine) it cannot explain the true nature of things nor establish causality (465a). Like rhetoric, which deceives the mind, like deceitful arts such as dithyrambic and tragic poetry, which seduce by flattery, it abuses the body; it substitutes a routine which has no rational basis for genuine medical science. We shall see later that poets (and orators) celebrate the deceit of cookery and readily adopt it as a metaphor of their own art.[35] Plato had already established the parallel, but in order to accuse dealers in both food and words of the same crime.

The criticism of food in Plato and the neo-Platonic tradition did not only relate to cooking. The spirit/matter dualism provided the general framework for a dichotomy which was largely accepted in the Renaissance between nutrition and reflection, between the stomach and the head. Such basic principles of philosophy also discouraged the Humanists from writing in favour of gastronomy. We only have to look at *The Republic*, where Socrates contrasts the legitimate pleasures of the intellect with vulgar physical satisfaction, to see this. To be in thrall to the demands of the stomach and to be content with food instead of acquiring knowledge is to fail in one's vocation as a man (585a–e):

> With eyes ever bent upon the earth and heads bowed down over their tables they feast like cattle, grazing and copulating, ever greedy

---

[34] See also ibid., 500–1.
[35] See chapter 5, Metaphors of bibliophagy, chapter 6, Satire and its cooking, and chapter 8.

for more of these delights; and in their greed kicking and butting one
another with horns and hooves of iron they slay one another in
sateless avidity, because they are vainly striving to satisfy with things
that are not real the unreal and incontinent part of their souls.
(*Republic*, 586a–b)

Only the mind can grasp what is authentic; gastronomic pleasure,
continues Socrates, is only an illusion, a ghost (*eidôla*). The
physiological section of the *Timaeus* also contrasts the power of
reason (*logoi*) with the false promptings of the stomach (*eidôla kai
phantasmata*) (*Timaeus*, 71a)

In the same passage, Plato says that there are four kinds of soul
in the human body, which are arranged according to a strict
hierarchy. There is the immortal soul in the head, the soul of
passions, between the neck and the diaphragm, the soul of food,
between the diaphragm and the navel and finally, below the navel,
the soul of carnal conjunction. Each faculty has its own separate
site so that there will be no interference between them and so that
the higher souls will not be debased by the lower ones. Above all,
the gods were wise enough to separate the higher soul from the
soul of food, 'housed as far away as possible from the counselling
part, and creating the least possible turmoil and din' (ibid., 70e). To
ensure that intellectual operations are of as high a quality as
possible, the miasma of the intestines is confined to the lower
depths. This anatomical belief was to have enormous repercussions.
In his brief and selective commentary on the *Timaeus*, Ficino does
not omit to comment on and stress this principle (*Appendix
commentariorum, in Timaeum Platonis*, p. 1478). In turn, several
sixteenth-century doctors were to reiterate this dualistic physiology.
One of these is the Spaniard, Juan Huarte:

It is quite impossible to find two such opposite activities . . . which
are so mutually inhibiting as reasoning and the decoction of foods. In
my opinion, this is because the former, which is just pure
contemplation, requires rest and only happens when there is peace and
the animal spirits are clear, whereas decoction is noisy and disorderly
and gives rise to a large quantity of vapours which trouble and cloud
the animal spirits so that the reasonable mind is in no state to see the
shape of things. (*L'Examen des esprits pour les sciences*, pp. 87–8)

The whole of this heavily polarized symbolism, laden with obvious affective and ideological values, goes beyond medical analysis: on the one hand, there is the airy lightness and the pure transparency of animal spirits (whose organic origin seems to have been forgotten), and on the other, the murky and degrading heaviness of visceral operations. This antithesis often provides medical doctrine with its structure and is firmly engraved on people's minds, contributing to the absence of gastronomy in Humanist treatises.

However, dietetics will fill the gap. If cookery is not worthy of scientific literature, the medical study of ingredients and of the relationship between diet and health certainly is. Such studies have the authority of the Ancients and are aimed at regulating food intake and processing pleasure. 'Gastronomy', now of a normative order, reverts to its etymological meaning: a rule for the stomach. Cookery is brought into the field of medicine and discourse on food becomes morally acceptable. The very title of Josse Willich's 200–page Latin treatise on cooking promises a typical rehabilitation of this sort: it is called 'The art of cooking, of food, of the preparation . . . of dishes and drink . . . A book especially useful to doctors, philologists and all those who wish to maintain health' (*Ars magirica*).[36] At the end of the work, an appendix designed to publicize the book enumerates the different specialists concerned with the question of food, using the characteristic order of the accepted hierarchy: first, the man of letters, because of the vocabulary; secondly the naturalist, on account of his study of living things; thirdly the doctor, for dietetics; fourthly the theologian, because of religious rules; and finally the cook, provided he remains subject to the laws of medicine!

Another German intellectual, Alban Thorer (Albanus Torinus), similarly rehabilitates cooking by bringing it under the aegis of medicine. As a medical student in Montpellier, he discovered, he says, a manuscript of Apicius's famous *De re culinaria libri decem*, and has arranged for it to be published.[37] The text is indeed worthy

[36] *Ars magirica, hoc est coquinaria, de cibariis, ferculis, obsoniis, alimentis et potibus diversis parandis, eorumque facultatibus. Liber medicis, philologis, et sanitatis tuendae studiosis omnibus apprime utilis.*

[37] This edition of Apicius, *De re culinaria libri decem* (Basle, 1541) also contains Platina's treatise, *De tuenda valetudine*, and a Latin translation of a treatise by Paulus Aegineta, a Greek doctor of the seventh century, *De facultatibus alimentorum tractatus*. The first edition of Apicius dates back to 1498.

of interest: it is a unique collection of Roman recipes, is relatively accurate and has no medical aim. This composite work has been attributed to a famous chef, who was apt to indulge in the greatest extravagance in order to satisfy his greed, inventing dishes of camel heels, peacock tongues, flamingoes and nightingales, and who was more concerned with sensuality than with health. But Thorer, the learned editor, quite improbably links it with the corpus of medical treatises. His argument is tenuous: whoever, he says, takes pleasure in eating and knows how to mix what is agreeable with what is useful in food, is guaranteed a healthy diet; Apicius's splendid feasts therefore represent a legitimate aspect of dietetics and of the cure of disease. This is a significant kind of appropriation: the Humanist, if he is to be interested in mere recipes, must have the support (however dubious) of medical science.

In the Renaissance, to write about food is therefore to discourse wisely on hygiene and diet. There is a vast bibliography of separate works, chapters of treatises on medicine or natural philosophy, translations or unpublished documents. Some generalizations will have to suffice here to show the main tendencies.[38] The dominant principle in all these works is the theory of the humours: a precise knowledge of the eater's temperament, the physical surroundings and the constitution of the food allows the correct proportions to be determined in each case, so that the balance of the humours is kept constant. The choleric temperament, dominated by heat and dryness, should, especially in summer, be given cold and wet foods, such as fruit, melon and marrow; on the other hand the winter diet, especially for someone who is cold and wet by nature, should favour hot, dry foods, like unwatered wine, roast meats and bread. This is why it is important to establish the exact composition (*natura*) of each food and its influence on the body (*vis, facultas*). These textbooks are organized as a consequence of this rule;[39] they are based on a series of entries which generally

[38] I am referring to general works and excluding specialized studies, for example on vines and wine, on dairy produce, on melons, etc.

[39] See B. Platina, *De honesta voluptate et valetudine*, C. Stephanus, *De nutrimentis libri III*, J. Bruyerinus Campegius, *De re cibaria libri XXII*, J. Willich, *Ars magirica*, A. T. Petronio, *De victu Romanorum*, B. Fiera, *Coena. De herbarum virtutibus, et ea Medica Artis parte, quae in victus ratione consistit*, and H. Eobanus, *Bonae valetudinis conservandae praecepta*.

give, for each food, the following details: a description of the product, probably with some terminological points; advice on storing it; and above all analysis of the effect of the food on health. The preparation of dishes – how to cook them, what goes with what, appropriate seasonings – is of course considered, but only in terms of their hygienic or therapeutic effect, so that criteria of taste take on secondary importance. Observations on climate play an important role – the season, the quality of the air, how dry or damp it is – since, in the Hippocratic tradition, it is universally recognized as forming an essential parameter in the chemistry of the humours.

There is a great similarity between these compilations. Most of the treatises are in Latin (a mark of the learned readership for whom they were destined) and, apart from their medical purpose, they also have a taxonomic and a philological one. They all convey more or less the same information, for the simple reason that they use the same sources. The famous eleventh-century *Regimen sanitatis* of the Salerno School, a frequently copied, imitated and interpreted textbook, continues to provide practical advice.[40] But the Humanists (so they say) have something better in mind than the mere perpetuation of the empirical, magical and moralizing medicine of the Middle Ages.[41] It is of course above all the works of the Ancients that they pass on, with the occasional complementary modern observation. The frequent references to Hippocrates and to Galen and his followers (even including Arab doctors) explain many of the common themes. Plutarch, Athenaeus and the masters of natural philosophy like Aristotle and Pliny the Elder also provide much information. In addition, Latin treatises on agriculture by Cato, Varro and Columella are a source of details on edible plants and animals. For here too, botanical and zoological knowledge, together with the general piling up of information, determines the works.

The great classic among so-called cookery books of the sixteenth century, *De honesta voluptate et valetudine* by Bartolomeo Platina

---

[40] It was printed in Italy from about 1470 and translated into French in about 1500. See Vicaire, *Bibliographie gastronomique*.

[41] Bruyerinus announces in his Dedication to *De re cibaria*: 'Salernitanorum nugae minime hic reperientur' ('You will hardly find here the trifles of the School of Salerno').

(1474), illustrates perfectly this order of priorities. The author was an educated man, librarian at the Vatican and editor of a monumental history of the popes. The book, which was frequently reprinted in Latin and in translation, is a collection of alimentary instructions in the spirit of the times. The intention of the book, at least in the first part, is resolutely dietetic, as the title of the French version makes clear: 'Platina in French . . . on . . . all meats and things which man eats, their virtues and how they are harmful or beneficial to the human body . . . '[42] The practical advice on cooking, when there is any, is decidedly pharmacological in nature, for, as Platina recalls, one must learn how to eat to live, and not live to eat. It is true that from book VI onwards the balance changes: the directives seem more like recipes and the medical advice is left to the end of each entry.

This hesitation is significant. However bookish and normative he may be, Platina does not banish the pleasure of eating; he just wants it to be subject to the rules of science. The title of the volume says it all: the *'honesta voluptas'* in question here is not that which desire inspires in immoderate people, but that which, through reasoned control of menus, brings about a feeling of well-being. Platina's programme is neither repressive nor austere. If he condemns the greedy and the debauched, it is in the name of an ideal of moderation and because health is a precondition of pleasure. As well as being a book on dietetics, *De honesta voluptate* is a moral treatise on the teaching of self-control. Moreover the book ends with a chapter called 'On easing disorders' and does not fail to mention Epicurus: knowing how to apply a rule (*ratio*) to one's passions and appetites and knowing how to moderate the joys of the table are a means of preparing for happiness. In the application of a carefully calculated diet, the body and the mind collaborate and pleasure and reason are in harmony. If Platina chose to write something other than a recipe book, he did so in the name of a higher form of hedonism.

---

[42] *Platine en françoys tresutile et necessaire pour le corps humain qui traicte de honneste volupté et de toutes viandes et choses que l'omme menge, quelles veztus ont, et en quoy nuysent et prouffitent au corps humain, et comment se doyvent apprester...*, Lyons, 1505, reprinted with the same title in 1509, 1528 and 1529. The 1586 edition removes the dietetic dimension from the title. The French translation of Platina was reprinted a dozen times during the sixteenth century. See Vicaire, *Bibliographie gastronomique.*

As I have said, then, the regulation of health through diet and the association of dietetics with not only health but also morality (which are themselves related) are themes to be found in classical literature and were not invented by the Humanists. The innovation of the Renaissance was less to do with practice than with the promotion and the propagation of this principle in learned circles as a subject for study. Dietetics become fashionable, a discipline which henceforth forms part of any decent man's culture. There is copious evidence of this. Erasmus does not disdain a lengthy exposition on his tastes and his conduct at table, any more than he hesitates to give advice on the healthiness of a menu.[43] Montaigne, when he wages war on medical dogmatism, does not think to challenge the principle that food affects health; on the contrary, he shows the interest he has in this – and the contemporary relevance of the question – when he explains in detail how he adapts his meals to his physiological requirements. Moreover, however independent his judgement, he observes closely and commentates scrupulously on the different phases of ingestion, digestion and evacuation:[44] this is typical of the gentleman who monitors his own body as a special 'experimental site' and makes control of his diet part of his everyday activities. Nutrition even becomes a subject for conversation in educated circles; it is acceptable at table to quote one's Platina and to show subtly that one is eating advisedly. Ponocrates discourses with his pupil on the dishes that are served and Francis I, when he summons learned men to share his meal, does so too.[45]

Gargantua comes a long way from the feasts of his childhood to the scientifically measured out meals of his adolescence. The ground covered in the first part of this book has been similarly extensive, ranging from literary works to learned treatises. We have seen on the one hand the exuberance of conviviality and the consumption of natural produce being set above all else, and on the other the moderation of right-thinking people and gluttony on trial. In fiction, we have seen celebrations of abundance and the

---

[43] See Bierlaire, 'Erasme, la table et les manières de table'.

[44] See *Essais*, III, 13 and the *Journal de Voyage*, and J. Starobinski, *Montaigne en mouvement*, chapter 4.

[45] As attested by Bruyerinus in his dedication to Michel de L'Hospital in *De re cibaria*.

PART II

When the fable comes to table

4

Table talk

Convivial speech

At court, and later in the salons, culture became a means to or a sign of power. The Renaissance court tended to prefer spiritual values and superior manners to the military virtues of feudal aristocracy. The ideal of heroic bravura henceforth had to compromise with the demands of politeness and good conduct – a process of domesticating the nobility which culminated, as is well known, in the great game that was Versailles. Here too, the stimulus is supposed to have come from Italy: the European elite, in the sixteenth century, borrowed models of urbanity and the laws of etiquette from the refined manners of the Italian principalities. The principles of civility, made known by Castiglione's famous treatise (*The Book of the Courtier*)[1] and then more widely circulated through many textbooks on *savoir-vivre*, progressively influenced everything, down to the detail of daily life.

In the system of fashionable manners, two aspects which were codified with particular care are relevant here: table manners – which have been discussed above[2] – and rules for good conversation. For the importance of courtesy and elegance demanded that one be a past master at speaking in public. A set of rules was quickly established on the art of adapting one's speech to a variety of subject matter and interlocutors, and on the tone and the formulae

[1] On the fashionableness of this treatise and the tradition it initiated, see Ossola, 'L'Homme accompli'.

[2] See chapters 2 and 3.

that were acceptable. The practice of using fine words became more widespread; formerly the preserve of masters of eloquence, preachers or Latinizing educationalists, it spread to the court and then to the town, and was an important element in the growth of a civil society. The campaign to defend and illustrate French usage was not only aimed at claiming the status of a literary language; it used all the resources of the lexicon and introduced refinements of style into the conversation of all civilized society. Mastering language became necessary as a mark of personal worth. Gentlemen learnt to perfect their speech at the same time as their manners, as Montaigne shows in his typical praise of the 'art of conversation' as the highest form of sociability.[3] In the Renaissance, in an increasing number of circles, social graces consisted of an art of living which was also an art of speaking.

These two kinds of politeness – the good manners of diners and the quality of the conversation – overlap in table talk. It is therefore logical that specialists in conviviality devoted themselves to analysing and controlling the conversation of eating companions. Precepts on table talk slip here and there into treatises on manners and into encyclopaedias on the meal as an institution. From Erasmus to Guazzo, from Stuckius to Bouchet[4] the same principles were repeated, principles which themselves go back to common origins in Cicero, Macrobius and above all in Plutarch. These theoretical statements are all the more effective for being frequently accompanied by practical application: the theory is expounded by the diners who, during descriptions of meals, reflexively lay down the law on the art of *sermones conviviales*.[5]

To put conversation on the menu and to commend it as a necessary spice to a meal is an essential part of the Humanist manifesto. Dialogue takes the pleasure of dining out of the realm of

---

[3] See *Essays*, III, 3 and III, 8. Montaigne was inspired by one of the most important theorists of conversation, Stefano Guazzo (see chapter 2, Manners and Mannerism). See also Pontano, *De sermone*.

[4] Erasmus, *De civilitate* and the *Convivia* (especially *Convivium dispar*) in *Colloquia*; Stuckius, *Antiquitatum convivialium*, III, 17 and 18; Guazzo, *La civil Conversazione*, and Bouchet, *Les Sérées, passim*. See also Rhodiginus, *Lectionum antiquarum*, books XXVI–XXX, *passim* and Puteanus, *Comus*.

[5] This practice is consistent with the genre of *Sympotika* (see chapter 6, Greedy grammarians).

pure sensation and allows reason to have a role. It is a question of the dignity of man:

> If dolts think that it is a great virtue to say nothing at table, pigs and other such beasts would by their lights be equivalent to the most noble people. (Tahureau, *Les Dialogues*, p. 137)

Animals gorge themselves in silence, whereas men must feed both the body and the mind. Words complement cooking; like a well-prepared sauce, they represent the specifically human contribution of a culture capable of keeping the excesses of nature in check. Everyone cries out for this additional refinement: moralists and doctors who condemn gluttony – 'therefore one must feed the soul and spirit more than the stomach' (*Dialogue des festins*, p. 3); followers of Plato, such as Plutarch, who contrast *deipnon* with *symposion*, dinner with after-dinner and physical with intellectual enjoyment, in order to gloss over the former and save the pleasure of discourse for the latter; or monists like Montaigne, who conversely defend the combination of food and words in the name of the unity of man: 'It is not a soul or a body that one is training, but a man' (*Essays*, I, 26; p. 72). Table talk returns to the diner ownership and awareness of his pleasure; it gives form to desire, it functions as a regulating force, and just when the appetite was in danger of taking over, it re-establishes man's unique role as a thinking animal.

The importance of this theme explains why convivial discourse should be carefully ordered and codified within the ceremonial of the meal. First of all, the constraining factors of the group, the desire to put everyone at their ease and to hear all voices in concert, set the tone. Out of consideration for others, two kinds of excess must be avoided: *garrulitas*, the kind of chatter that monopolizes attention, and *taciturnitas*, a laconic tendency which makes the atmosphere cold. During a meal, conversation should erase differences, remove hierarchy and overcome inhibition; conversation will flow freely and everyone will have an equal share in it. Thus topics will be chosen to suit everyone's knowledge and tastes. There will be laughter, but no mockery, there will be jokes, but no provocation. Always striking the right note and remaining 'elegant, urbane and ingenious' (Stuckius, *Antiquitatum convivialium*, p. 379r.) is a subtle art.

Like public speaking, convivial conversation implies a knowledge of psychology and postulates an accurate perception of one's partners. A micro-society is formed around the table in which the speaker can sense the effect of his or her words. A whole system of rhetoric is in operation, but it is one which seeks more to seduce than to persuade; the skill here lies in being able to hide one's ability in order not to be oppressive or intimidating. The good guest is at pains to please and gets on well with people, for nothing enhances the joy of a feast more than friendship and trust: 'the most truly god-like seasoning at the dining-table is the presence of a friend . . . not because of his eating and drinking with us, but because he participates in the give-and-take of conversation' (Plutarch, *Table Talk*, vol. IX, p. 5). Cicero's archetype of *sermones familiares* – an intimate dialogue in a welcoming atmosphere – had a great influence in defining this ideal of plenitude and sociability.

For the sake of pleasure, and so that everyone can participate, one must be wary of serious or difficult questions. Theorists never tire of saying that a gentleman should not try to rival pedants. So that the discussion stays pleasant and accessible to all, practical subjects should be chosen that have a useful application without being tiresome. Not that philosophy should be banished from dining rooms; it can be admitted provided it is watered down and fits in with the general conversation. It does not have a privileged place, but mingles discreetly in the discussion and is careful to remain within the grasp of all the guests. Besides, is it not the height of wisdom to converse with the uninitiated, to adopt a playful air and to accept the challenge of laughter? This idea will be generally recognized as coming from Plato's *Symposium*: Plato did not fear for philosophical discourse in the face of the bold Dionysian challenge:

> As for philosophy, however, in so far as it treats of man, his duties and functions, all sages have agreed that its conversation is too charming for it ever to be denied admission to feasts or to sports. When Plato invited Philosophy to his Banquet, we see how pleasantly she discoursed to the company, in a fashion suitable to the

time and place, although this is one of his loftiest and most salutary
Dialogues. (Montaigne, *Essays*, I, 26; p. 72)

At table, philosophy accepts the company of the anecdote and the
practical joke. It abandons systematic analysis in favour of random
remarks and chat about this and that. 'Miscere sermones', advises
Erasmus (*Convivium dispar*, in *Cinq Banquets*, p. 133): move
freely from one register to another and from one topic to another,
so that everyone can find something of interest. As it is the child of
circumstance, table talk adopts the uncontrolled and disjointed
character of improvisation. *Varietas*, medley and mixture are the
remedies recommended to diners to relieve the boredom of
regimented conversation.

Enjoyment is so important that jokes, banter and witticisms are
all allowed as long as they remain within the bounds of good taste.
To dispel melancholy on the one hand and gravity on the other,
good guests will talk freely of frivolous things, they will make
puns, crack jokes and pose riddles. The perfect guest is an amateur
who can talk about everything and nothing, can be serious and
frivolous in turn and can wrap up profound thoughts in amusing
turns of phrase. It is true that this ideal of easily digestible and
apparently artless speech goes beyond the field of table talk; it
reflects the search for gentlemanliness and the model of wit which
became accepted as norms of elegance even before the seventeenth
century. By affecting lightness and grace, discourse concentrates
on effect; soon it is reduced to a matter of tone, and manner
replaces substance.[6] The social form of convivial style contributes
to the creation of a system of *savoir-vivre* which far surpasses the
organization of symposiac enjoyment.

The role of dialogue is so important in the ceremonial of meals
that treatises go far beyond general recommendations and provide
topics and even ready-made formulae for use in meal-time
conversation; they lay down not only how to speak, but what to
say, what ingredients to add to the discussion; they provide the
code but also the content: they deal not only with the cooking but
also with the victuals. When Macrobius, for example, recommends

---

[6] This evolution is very marked in Guazzo (see chapter 2, Manners and
Mannerism).

the making of jokes at table, he adds a vast collection of witticisms, like a store to draw from to amuse one's companions.[7] When Plutarch, Athenaeus and their imitators expound the ins and outs of the *ars convivatoria*, they also do more than pronounce some simple rules: they also provide material suitable for use in conversation, since talk about meals can always serve as talk at meals, given that it is so natural and common to speak about food when one eats. Table talk is inclined to be reflexive: this is a constant factor, as anyone can verify.

This double function is illustrated in a textbook called *Mensa philosophica*,[8] which was popular at the end of the Middle Ages and was frequently reprinted in the sixteenth century. At one level each of its four books provides advice on how to behave at table. Well supported by erudite quotations – from doctors in antiquity and philosophers from Arabia – the treatise gives a mass of information on diet from both a practical and a scientific point of view: what to eat, how to eat, etc. (ibid., books I and III). But to help the diners adapt their discourse to their interlocutor, the work also provides an interesting typology of characters – a series of stereotyped portraits arranged by social class and designed to anticipate all possible encounters (book II). Finally, it recalls the usefulness of laughter and, following Macrobius's example, quotes a number of jokes which are as suited to aiding the digestion as they are to maintaining good temper (book IV). The shift from one level to the other is perceptible throughout: the *Mensa philosophica* is as much an anthology of table talk as a textbook about good conduct. The best advice on health and the most accurate psychology are worthless without the support of a certain type of discourse, which can be learnt. The smooth talker is cunning and perhaps only pretends to improvise: he may have found his ideas, duly listed and with ready-made and precise accompanying effects, in books like the *Mensa philosophica*. The charm of the *sermones conviviales*, elaborate, premeditated and tested by tradition, is not innocent.

Moreover, the *Mensa philosophica* is firmly part of the rhetorical tradition of *inventio*. It is a compilation of clichés drawn from the

---

[7] See the series of *dicteria* in book II of the *Saturnalia*.
[8] This treatise is attributed to Michael Scott (thirteenth century).

great authors, resembling the many catalogues of quotations, of *exempla* and of memorable thoughts, and it provides a store of motifs to decorate a book, a speech or a conversation. The classifications used to divide up the material, which is arranged by question and answer or organized into methodically arranged chapters – serve as an *aide-mémoire* and confirm that the book has a practical aim: like a list of topics, the book contains a judicious classification of snippets of texts and extracts hallowed by tradition or by the presence of famous names, which are designed to be imitated. Apart from its specific aim (to set out what to say at table), it is therefore a conversation manual that is sufficiently large and varied to be used on other occasions, and takes its place among the anthologies which were widely circulated in schools in the Middle Ages and the Renaissance. It is however significant that this wide-ranging handbook is based on table talk. To help a speaker to enrich and ornament his conversation, the author imagines him discoursing at table. It is as if the convivial scene was a privileged place in which to learn the art of fine speech. The relationship is reciprocal: one learns to speak at table and the table teaches one how to speak. There are many close affinities between the speaking mouth and the eating mouth, between alimentary and linguistic didactics. The rest of this book is devoted to examining precisely this network of relationships between food and words.

A mouth full of words

Up to now I have studied meals and table talk as social institutions and cultural signs. We have seen the ethical perspective or the didactic objective legitimizing pleasure by channelling it in certain ways. So far, the theme of conviviality has had a normative aim; in the name of politeness and elegance, it dictates how to behave and how to speak. Discourse, subordinated to the elaboration of a strictly codified ceremonial, is allowed to participate in the feast provided it stays within the bounds of what is reasonable; it is evidence of undiluted vigilance among the aromas of each dish, and functions as a means of control. But this scale of values is not universal: one only has to move into the realm of the popular festival, the tavern table or Dionysian revels to see that words and actions, no less codified, adopt a variety of styles whose meaning lies in their powers of transgression. Some meals support the social fabric, but others subvert it: some tipsy words enhance the power of dialogue, others break it down.

Like wine and hunger, feasts are ambivalent; wisdom and folly, order and disorder, moderation and excess exist side by side in them. While Thalia the Muse presides at banquets she makes sure they are harmonious;[9] when Dionysos comes, morality shifts and instinct is liberated. Since time immemorial moralists have recognized (if only to exorcize it) the latent power of subversion generated by the pleasures of eating. Discourse, which also has a dual nature, moves from sobriety into delirium, from social polish into wild impulse. At any moment, drunken and deranged speech can invade the disciplined discourse of the diners. Plutarch, in his treatise on banquets, speaks for many other writers: Bacchus is 'the Looser and the Liberator of all things, and . . . especially he unbridles the tongue and grants the utmost freedom to speech' (*Table Talk*, vol. VIII, p. 11). Wine frees the tongue, removes inhibitions and reveals the innermost being: 'it shakes out the folds as it were, where duplicity and rancour lurk in the mind, and reveals every trait of character and every secret feeling in transparent language' (ibid., vol. IX, p. 101).

This is the chink through which symposiac literature plunges. In the same way that it gave form to the imaginary representation of the feast,[10] it welcomes and exploits the fantastic verbal possibilities of uninhibited discourse. Whereas philosophers and masters of good conduct only admit the existence of this vertiginous potential the better to control it, poets and storytellers allow it to be fully realized. Since the setting of the meal stimulates volubility and, better still, contains potentially all the ways in which language can run riot, the literary text, in as much as it is concerned with words, finds in it a marvellous opportunity for experimentation. Transposed into fiction, table talk can achieve its

---

[9] 'To turn to desire, Thalia converts our concern for food and drink from something savage and animal into a social and convivial affair. That is why we apply the word *thaliazein* (merry-making) to those who enjoy one another's company over wine in a gay and friendly manner, not to those who indulge in drunken insults and violence' (Plutarch, *Table Talk*, vol. IX, p. 287).

[10] See chapter 1, The feast of the gods.

full imaginative and inventive potential,[11] especially in an age like the Renaissance when French was still unstable and flexible, leaving the writer a great deal of room for manoeuvre.

This is the field I wish to explore from now on. Let us take the high road and start with Rabelais.

Conversation is rarely lacking in Rabelaisian feasts. Indulging oneself without company and laughter would be to go against the laws of Pantagruelism. For blow-outs and drinking bouts help strengthen social relations; the table is not only a place for eating food, it is also, for the giants and their companions, the ideal setting for conversation. They love food but are also loquacious, they like to tell jokes while drinking and they fill their mouth with words as much as with food. Sometimes their conversations are only briefly recounted by the narrator, but often they are reported at great length, and this is when the astounding wealth of table talk bursts forth in the euphoria of continually reinvented words. The trust between the companions and the good humour created by wine inspire the diners to brilliant and copious discourse. Only rarely has writing as a creative force and a laboratory for research into sound felt so much at home: the prolixity of the speakers, the exuberance of their rhetoric and their comic verve arouses a tremendous range of language and style. Convivial discourse bubbles on a sea of words, it proliferates from chatter to digression, it yields to a voice which never tires of telling stories and laughing and which never stops testing its ability in the exercise of virtuosity.

Rabelais's verbal energy is not, of course, limited to meal scenes. Wordplay, stylistic acrobatics and the way in which the narrative is taken over by the imagination of uninhibited language do not belong exclusively to any one theme. Feasts simply give it a special setting. We only need recall a few of them to see this.

In the wings of the Picrocholine war, a sumptuous table is laid: Grandgousier is wining and dining his son's friends, and military episodes alternate with the joys of good food (*Gargantua*, chs. 39–

[11] The liberation of the power of words in literature goes directly against the condemnation of the abuse of language and the denunciation of the dangers of speech in the moral tradition. See for example Erasmus, *Lingua*, or the chapter entitled 'That there is nothing in the world which does more harm to man than language' in Du Verdier, *Les diverses Leçons*, pp. 191–5.

41 and 45). The aggressors are uncouth people who know neither how to live nor how to eat together. They have refused the gift of cakes, spoilt the harvest and refused an invitation to share food as a sign of peace; their greed does not provide an opportunity for *rapprochement*, but rather incites hostility and leads to pillage. The monks also pervert the pleasures of eating and of conviviality: 'they eat the world's excrement, that is to say, sins; and as eaters of excrement they are cast into their privies – their convents and abbeys that is – which are cut off from all civil intercourse, as are the privies of a house' (ibid., pp. 125–6). Conversely, Gargantua and his friends prepare for action by feasting; they mitigate the fury of combat through the charms of the banquet. Like the warriors in the Dipsodes war in *Pantagruel*, they substitute pranks and feasts for the violence of war. They like 'banqueting joyfully all together' (ibid., p. 136), and plan their strategy with the aid of a bottle. Above all, they revel in saucy stories and witty remarks: 'This leveret's thigh is good for the gout. Talking of trowels – why is it that a young lady's thighs are always cool?' (p. 124). While the dishes are being finished off, jokes and spoonerisms break out at an astounding rate. Friar John particularly, a big eater and great talker, is extremely voluble; the banqueting hall echoes with his jokes and puns; he recounts endless anecdotes, blathers on and just talks for the sake of it. When he is asked why he has 'such a handsome nose', he replies: 'According to true monastic reasoning it was because my nurse had soft breasts: when she suckled me my nose sank in, as if into butter' (p. 127). One could quote endlessly from the witticisms which come to his lips as abundantly as does the food. He is a past master of dinner-table rhetoric, unmatched in loquaciousness except perhaps by Panurge, that other immoderate talker and big mouth.

The interaction of the two oral activities, eating and speaking, also dominates the feast of the Drunkards (ch. 5). The carnival is in full swing, people are full to overflowing, flagons are passed round and the baby Gargantua, who as we know came into the world in the middle of a feast, is in a tearing hurry to begin to talk, in order to wet his whistle: 'As soon as he was born he cried out . . . "Drink! Drink! Drink!", as if inviting the whole world to drink' (p. 52). It is however the company, among the barrels and the hams, whose verbal debauchery is the most astonishing. As in the best symposiac tradition, the Drunkards talk about food and drink while eating and drinking – but in delirious language. Taking learned phrases borrowed from various kinds of professional jargon, they invent all kinds of incongruous expressions by the use of ambiguity and spoonerism. They give new, clandestine and comical meanings to old words. Parody subverts and revives set formulae and language is treated like phonetic material to be manipulated. In this polyphony of discordant voices, even the constraints of communication seem to be removed: the joyful shout, the playful use of sound patterns and lexical transformations – verbal concoctions as a whole – are an end in themselves.

There is not always euphoria and unanimity at the table of Pantagruel and his supporters. In *The Third Book*, there is a banquet of educated men (chs. 29–36) which is full of misunderstandings and gives pleasure to no one, and where the guests do not reach agreement of any sort. And in *The Fourth Book* especially bodies weigh more heavily and joyful over-indulgence bcomes bulimia; food, associated with violence and excess, takes on a pathological character.[12] Splendid food and wordplay have become suspect. During their voyage Pantagruel's comrades, more interested than ever in their stomachs, often reduce phenomena to mere sensory messages or objects that, in their greed, they want to consume. Friar John lurks in the kitchen, does battle with the Chitterlings and organizes meals; Panurge obeys his instincts and becomes a victim of his intestines when he ends up disgracing himself by soiling his shirt. The episode with Messer Gaster in *The Fourth Book* recalls with good reason the tyranny of the stomach: in the world of the friends, as among the strange populations of the islands, physiology and food often dominate: 'And all for the sake of the belly!' (*The Fourth Book*, p. 572). But the alliance of table and fable loses nothing by this: whatever the moral objections, it is in the semantic field of the body and cookery that language achieves its greatest heights. The contrast with the frugal, laconic Pantagruel also reinforces, conversely, the parallel between food and talk. Here, greed for food and taste for speech go together. Through their puns and etymological configurations, their onomato-

---

[12] On various aspects of food in *The Fourth Book*, see Jeanneret, 'Alimentation, digestion, réflexion dans Rabelais', and 'Quand la fable se met à table. Nourriture et structure narrative dans *Le Quart Livre*'.

poeia and synonyms, the companions manipulate words, explore the potential of sound links to produce meaning and study the semantic associations this creates. Morally, their appetite is reprehensible, but their volubility redeems them: it is they who, by their lexical vividness, their incongruous outspokenness and their love of language, generate some of the richest pages of *The Fourth Book*.

The stylistic fecundity of the convivial theme is not confined to table talk. The narrator's voice, and with it the whole narrative, becomes animated whenever the semantic field of food is entered. Gastrology offers the writer a field of literary experimentation and innovation in which Rabelais excels – to the extent that, when the fictional overflowed into the historical, he was assimilated with his characters and acquired his legendary image as a jolly toper, as someone with an ever-open mouth, and has been seen through the ages as the archetypal glutton.[13] Without wishing to establish an exclusive relationship between food and linguistic ingenuity here either, I shall suggest two obvious causes for this complicity between writing and eating, between stylistic virtuosity and the alimentary imagination.

The vocabulary of food and cooking enriches discourse enormously, bringing a virtually infinite terminology from popular and dialectal sources which is passed on orally and is rarely used in written works. When one speaks of gastronomy, one is also allowed to use expressions from low style which are less bound by rules than the formal and selective language of high literature. But there is more to it than the simple imitation of paradigms from this subculture. Like the vocabulary of the body (the organs, natural functions, sex), that of food and the stomach, in as much as it is outside literary convention, has a sort of mobility and malleability that Rabelais exploits to the full.[14] The linguistic field of food invites numerous manipulations where the words take the initiative: hence the coining of new words by grafting on parts of others, by going back to their roots, or by metaphor. The vocabulary of the kitchen also lends itself to comic analogies and to surprising

---

[13] As in Ronsard's comic epitaph (see chapter 5, 'My salad and my Muse'). See also the chapter entitled 'Rabelais' in Hugo's *William Shakespeare*.

[14] See Bakhtin, *Rabelais and his World*. Echoes of this seminal work will be found in the pages which follow.

transfers into other semantic fields, such as organic life ('If he shat, it was toadstools and morels' – *The Fourth Book*, p. 519), erotic pleasure ('rubbing his bacon' – *Pantagruel*, p. 240), or military activity (the 'culinary battle' against the Chitterlings – *The Fourth Book*, p. 533), not to mention literature ('smelling out . . . these fine and most juicy books' – *Gargantua*, p. 38) and parody (*'De moustarda post prandium servienda'* – *Pantagruel*, p. 188), etc.

But it goes beyond isolated figures: many of the episodes in *The Fourth Book* seem to be the product of alimentary themes, whether they be taken at face value ('They live on wind', *The Fourth Book*, p. 540), narrativized (the battle of Lent and Carnival) or allegorized (the episode of Messer Gaster). The 'culinary battle' (ibid., ch. 39) against the Chitterlings is typical of this: the story of a military campaign with its strategy, its diplomacy and its noble deeds is constructed (through semantic sliding and extending metaphors) around a tale of sausages, butchery and chefs. As if to extract every last drop out of culinary vocabulary, the narrative lingers on one of Rabelais's famous lists (ch. 40) in which his verbal virtuosity and love of words are expressed through columns and columns of lexical variations on a given theme. Here it is the names of cooks, which not only amusingly reflect their jobs but also take pleasure in rifling the vocabulary of the cutlery drawer and the larder: Soupspoon, Mortarpestle, Soursauce, Antibacon, Urelelipipingues, Saltgullet, Blowguts, etc. It is doubtless not a coincidence that two of the three other lists in *The Fourth Book* also take their litany from the area of food: the anatomy of King Lent, in which the digestive organs and the strangeness of the monster's diet are described (chs. 30–2) and the foods offered to Gaster, one menu for feast days and another for fast days (chs. 59 and 60). The latter is a further example of the lexical exuberance whose importance is clearly revealed by François Rigolot:

> The sumptuous menu which, according to the logic of the story, should have served to criticize the gluttony of the Gastrolaters, is in fact a colourful defence of gastronomy and is enhanced by verbal discoveries which are as mouth-watering as the foods they describe . . . The jovial language gives the lie to the moralizing intention . . . The appetite is being celebrated through the joy of language. (*Les Langages de Rabelais*, pp. 155–6)

A list from *The Fifth Book* takes the experiment even further by creating (untranslatable) imaginary dishes out of deranged and disparate language: 'Des estroncs fins à la nasardine . . . des cornicabotz . . . des cornamcuz revestuz de bize . . . de la mopsopige . . . de la pétaradine . . . des spopondrilloches' (*The Fifth Book*, ch. 33 *bis*).[15] This is no longer referential: all that is left is a *verbal* concoction.

A second source of literary dynamism which is equally obvious in Rabelais comes from the burlesque. The mechanics of this are simple: food and drink belong to generic and stylistic registers that are traditionally vulgar: to associate them with serious and noble themes is to upset the accepted hierarchy, to join two orders which are conventionally separate and to confuse the normal relation between form and content. This incongruity produces a crack in the system and generates comedy; furthermore, it gives received vocabulary and discourse a shock which gets rid of the cobwebs and revitalizes them. Master Janotus, having duly swilled his wine, comes to claim the bells of Notre-Dame, his sausages and his breeches (*Gargantua*, chs. 19 and 20). He mixes solemn scholastic formulae from theology, liturgy and the law with less noble pleas dictated by his appetite. He jumps from Latin to French through dog Latin and Latinized French, mingles educated discourse with street jargon, and adopts a noble, eloquent style although he is unaware of even the basic principles of rhetoric. The greedy, garrulous tongue is in full flood; wine and hunger give the pompous scholastic discourse a surprising vividness. Friar John does something similar at Grandgousier's feast (ibid., chs. 39–41): he reserves his best jokes and grossest puns for monastic life; conventual rules and ecclesiastical ritual and language all dissolve into laughter and bawdiness through the licence of table talk. This comical perversion of standard formulae is no less bracing for being traditionally found in colleges and monasteries.

There are many examples: parody is everywhere in Rabelais and cooking is one of its most favoured springboards, as during the battle against the Dipsodes (*Pantagruel*, ch. 27). To commemorate his friends' military prowess, Pantagruel sets up a trophy covered

---

[15] Included in the French edition only. See also the list of fanciful foods in *Le Disciple de Pantagruel*, chapter 14.

with warlike insignia and writes a high-falutin and edifying epic poem on it. Panurge replies to this by putting up another trophy that is absolutely symmetrical, but dedicated to good food. It is covered in gastronomical emblems and celebrates, in similar verse to that of Pantagruel, the joys of drink. The clichés of chivalry and honour interact with the language of digestion: war is demystified by this comic juxtaposition and acquires a human aspect. The narrative goes on

> Then said Pantagruel: 'Come, my lads, we have brooded here too long on our victuals. It is no easy thing, as we know, for great feasters to perform great deeds of arms. But there is no shade like that of banners, there is no smoke like that of horses, nor clattering like that of armour.'
> At this Epistemon began to smile and said: 'There is no shade like that of kitchens, no smoke like pie-smoke, and no clattering like that of cups.' To which Panurge answered: 'There is no shade like that of curtains, no smoke like steaming breasts, and no clattering like the sound of ballocks.' (Ibid., p. 255)

The stratification of the discourse does not cancel out epic dignity, but rather reactivates it. The culinary and sexual motives which are introduced under the heroic give men new dynamism. The blurring of accepted hierarchies, although morally and aesthetically suspect, is a literary bonus.

This tone is set in the first chapter of the first book (ibid., ch. 1). It will be recalled that the chronicles of Pantagruel open with a myth of origin which tells of the formidable appetite of primitive man and how an excess of greed led to their grotesque bodies.[16] Now the meaning of this episode derives from a parodic impulse. Among the many references to the Bible in these pages, the catalogue of comic names and relationships is a parody of the genealogy of Christ according to the Gospels (Matthew 1: 1–16 and Luke 3: 23–38). Similarly the first chapters of Genesis are given an unexpected twist, and it is around Rabelais's feast of medlar fruits and the ensuing indigestion that this revolves. In the Bible story many prohibitions surround food: the forbidden fruit of the tree of knowledge, the sterility of the soil, thankless toil in

---

[16] See chapter 1, The al fresco meal.

the fields. But Rabelais, proud of the stomach's legitimacy, rewrites and overturns the venerable story of the Fall. Gluttony allows no prohibition; bodies, full to the brim, certainly swell up out of all proportion, but their growth is healthy, since it enlarges the vital organs and gives rise to the race of giants. What in the Bible is a first step towards death initiates here the conquest of life.

Such a transformation clearly goes a long way beyond any burlesque prank. Superimposing the new text on the old provides a contrast which allows the expression of a better world – a world with no other law than that of pleasure. In the Land of Cockaigne, evil does not exist, nor does the knowledge of sin nor the loss of paradise; wrongdoing is erased. By exploiting parody, Rabelais substitutes for the moral and guilt-ridden version of the origin of man a fable of sensuous but innocent humanity, at one with nature and intent only on satisfying its desires. Everything starts with a feast because the narrative finds in it suitable material for the theme of the regeneration of forms and values. Here too, the discourse of good food and obedience to nature stand received hierarchies and ideas on their heads. Not that parody nullifies or invalidates the biblical references: it merely adds a new dimension to them. In this way a unitary and dynamic system beyond traditional dualism is outlined, a system in which the material and the spiritual, the vulgar and the sublime have equal status. The language of food tends to replace the static and vertical disjunction created by adverse poles with an integrated axiological and literary order which brings opposites together.

By exploiting the ambivalence of the alimentary theme – as an upholder of the law and as an expression of natural desire, something which is both prohibited and sensual – parody permits the obvious to be confounded. The signs of food shift, they have surprises up their sleeve and they challenge established morality. Herein lies perhaps the source of that feeling of well-being and of infectious joy which one gets from reading about meals, at least in *Gargantua* and *Pantagruel*. After these first two novels, however, antinomy re-emerges, stomachs get weightier and their regenerative powers are dulled.

Philologists or logophiles?

Meals do not only inspire linguistic experiment on the part of diners and storytellers. A taste for words in discourse on food tempts and enlivens even the most serious writers, namely scientists and philologists. It is as though the language of food is flavoured by its theme and acquires a special piquancy, even in the most unexpected and least frivolous contexts. This is the spirit of table talk invading the austere sphere of science.

The naturalist Pierre Belon, in his *Histoire de la nature des oyseaux*, devotes a chapter to the food and table manners of the Ancients and Moderns. Anthropological information takes up several paragraphs, but it is above all the vocabulary of the kitchen which attracts his attention: starting from a 'little book called How to make a notice for a banquet', Belon's aim is to collect all the words and all the turns of phrase suitable for putting on a menu: and he draws up an enormous (and untranslatable) list of almost two hundred items, in which naming becomes as sensuous as tasting the dishes themselves:

> Lions de blanc chapon . . . Gelee en poincte de diamant . . . Oysons à la malvoisie . . . Pieds à la saulce d'enfer . . . Gelee·embree, Gelee moulue, Gelee blanche picquee . . . Angelots de gelee . . . Sallades de poires de bon crestien . . . Gauffres coulisses . . . Estriers de pruneaux . . . Soleil de blanc chapon . . . Connins à la grenade . . . Papillons de marrons . . . Pastez de becasse au bec doré . . . Fontaine de gelee . . . Neige en romarin . . . Formage plaisantin . . . (*L'Histoire de la nature des oyseaux*, pp. 64–5)

There is nothing to choose between Belon's list and Rabelais's: moreover it refers us back to the *The Fourth Book*, to fill in its gaps. This is a bizarre complicity between the discourse of science and the discourse of fiction which combine their resources to give the reader an appreciation of culinary vocabulary. Furthermore Belon recognizes that his aim is to defend and illustrate the French language as much as to contribute to natural history: 'We believe that other nations cannot name as many foods in their language as we can in French' (ibid., p. 65).

This shift from encyclopaedia to lexicology in Belon's work can be explained by the fact that the names of foods in the vulgar language come mainly from the oral tradition and had not yet been recorded or fixed through writing. Treatises on nutrition and research into the ceremonial and the ethics of meals are mostly in Latin, as we have seen.[17] Gastrology is still reserved for learned people; it derives from academic language which has been tested through the centuries and guarantees easier communication. Even here though, terminology, far from functioning as a transparent vehicle, occupies centre stage. So let us turn again to these books of convivial erudition and let us watch them examine words just as much as things.[18]

Of course, this concentration on terminology is a normal philological reflex which is widespread among the Humanists. As we have seen, they are interested less in practical application than in the organization of information on the dietetic and ceremonial heritage of the Ancients. Their semiology is an archaeology, and their symposiac didactics are based on a mass of readings which are deciphered and then rigorously classified. Working as they do from Latin and Greek documents, how could they avoid studying words, their meanings and their use? Justus Lipsius devotes a large part of his study of Roman banquets to the preliminary problems of drawing up accurate texts, since it is clear that access to historical truth necessitates finding the most correct version.[19] Above all, everyone agrees that to understand the sources accurately one must carry out a critical analysis of the means by which the information is conveyed: the vocabulary. Without philology there would be no encyclopaedia. Knowledge of man comes to us through knowledge of antiquity: and knowledge of antiquity comes to us through a carefully interpreted terminology.

[17] See chapters 2 and 3.

[18] The ensuing remarks are based on the following treatises: a) studies of classical banquets: Bulengerus, *De conviviis*, Ciacconius, *De triclinio*, Lipsius, *Antiquarum lectionum*, Stuckius, *Antiquitatum convivialium* and Rhodiginus, *Lectionum antiquarum*; and b) studies of classical dietetics: Torinus's edition of Apicius, *De re culinaria*, Bruyerinus, *De re cibaria*, Stephanus, *De nutrimentis*, and Willich, *Ars magirica*.

[19] See *Antiquarum lectionum* book III: 'In quo conviviorum veterum ritus proponuntur: in eam rem varii scriptores emendantur, explicantur' ('In which the customs of antique meals are related: on the same topic, different authors are corrected and explained').

There remains the question of priorities; should one examine the *verba* the better to understand the *res*, or use the *res* as an opportunity to study the *verba*? Albanus Torinus, the German editor of Apicius's Latin recipes, recognizes this problem; the special language of this cookery book, he says, might well nowadays interest 'logophiles more than philologists' (Dedication to *De re culinaria*), lovers of words rather than lovers of science. Another German scholar announces from the start that he is going to devote his treatise to the lexical system of cookery as much as, if not more than, to information about foods; he presents himself as a *grammaticus* and a *philologus* working on *verba coquinaria* (Willich, *Ars magirica, passim*). By now it is unclear whether the pleasure lies in the images of foods as conveyed by words or in the signifier, which has its own savour. The imaginative or libidinal element inherent in discourse on food has surreptitiously filtered into scholarly writings.

These treatises are designed to ensure that language is treated systematically. The priority is to specify as closely as possible objects from long ago: ingredients, dishes, utensils, the service and gestures. A new methodology is introduced to provide precise definitions: terms with similar meanings are collected, apparent synonyms are examined and, by studying lexical groups, etymology and derivation, scholars try to give each term a specific sense. In order to explain the meaning of one word by using others, authors also have recourse to translation: either comparing classical languages like Latin, Greek or sometimes Hebrew, or referring to modern languages such as French, Italian, German, and so on. In this way they are moving towards a global view of any given nomenclature: an understanding of each of the terms in the system allows one to establish distinctions of meaning, or analogies, and finally to classify the objects studied according to a taxonomy which is sometimes very sophisticated. Thus the often polyglot terminology of the art of the table is fixed – a process of definition to which lexicographers will refer in the future.

It is true that classical theorists of conviviality, especially Athenaeus and Macrobius, set the example in this field: the documentary interest in their compilations is always linked to linguistic enquiry; they pass on vast amounts of information, but they are also grammarians who attach prime importance to the history of words and their derivation, morphology and precise meaning. At the banquet of *The Deipnosophists* and at that of the *Saturnalia*, the array of dishes inspires a linguistic commentary from the guests. When the dessert is brought in 'Symmachus, handling some nuts, said: "I should like to hear from you, Servius, the reasons for, or the origin of, the many different names given to nuts" ' (Macrobius, *Saturnalia*, p. 245) and so on. Guests at the banquets of Athenaeus and Macrobius – I shall return to this later[20] – are logophiles rather than gastronomes. They feed on a 'long feast of words' (Athenaeus, *The Deipnosophists*, VIII, 354d; vol. IV, p. 105). Even for them, eating, talking about food and manipulating language are interdependent activities.

This affinity appears in other forms in Erasmus. Some of the *Colloquia* base the teaching of Latin formulae and the refinement of style on table talk; the meal, as we shall see, therefore becomes a laboratory for the study of language at work.[21] As will be recalled,[22] the treatise *De civilitate morum puerilium* had a powerful effect on the popularization of good manners; it too associates knowing how to eat with knowing how to speak. Widely used as a school textbook, it served to inculcate into children not only rules of good conduct but also examples of good Latin. Tutors were aware of the form of the message as much as of its content and used it for exercises in grammar, vocabulary and style. This is shown, for example, in an index of 'Phrases sive Formulae loquendi, e Libello de morum puerilium Civilitate, cum ad elegantiam, tum ad meliorem constructionem'[23] in an edition of 1678. This is a Humanist project *par excellence*: preparation for social life and the study of philology in the same lesson, based on the same book. While one refines one's behaviour, one perfects one's speech; here, too, *res* and *verba*, conduct and language, go hand in hand.[24]

---

[20] See chapter 6, Greedy grammarians.

[21] See chapter 7, Erasmus: feasting on words.

[22] See chapter 2, Civility.

[23] 'Phrases or forms of speech, from the book about the politeness of children's manners, to be used as much for elegance as for improvement in construction'; quoted, with additional details, in Bierlaire, 'Erasmus at School'.

[24] The same combination of lessons on table manners and lessons in Latin can be found in J. Sulpitius Verulanus's textbook, *Doctrina mensae*.

In his essay *On the vanity of words* Montaigne ironically describes his meeting with an Italian

> who was chief steward to the late Cardinal Caraffe until his death . . . He expounded on the culinary art [*science de gueule*] with solemnity and scholarly bearing as though he were telling me about some great question of theology. He described to me the difference in people's appetites: that which they have on an empty stomach and that which they have after the second and third courses; the means to simply please and the means to stimulate and titillate the palate; the way he made his sauces, first in general terms, then by describing the quality of the ingredients and the effects they have; the different vegetables according to the season, those which should be cooked and those which should be served cold, how to decorate and enhance them so that they are pleasing to the eye . . . And all this was embellished with rich and magnificent words of the very sort used to speak of the government of an Empire. (*Essais*, I, 51; p. 306)

Everything is here, from the stylization of the meal to the stylistic exercise of describing meals. On the look-out for excesses of rhetoric, Montaigne perceived that the '*science de gueule*' operates on two levels: the scientific construction of a menu and of ceremonial, and then the eloquent but no less sensuous account of all this. As if by chance, the master of oral pleasures is also careful over the language he uses, and he loves words. The pleasure of a refined meal and the supreme mastery of taste culminate in 'rich and magnificent words'.

In this chapter, I have drawn on material from very different fields: the social codification of table talk, the literary use of the meal scene and learned discourse about conviviality. In each of these registers, however, we can see how the awareness of language is heightened when it refers to food. Tongues are untied when feasts are imagined and when the splendours of the kitchen and of fine food are described, and the accompanying words, whatever their status, thereby gain in savour.

5

Eating the text

Storytelling while eating

'Edere et audire' (Erasmus, *Convivium fabulosum*, in *Colloquies*, p. 257), to eat and listen: in Erasmus's *Fabulous Feast*, this is the goal of a few friends sitting around a table. Theirs is a double pleasure: they take in stories while eating their supper.

This narrative theme reflects a situation which was part of everyday life for the people of the time. In the refectories of monasteries and colleges, meals were accompanied by readings. The auditory memory absorbed textual sequences while the body took in its commons. The ambiguous meaning of the word *collation* in the language of monks is very significant: the term denotes a sermon given after a meal, but also the meal itself, as if listening and eating, discourse and digestion were identical operations.[1] The educated elite in the sixteenth century had a similar practice: at the king's table, and subsequently at the table of nobles converted to Humanism, one was also entertained or instructed by texts read around the table. Francis I's reader had an important role at court and often embellished meals there. Sometimes learned men or poets were also invited, and between courses their conversation provided the monarch with scraps of that culture he loved so much. It is probable that the Renaissance princes who regularly put readings, recitations or songs on the

---

[1] See the entry on *Collation* in Littré's dictionary and *Quatre sermons joyeux*, p. 16.

menu at their feasts owed a large part of their knowledge of literature to this method of communication.[2]

This phenomenon had been almost universal since antiquity. For learned people and for the illiterate, in private reading and in public readings, the book was seen as an auditory message carried by the voice and as part of the oral tradition. Of course, the circumstances of such recitations varied, but in many circles the meal provided an appropriate setting. Moreover, it was not only written texts that were propagated in this way; epics, songs, popular tales and so on were also frequently passed on at table; from Homeric Greece to the French countryside, during celebrations or wakes, groups of friends gathered together to tell each other stories or to listen to a professional telling them. Whatever the variations, one custom remained which affected the status of literature: the reception of books and ingestion of food were often linked. Food for the mind and food for the body, absorbed and digested together, joined in a single physiological experience.

Because it was part of everyday experience and charged with symbolic value, this conjunction provided literature with a special *topos*: one or many narrators reading, reciting or telling a story to their table companions. This scenario derives from the common device of narrative on two levels: the story represents a fictional author and public, revealing the conditions of its own production and reception. The range of possible subjects is vast: edifying or frivolous themes, academic questions or fairy stories can all be used to add a finishing touch to the description of a meal. As for the form, it varies according to content: serious themes are normally treated in dialogue, so that a variety of voices can offset the weighty material; monologue is reserved for entertaining stories that give rise to laughter or fantasy. One way or another, the recreational role of symposiac literature is respected. In the following chapters,[3] I shall examine the techniques whereby the meal scene enlivens or vulgarizes traditionally serious subject

---

[2] Ronsard, for example, writes that his lute 'knows how to entertain Princes at their table' (*Oeuvres complètes*, vol. II, p. 156). He also shows that his poems were sometimes read at the king's table, when he reproaches a secretary of the court saying: 'you dare to laugh at my poems in the middle of meals . . . And you clumsily read them all wrong' (ibid., vol. XV, p. 122). See also ibid., pp. 136–41.

[3] See chapters 6 and 7.

matter. In the pages which follow now, I shall concentrate on the use of entertaining fables.

Among those Renaissance stories structured around the illusion of oral recitation, volumes of tales in the tradition of Boccaccio form an impressive corpus. A group of friends enjoy themselves telling each other stories; according to a carefully drawn up contract, each participant takes it in turn to speak, with interspersed conversations between the listeners of varying importance. The setting of the recitation is always described in detail – the causes and effects of the narration, the site of this exchange, and the social identity of the storytellers. It is here that the meal, as a privileged opportunity for oral pleasure, should come in: but in fact it is elided. Boccaccio's *Decameron*, the archetypal work in a long series of collections of short stories, is a good example of this.[4] The happy band of friends, having escaped from the plague in Florence, does not deny itself anything which could provide a feeling of well-being in the daily timetable it has fixed for itself. Among the entertainments that precede or follow a storytelling session, sumptuously laid tables and picnics in groves of trees contribute to the festive atmosphere. But the friends search out marvellous landscapes – a *locus amoenus* – where the body is at rest, in order to listen to each other. They are too polite to speak with their mouths full; their concern for refinement and the impeccable courtesy at play in their activities rules out any pleasure that is too sensual. As in the tradition of the Platonic *symposion*, the mouth that speaks and the mouth that eats are dissociated; the needs of the stomach merit only a passing mention, nobler preoccupations of the mind taking up all the space.[5] The sensuality of the flesh is displaced into the stories where, with all rules of decency removed, immodest people give full rein to their instincts, providing the storytellers

---

[4] Apart from a few variants, most collections of French tales, like those of Jeanne Flore, Noël Du Fail, Des Périers, Jacques Yver, Gabriel Chappuys and Etienne Tabourot, generally share this tendency. Even the promising title of *Le Cene* (The Supper) by the Florentine writer, A. F. Grazzini, is deceptive. See O. Löhmann, *Die Rahmenerzählung des Decameron, ihre Quellen und Nachwirkungen*, and G.-A. Pérouse, *Les Nouvelles françaises du XVIᵉ siècle, images de la vie du temps*.

[5] Meals are also mentioned in several philosophical dialogues (either at the beginning or in an interlude), but the meals and the guests are not described. See the end of book I of Thomas More's *Utopia*, and the end of Tahureau's 'Premier dialogue'.

with an inverse and self-satisfying reflection of their own refinement.

If not to Boccaccio, narration at table can trace its origins back to another written tradition. Two complementary models – the Homeric and the Horatian[6] – give the authority of classical literature to a form of interchange which is already sufficiently legitimized by the customs mentioned above.

The convivial institution in Homer's world gives society its essential focal point and provides the narrative with the nexus where many episodes coalesce or resolve themselves. Guests are always given a welcoming meal at which, around jugs of wine and steaming meats, trust is established and stories are exchanged; dialogue ideally starts at table, after which it can continue freely elsewhere. But the role of discourse in the alimentary ceremony is not confined to conversation. To put the finishing touch to a banquet, a bard arrives to recite a heroic tale. The feast scene in the palace of Alcinous is typical: the blind Demodocos, sitting 'in the midst of the banqueters' (*The Odyssey*, book VIII, p. 261), recounts alternately episodes from the Trojan War and the story of the love of Aries for Aphrodite. Moved by this song, Odysseus has a choice cut of meat brought in for the bard, and then says to Alcinous, who has asked him now to reveal his identity:

> I declare that there is no greater fulfilment of delight than when joy possesses a whole people, and banqueters in the halls listen to a minstrel as they sit in order due, and by them tables are laden with bread and meat, and the cup-bearer draws wine from the bowl and bears it round and pours it into the cups. This seems to my mind the fairest thing there is. (Ibid., book IX, p. 303)

Putting his seal of approval on the location and the style of the symposiac utterance prepares the way for Odysseus's own intervention: he takes the place of the bard and tells the guests, who are still seated at table, the story of his tribulations, from his departure from Troy to his arrival at the Phaeacians, a long tale of four cantos which forms the central part of the *Odyssey*.

This scene was to give the banquet narrative its credentials and

[6] A third antique model, Petronius's *Satyricon*, could have been mentioned here; but see chapter 3, note 9.

became a model in the classical epic tradition. Virgil imitates the sequence, although the convivial setting in the *Aeneid* (books II and III) is only partially present. Dido gives a splendid feast for Aeneas; but the dishes have to be removed before Iopas sings and the Trojan prince speaks deep into the night of the fall of Troy and his voyage to Carthage. Ronsard uses the same device in *La Franciade* (II, 927–1096),[7] but here too the stories come after the meal. The dual potential of the mouth, which Homer had unified in one all-embracing celebration, is dissociated by his followers; the meal becomes a mere ornament, epic storytelling becomes more refined and breaks down the interdependence of feasts and words.

Ronsard does, however, celebrate the coming together of meal, wine and song in the more light-hearted register of his *Folastries*, invoking Homer's model itself and paraphrasing the words spoken by Odysseus at Alcinous's:

> Verily we do not revere enough
> The divine inventions of Homer
> Who says there is
> No greater pleasure than
> To be with friends at table
> While a sweet minstrel
> Feeds the ear with song
> And while the quenching cup-bearer
> Sends the full cup
> Around the group.
>   (*Livret de Folastries*, VII, 1–10)[8]

Like Rabelais, Ronsard revitalizes the Horatian *topos* of Homer as a 'merry boozer' (ibid., line 11),[9] and in the same *Folastrie* 'Homer' ('Homère') twice rhymes with 'dinner' ('bonne chère')! At a time when the Pléiade were trying to revive the classical combination of poetry and music and when the poet, to be worthy of the name, was supposed to hum his text while writing it, and then recite it accompanying himself on the lute, the model of the Homeric bard

[7] In *Oeuvres complètes*, vol. XVI, pp. 140–9.
[8] Ibid., vol. V, p. 42. See also *Folastrie* VIII.
[9] See Horace, *Epistles*, I, 19, line 6 and Rabelais, Prologues to *Gargantua* and *The Third Book*.

obviously had particular prestige. Through a kind of mimetic enthusiasm, the narrator of the *Folastrie* describes himself as a 'rhapsodist' (ibid., line 19) and soon starts to compose on his lyre (lines 69–76). It is true that later in the poem the model becomes more introverted, as the narrator represents himself as old, alone and isolated from social gatherings, but capable of creating, thanks to the bottle and to reading other poets, a new kind of conviviality which inspires further cantos. The voice of books replaces those of fellow guests and his public deserts him, but the mutual relationship of wine and poetry, of table and fable, remains.

This shift in the Homeric model is probably attributable to the influence of Horace. Whereas Odysseus tells his story at the king's table, and whereas the storytellers in Boccaccio are nobles used to marvellous palaces, Horace sings of the joys of the intimate, rustic meal. His *Odes* are variations on the same exhortation: let us leave the troubles of the town behind and make merry or make love with a few friends among goblets, flowers and perfumes. Drink loosens tongues and inspires songs; the exuberance of an intimate conversation inspires poetry. It is true that these convivial scenes, except for one famous satire (II, 6), contain no reported narratives; Horace sketches dialogues and evokes a world buzzing with *fabulae* – the Latin word does not distinguish between conversations, remarks, narratives, tales or plays – but these are stories that others will tell later, learning from Horace's example. For the Horatian feast, a favourite *topos* among Renaissance poets, also legitimizes the banquet narrative and associates literature with the pleasures of the flagon.

The scenario of sharing good food and good stories allows various sixteenth-century authors to enliven their material and to organize it without subordinating it to a rigid structure or to a single tone. It provides the opportunity for Erasmus to bring in snippets of books he has read, humorous examples and funny anecdotes, etc.[10] It provides an excuse for Guillaume Bouchet to make his compilation seem like all-night discussions around the family table as in days gone by, and to parade all sorts of 'entertaining stories and amusing twaddle' (*Les Sérées*, vol. I, p. xi)

---

[10] Especially *The Fabulous Feast* and *The Sober Feast* (*Convivium fabulosum* and *C. sobrium*). See chapter 7, Erasmus: feasting on words.

among the serious material and the erudite comments.[11] But the convivial scene in these texts is often engulfed in a mass of documentary information which eclipses references to meals. Let us return to our main theme and turn to Rabelais, who exploits the device of the meal-time story to the full, and even uses it as a model for the reception of his work itself.

'Our after-dinner entertainments'[12]

The lord of Basché, who appears briefly in *The Fourth Book*, knows how to set about telling a story:

> My Lord of Basché called his wife, her ladies and all his people out into the arbour of his private garden. Then he sent for the luncheon wine, and for plenty of pasties, hams, fruit, and cheese to go with it, and they all drank together in high glee. At the end of the meal he told them this story. (Rabelais, *The Fourth Book*, p. 478)

This is an exemplary scene: a community gathers together – to defend itself against the outside world – around a meal and a story. 'Relating' happens here in both senses of the word: telling a story and feeling close to others, basing a pact of solidarity around the narrative exchange. The attraction of the fable is heightened by the charm of the direct relationship between the narrator and his audience; the shared food, the pleasant decor and the immediacy of the narrative voices all contribute to the double magic of the oral, the relationship between fellow men and between them and natural produce.

But Rabelais has a more important use for this *topos*: he builds his own narrative strategy on it. As we know, there are two levels in the novels: the story of the giants is introduced by a scene where the narrator and the narratee together act out the ideal relationship between the author and the reader. In each prologue an imaginary setting is provided for the production and reception of the text, a contract between the author and the reader is drawn up and the tone is set: the story can only begin after this preliminary

---

[11] See chapter 7, Guillaume Bouchet: stuffings.
[12] Rabelais, Prologue to *The Third Book*, p. 285.

programme and this meeting of the partners in the exchange. Now it is here, in the very structure of narrative communication, that the paradigm of the banquet enters the picture: as soon as he opens the book, the reader is invited to eat and drink. To enter the world of the fiction, the rite of passage is a simulation of conviviality. This is what I shall now show by considering the five prologues.[13]

In each of them a voice is heard, an *I* who addresses his listener in the second person as though he or she were present. Everything is arranged to simulate oral communication, an exchange between living people. The receptor, it is true, does not speak; the model is more like that of a dramatic prologue or a public recitation – a monologue punctuated by apostrophizing, to establish a relationship with the public and to invite its participation. Be that as it may, the pretence of a direct confrontation between 'myself, who address you' (*Gargantua*, p. 41) and 'you, my good disciples' (ibid., p. 37) is a constant feature of all five prologues.

In three of them (*Gargantua*, *The Third Book*, and *The Fifth Book*), the receptors are described as drinkers ('most noble boozers . . . ' – *Gargantua*, p. 37). They are invited to sit at table to follow the story which is about to unfold, because listening and tippling go together well: 'I will tell you a story about him [Diogenes] presently, while we start on the wine – Drink up, my boys – and I start my argument. Now listen to me!' (*The Third Book*, p. 281). The fiction of the sozzled listener in fact goes beyond the prologues and reappears from time to time in the course of the narratives (*Pantagruel*, ch. 1, *Gargantua*, ch. 1, *The Third Book*, chs. 1 and 51, etc.), as if to ensure throughout that reading remains under the aegis of taste and physiology.

On the other side, the narrator naturally wears the same mask: 'For I have a slight headache, and I clearly see that the registers of my brain are somewhat confused by this new September wine' (*Pantagruel*, p. 277). The prologue of *The Third Book* (along with that of *Gargantua*) pushes the logic of this kind of enunciation the furthest. To the producer, drinking and telling stories are one and the same: 'As I drink I here deliberate, discourse, resolve, and conclude. After the epilogue I laugh, write, compose, and drink

---

[13] Although the authenticity of *The Fifth Book* is far from certain, I shall refer to it from time to time without prejudice to the question of authorship.

again' (*The Third Book*, p. 284). He drinks and, drawing wine from his barrel, hands drink around, creating with his listeners a company of merry boozers. He presents himself as the organizer of a feast, a 'faithful steward' (ibid., p. 285). Literary exchange seems naturally to take place around a table where wine is flowing, a recurrent scenario for the origination of the narrative and an ideal setting for its consumption.

The guests are brought closer when wine is circulating and when everyone is listening to a story. The pact with the reader which is made in the prologues ensures agreement between both parties on basic principles: the paramount importance of laughter, pleasure and good food, rejection of constraints and loyalty to friends. Physical suitability is not enough to enter into the world of the fiction: a common ethos must be defined. From his public, the narrator immediately banishes parasites and hypocrites (Prologue to *The Third Book*), critical people who know neither how to live nor to read, and the slanderers who 'seeing all those people so eager to see and read my writings . . . spat in the basin' (*The Fourth Book*, Prologue of 1548). It is no coincidence that the prologues regularly refer to the ideal of Pantagruelism and provide the most elaborate definitions of that art of living happily and confidently: 'they will never take in bad part anything that they know to spring from a good, honest, and loyal heart' (*The Third Book*, p. 286).

The structure Rabelais perfects here is repeated (significantly) in one of the anonymous tales which carried on the fashion for stories about giants, *Le Disciple de Pantagruel*. Here it is from within the plot that the reader receives the invitation to share the characters' feast: 'If you would like to come, we will give you some' (ch. 18, p. 49). Good food, from then on, is not only virtually the sole theme in the fiction: it also moves outside the text to become the real mediator of the message; unless, conversely, it invites the participation of the public in order to destabilize it by plunging it into its own phantasmagorical world. When the sailors return laden with food from their voyage, they again appeal to the reader: 'We will give you fruits . . . which we have brought and we will fill you full of tales' (ch. 31, p. 84). Reading therefore becomes one more illusion, albeit a most nourishing one.

Rabelais also uses the *topos* of the banquet to provide continuity between the level of the story and that of its narration, in that the partners in the narrative interchange, who eat, drink, and laugh, are of course close to the characters of the tale. They adopt the same values and they are part of the same field of reference. For example, the homology of tone and theme eradicates any disjunction between the prologue to *Gargantua* and the Drunkards' Fair (*Gargantua*, chs. 4–5). One particular concatenation in the latter episode illustrates this device well; the narrator tells his audience: 'and if you don't believe it, may your fundament fall out!' and immediately follows this, referring to Gargamelle, with: 'Her fundament fell out' (ibid., p. 47): the reader and the character, the instruction to the reader and the fictional event are one and the same. There is a similar mirror effect at the end of *Gargantua*; Friar John is talking about tennis: 'After the game they refresh themselves before a clear fire and change their shirts, and they are glad to feast . . . and here's good cheer!' (p. 163). The book ends by coming back to the initial theme of the prologue; thus it encompasses the time taken to tell the story and all its actors, the narrating and the narrated, in the space of a meal – a means of returning to the point of departure and of recalling that everything had started with the pronouncement of a convivial word.

The symposiac paradigm, so neatly expressed here, sets out a clear programme: it removes the book from the curse of solitary reading, it rejects the anonymous and distant relationship between the reader and the written word (which is further aggravated by the circulation of printed matter) and exorcizes this unnatural tendency by reviving the old myth of narration as 'after-dinner entertainment' (*The Third Book*, p. 285). The accepted form for the transmission of the story is therefore table talk; the narrative is the product of a recitation, an oral event in a concrete setting. Two strategically placed references show the importance Rabelais attaches to this model. From the start of the prologue, *Gargantua* situates itself in the tradition of Plato's *Symposium*: it immediately takes its authority from the original work of symposiac literature, the prototype of narrative interchange accompanied by drinking. Later, the *Third Book* complements this by reserving its first reference to a classical text for Plutarch's *Symposiaka*, another major source in the development of the genre: this is a further sign of Rabelais's loyalty to the tradition of classical banquets.

The extraordinary linguistic virtuosity of the prologues brings further confirmation of this. As we have seen in the preceding chapter, diners, in Rabelais, are not content just to talk in their cups; they are amazingly loquacious and their verbiage is as prodigious as their appetities. Now drink also loosens the tongue of the narrator, to such an extent that the prologues (particularly those of *The Third* and *Fourth Books*) are without doubt the most stylistically adventurous and inventive parts of the whole work, in which Rabelais reaches the height of his art as a storyteller and a craftsman of language. Rabelais's verbal devices do of course simulate spoken communication: the narrator addressing the reader, with apostrophes, questions and insults; free association of words; imitative harmony; playing with the sounds of language, and so on. The prologues are not meant to be read, they are meant to be listened to as shouts and general auditory phenomena. But Rabelais's experiments surpass the usual collection of auditory effects. Puns, paronymy and etymological figures all uncover vast stores of meaning in the signifiers; preposterous or obscene ambiguities now and then provide the very impetus for the text – for example, the erotic modulations on Ballocker's hatchet in the prologue to the *The Fourth Book*. Working on words again implies playing with accepted discourse to instil it with burlesque significance, as in the parody in the prologue to *Gargantua* on the question of interpretation. To which we can add a supreme example of verbal energy and narrative impudence – the famous series of synonyms on the defence of Corinth (Prologue to *The Third Book*). The narrator, as if carried away by his words, opens the floodgates of the dictionary, first pouring out a stream of vocabulary about war, and then, in sixty-four verbs, describing Diogenes tormenting his tub. Such openings, interspersed with sound-play and verbal extravagance, do more than evoke the genre of the banquet through image or intertext. They set the tone of table talk and realize the full potential of meal-time discourse.

'My salad and my Muse'[14]

The mask Rabelais dons in his prologues, as an author of conviviality and good living inspired by drink, gave rise to a myth

[14] Ronsard, *La Salade*, line 38, in *Oeuvres complètes*, vol. XV, p. 78.

which lasted for centuries after his death. Ronsard's famous *Epitafe de François Rabelais* (1554)[15] is one of the first examples of this. This text is worth examining in some detail: although it takes Rabelais at his word and turns portrait into caricature, it also bears witness to the popularity of the symposiac theme among the poets of the time, despite their concern for differentiation.

To many commentators the *Epitafe* seems insulting: the image of the drunken, greedy and clownish author, wallowing among tureens and reduced to a gaping mouth and a ravenous stomach, has been interpreted as a polemic in which the poet denounces the novelist.[16] Other critics, on the other hand, have seen it as a farcical epitaph like so many others, as a jest without acrimony or hostility.[17] A closer understanding of the theme of food in Renaissance literature might lead to a better appreciation of it. First of all we must recognize that Ronsard is only reproducing, in a slightly exaggerated way, the physiognomy that Rabelais himself sketched out. There are also other ways in which the potential outrage is defused. Ronsard may have read in the Greek Anthology (which was then highly respected by young poets) epigrams in the same vein as the poem about Rabelais dedicated to Anacreon, who was also commemorated by a vine on his tomb or by juicy offerings; as Laumonier says, the comparison between Rabelais and Anacreon was in fact rather flattering.[18] Above all, the description of Rabelais is surprisingly similar to the portrait Ronsard liked to give of himself at the same period – the beginning of the 1550s. Imbued with models provided by Horace and Anacreon, he happily depicted himself as a reveller, a *poeta vinosus*. He too uses food and drink and bases on them the myth of the poet inspired by the pleasures of the table. One can therefore speculate that Ronsard is not seeking to insult Rabelais in the epitaph, but rather to associate him with the imaginary feasts and

[15] Ibid., vol. VI, pp. 20–3.
[16] See S. F. Will, 'A Note on Ronsard's *Epitafe de François Rabelais*'. See also the works by Pierre Bayle and Jules Michelet, as well as A. Lefranc, J. Boulenger, L. Sainéan, H. Chamard, J. Plattard and M. de Schweinitz referred to in this article.
[17] See Sainte-Beuve, Marty-Laveaux, H. Vaganay, P. Villey and P. Laumonier: references can again be found in the article by S. F. Will.
[18] See *Anthologie grecque*, vol. I, pp. 23–33, quoted by P. Laumonier, 'L'Epitaphe de Rabelais par Ronsard', p. 213.

the fashionable tone of the new poetry. It is probable that he had an imperfect knowledge of Rabelais's work:[19] but it is much less likely that he denigrated it on account of its taste for revelry.

Several groups of poems in Ronsard's collections of 1553, 1554 and 1555 are arranged around the theme of carousal, and here we find unexpected similarities with the mythical image of Rabelais.

One of these cycles is obvious: the various poems to the glory of Bacchus and the vows of allegiance which are numerous in Ronsard at that time: 'As a poet, I prefer The good Bacchus to all the other gods' (*Epitre à Ambroise de La Porte*, lines 51–2).[20] The series of the *Bacchanales* (1552), the *Dithyrambes* (1553) and the *Hinne de Bacus* (1555)[21] is complemented by other pieces or fragments describing country feasts as a privileged meeting place for poets, the site *par excellence* where song is part of communal entertainment. It is the opportunity for Ronsard to develop his deliberately trivial comic mask, distinguishing himself from his more nobly inspired companions:

> But I whose base Idea
>   Is not elevated
> To such a pitch [as that of cosmic poetry] . . .
> Instead of such marvels,
>   I shall hang
> Two bottles on my backside.
>   (*Les Bacchanales*, lines 61–9)[22]

These sentiments match those of Rabelais's prologues. The resemblance is particularly striking in the *Bacchanales*, the tale of young poets picnicking with their master, Dorat, at Arcueil. They laugh, gambol, and make merry. Bacchic enthusiasm, fed by wine and food, takes on the appearance of popular jubilation, and literary activity, mixed in with the joys of eating, is at its height. This text, in which Ronsard talks of himself and his friends, and the *Epitafe* in which he talks about Rabelais, have many words in

---

[19] See lines 37–43 of the *Epitafe* with their approximate data and factual errors.
[20] In *Le Bocage*, 1554; *Oeuvres complètes*, vol. VI, p. 12.
[21] Respectively ibid., vol. III, pp. 184–217; vol. V, pp. 53–76; vol. VI, pp. 176–90. On this series, see T. Cave, 'Ronsard's Bacchic Poetry: from the *Bacchanales* to the *Hymne de l'autonne*'.
[22] In *Oeuvres complètes*, vol. III, p. 188.

common, such as 'cup', 'flagon', 'saveloys', 'ham', 'paunch', 'fat', 'smear' and 'frog': terms which are fairly rare in poetic language and reveal a relationship between the two texts, appearing to indicate that Ronsard and Rabelais share a common physiognomy and vocation.

The *Livret de Folastries*,[23] written at the same time, confirms this Rabelaisian side of Ronsard. Everything in this collection – motifs from popular farce, licentious or burlesque themes, parody of high literature – tends to exploit low genres and to illustrate the interdependence of the erotic, the Bacchic and the poetic. The drunkard, Thenot, sets the tone: one evening at a cabaret,

> in the middle of the feast
> Having already poured a thousand glasses
> Down his wide gullet,
> Having greedily swallowed
> Without chewing many salt hams,
> Having gnawed a thousand sausages,
> A thousand pasties full of spices . . .
> (*Le Nuage, ou L'yvrogne*, lines 2–8)[24]

he starts to describe a fantastic, frenzied vision, whose verbal extravagance would have impressed Rabelais.

Alongside the Bacchic cycle and the *Folastries*, the same tone can be found in the series of poems dedicated to Jean Brinon,[25] a man fond of good living and a friend of poets. Ronsard conspicuously puts himself under the patronage of a man who links the pleasures of good food with those of art; at his splendid table, among the entertainments and the luxury of his banquets, Brinon talks to 'learned people' (*Le Houx*, line 218).[26] As at the Bacchic feasts (but with better manners, since here one is in a more refined circle), the mind and the body, the mouth that speaks and the mouth that eats, take their pleasures together.

This same ideal is found again in the group of poems addressed to Corydon. This interesting character is a fictional valet, a wine

[23] This appeared anonymously in 1553; ibid., vol. V.
[24] Ibid., vol. V, pp. 47–8.
[25] See the *Meslanges* of 1555; ibid., vol. VI.
[26] Ibid., vol. VI, p. 144.

waiter, a great organizer of alimentary pleasures, whom Ronsard (also in 1554–5) introduces into his imaginary biography. But Corydon is more than a mere orchestrator of drinking bouts and feasts. He is also the poet's accomplice and is a further symbol of the links between feasts and words (*Oeuvres complètes*, vol. VI, pp. 102–7), for example when he is asked to bring together for a literary banquet a squadron of men of letters to toast Henri Estienne and the discovery of Anacreon (ibid., vol. VI, pp. 174–6); or when he invites Belleau to taste 'milk reddened with many strawberries' and, in another profoundly literary act, to praise one's mistress by drinking 'as many glassfuls as she has letters in her name' (ibid., vol. VII, pp. 130–1); or finally when he receives the order to close the door because 'I want to read Homer's *Iliad* in the next three days' (ibid., vol. VII, pp. 182–3). Moreover, this functionary comes straight out of Virgil's *Eclogues* where he twice appears as a poet who sings as naturally as he eats and breathes (*Eclogues* 2 and 7).

Following the example of Rabelais, Ronsard is also searching for his own image and seems to look for it, at this point of his career, in the myth of the writer as a lover of the good life. Such a choice can easily be explained: he had alienated many of his public by treating sublime themes in his first works – Pindaric odes and the *Amours de Cassandre* – and by claiming for himself knowledge of the Greeks and the gift of prophecy. Around 1552–3 came the inevitable conversion, as described by Ronsard's biographers. But the way in which the theme of food and the Bacchic model contributed to this has been underestimated. The advantage is obvious: by assuming the image of the drunken poet, Ronsard is trying to retain (through a compromise) both his classical sources and the myth of inspiration. Without denying the prestige of the Ancients, nor his desire for originality, he returns to more familiar themes; he dons a mask which derives its credentials from mythology, but which also goes back to the popular tradition, belonging to the world of revelry as much as to the world of books. Bacchus and the drunkard Thenot enhance each other, the former gaining in credibility, the latter in a kind of dignity.

The choice of new literary models also contributes to this process of acclimatization and domestication, to this grafting of the academic on to the vulgar. We know that, at the same time,

Ronsard was turning to the Greek Anthology and the Pseudo-Anacreon, to Catullus, Horace and their neo-Latin imitators. Never ceasing to search out and recycle classical material, he found in these authors drinking songs, evocations of rustic festivities and comic motifs which could be combined with themes from the vulgar language which were more acceptable to the public at large. His tales of drinking bouts and revels retain a Greek flavour; they enjoy the authority of the erudite and preserve the ideal of Dionysian frenzy, while at the same time adopting the tone and subject matter of the old French school. This is a twofold movement towards naturalization: thanks in part to the theme of food, the strangeness of the classical material is domesticated and takes root in local tradition, in the decor of everyday life, in the discourse of the body and the imaginative world of physical pleasures.

The marrow bone

There is more to say on Rabelais and his prologues (from whom, as I have argued, Ronsard is not so different). For the theme of food does not only affect the figure of the narrator and his relationship with the audience, it also determines a network of metaphors which relate to the book, its production and its consumption.

The prologues to *Gargantua* and the *The Third Book* contain extensive variations on this analogy – writing, drinking and eating are part of the same referential order and of the same spatio-temporal register: 'Ennius wrote as he drank, drank as he wrote. Aeschylus . . . used to drink as he composed, to compose as he drank. Homer never wrote on an empty stomach. Cato never wrote except after drinking' (Prologue to *The Third Book*, p. 284). The fictive 'I' claims this simultaneity of activity for himself – writing is indissociable from bodily functions:

> For I never spent – or wasted – any more – or other – time in the composing of this lordly book, than that fixed for the taking of my bodily refreshment, that is to say for eating and drinking. Indeed, this is the proper time for writing of such high matters and abstruse sciences. (Prologue to *Gargantua*, p. 39)

Among the various identities he assumes when introducing himself to the reader, this is the most persistent: the tipsy poet writing (or rather speaking) his book at a tavern table and, following the Horatian *topos*, working more by the scent of wine than by the light of an oil lamp. In this depiction there are probably traces of the myth of Dionysian inspiration and of the neo-Platonic theory of frenzy – wine as the mediator of truth and drunkenness as an image of divine possession; the references to Plato's *Symposium*, to Silenus and to Bacchus at the start of the prologue to *Gargantua* all indicate this. But the metaphor is largely secular, and taken at face value it makes a case for a materialistic and playful theory of literature. Whereas Ronsard oscillates between one pole and the other, Rabelais prefers the immediate joys of conviviality to sacred enthusiasm. He substitutes for the myth of art as expression of the metaphysical the myth of art as product of the body and as profane recreation.

The network of analogies extends from the writer as eater, drinker or host to the book as a consumable product and to reading as ingestion. Wine provides one group of metaphors. If the listener is invited to drink, it is not only so that he should be merry and so enjoy listening more (which would be a simple relationship based on contiguity), but also because drinking functions as an appropriate image of reading – a more complex relationship based on similarity, underpinned by shared themes to do with pleasure, health, fraternity and profusion. As for the book, it is a bottle covetously uncorked: 'Have you ever picked a lock to steal a bottle?' (*Gargantua*, p. 38); and it is also a breviary from which one drinks (*The Fourth Book*, Prologue of 1548). The prologue to *The Third Book* exploits at great length the extended metaphor of the volume as a barrel, and *The Fifth Book* explores with rare subtlety the symbolic variations on the 'Holy Bottle' as a repository of wisdom and knowledge (*The Fifth Book*, chs. 44–7).

The burlesque device at work in these liquid images – the transposition of reading (and the literary operation as a whole) into the realm of the material and the physiological – clearly determines Rabelais's choice of references to the parallel sphere of solid nourishment: 'these fine and most juicy books' (*Gargantua*, p. 38), 'a great, greasy, grand, grey, pretty, little, mouldy book' half-eaten by 'rats and moths' (ibid., p. 42). The prologue to *The Fifth Book* contains a metaphor which, as far as hierarchies of taste are concerned, is also vulgar: the 'jolly and fruitful books' are so many 'beans' (p. 602), germinating beans or beans in a pod, beans that are shelled and eaten. The famous comparison with the 'marrow bone' (*os médulare*' – *Gargantua*, p. 38) makes the comparison of the book and fatty matter complete; the marrow (*medulla*) the traditional image of hidden meaning, regains its common meaning here. It provides the most effective representation of reading as sensory excitement and alimentary enjoyment, particularly because of the comic comparison between the reader and a gourmet dog searching for the marrow, and the colourful series of verbs that this comparison gives rise to (to gnaw, to break, to lick, to smell, to sample, etc.).

The activity of eating interests Rabelais as much as what is being eaten: appropriation by touch, smell, taste, chewing and absorption. Whereas other authors prefer to develop the culinary metaphor – the book as a dish which is concocted and simmers away[27] – here the stress is on ingestion – the book as a dish that is savoured and eaten: the work of production gives way to the pleasure of consumption. The reader–eater takes possession of the object being read, assimilates this foreign body and makes it part of his own being. Rabelais here uses a commonplace from the Latin theory of *imitatio*: reading is a process of nutrition and digestion; it appropriates earlier texts, recycles them and remakes them in order to feed the new works.[28] In such a context it is easier to understand the association between the act of writing (and reading) and swallowing, since writing, in the theory of *imitatio*, is the logical consequence of reading. To compose is to collect, to transpose and reorganize fragments of one's heritage; it is to absorb and digest books from the past; it is therefore to eat and to drink.

The traditional representation of *imitatio* may give the metaphors for literary exchange in the prologues a credible conceptual framework, but it does not exhaust their meaning. Rabelais does more than just repeat the classical *topos* in a burlesque tone: he reinvigorates it and gives it new scope. It would be wrong to treat

[27] See chapter 8.
[28] See Metaphors of bibliophagy, below.

these images of bibliophagy lightly and deny their force by assigning them to the storehouse of rhetorical cliché. They seem frivolous, but in fact set off a fundamental re-evaluation of the status of literature in everyday life. This is better understood when seen in its cultural context. Oral transmission, or at least what is left of it after printing became widespread, still dominates mentality and custom;[29] the written document is rarely dissociated from the voice that pronounces it. In these conditions, the word is considered as a sound, articulated and accentuated through the physical role of the sender in producing his own message. The text is not only addressed to the intellect; it is a global event which requires the participation of body and mind. Communication is perceived not only in terms of abstract ideas but just as much as a physical impulse which modifies the whole person and is part of organic life. The same is true of knowledge, which is still associated with an act of sensory perception. Learning involves bringing a tangible object from the outside to the inside, growing as a consequence of what one consumes and absorbing it into one's whole being. Memory stores anything but abstract signs; it is full of words heard, spoken and recited: it is a muscular and acoustic memory which feels sounds, chews them and stores them like organic matter.

The imaginative transfer of the book into the realm of food inspires yet further metaphors (but are these really metaphors?): 'Lay up a fair store of [books] . . . you must not only shell them, but gulp them down as an opiate cordial and absorb [*incorporez*] them into your systems' (Rabelais, *The Fifth Book*, p. 605). When he is about to have the Holy Bottle revealed to him, Panurge swallows down the contents of the book of Truth. Bacbuc the priestess uses the same verb as Rabelais, *incorporer*:

'The philosophers . . . feed you with fine words through the ears. Here we literally take in [*incorporons*] our teaching orally, through the mouth. Therefore I do not say to you: Read this chapter,

[29] See especially M. McLuhan, *The Gutenberg Galaxy, the Making of Typographic Man*, W. J. Ong, *Orality and Literacy. The Technologizing of the Word*, J. Leclercq, *L'Amour des lettres et le désir de Dieu. Initiation aux auteurs monastiques du moyen age*, and, in another context, M. Jousse, *L'Anthropologie du geste. II. La Manducation de la parole*.

understand this gloss. What I say is: Taste this chapter, swallow this gloss. Once upon a time an ancient prophet of the Jewish nation swallowed a book and became a learned man to the teeth . . . Here, open your jaws.'

Panurge opened his mouth wide, and Bacbuc took the silver book – which we thought really was a book because of its shape, which was that of a breviary. But it was a true breviary and natural flask, full of Falerian wine, which she made Panurge swallow. (*The Fifth Book*, p. 704)

It is justifiable to see this imbibing of the book as matter as more than the simple illustration of the saying *in vino veritas* or the emblem of literary *imitatio*. The book is communicated as words are, and words are received as physical substance, as present and as tangible as the things they denote. The reception of the message is ingestion because it implies osmosis and the fusion of two bodies. The reader–eater not only swallows the fruits of the earth, he savours words and consumes texts which touch him, nourish him and transform him. In the same way, Rabelais the doctor often claimed that his book had therapeutic powers, entertaining the reader to restore his health, a carefully administered dose of Pantagruelism putting the patient back on his feet. Here again he is crediting language with a real influence on the body. Reading is a feast, in that it affects the whole being: it is an experience which is physical and psychological, material and spiritual. At table, in close association with food, the materiality of discourse, the physiological reality of utterance and hearing and the incorporation of words become obvious. At least this is what the narrator wishes: 'Read joyfully on for your bodily comfort and to the profit of your digestions!' (*Gargantua*, p. 39).

Metaphors of bibliophagy

Alimentary metaphors are innumerable, polymorphous, unsystem-atizable and ubiquitous in everyday language. They proliferate, amongst other areas, in discourse on literature. From Pindar to the Bible, from rhetoric to the Cabbala, symbolic variations on the 'edible' book or on the 'nourishment' provided by doctrine are too numerous to mention, and I will not attempt here to list all the forms this analogy takes. I shall limit myself to the clusters which were the most relevant and the most common in the Renaissance.[30]

According to Latin etymology, a satire is a dish of mixed ingredients, a salad, a macedoine, a salmagundy or a pot-pourri: a composite genre derived from diverse other forms.[31] In French, *farce* has a culinary sense (forcemeat) as well as a literary one – probably originally denoting a little comic interlude 'stuffed' into a serious performance. Although they do not necessarily use these particular examples, metaphors of writing as an art in which raw material is mixed together and simmered are common. A book may be described as being concocted according to a clever recipe, or an author may think of himself as a cook as, for example, Montaigne: 'all this medly [*fricassée*] which I am scribbling here' (*Essays*, III, 13; p. 361). The analogy gives the work of writing a festive and often burlesque character: the text is ordered like a menu, the elements of style are measured out as in a sauce, and the tale contains a variety of ingredients, like a stew.[32]

From culinary images for the genesis of the work, it is natural to move on to the consumption of the literary meal: 'I have always thought of poetry as a sumptuous banquet to which everyone is welcome' (Du Bellay, Preface 'Au Lecteur' to *L'Olive*).[33] This image, inspired by the Bible, perhaps owes its popularity to Dante's *Convivio*, which contains an extended metaphor of this type: the poet has gathered crumbs from the 'table where they feed on the bread of angels' (*The Banquet*, I, 1, 7; p. 14), and out of them he has created a banquet, in vulgar language, for the profane: songs are the meat and the commentaries are the bread. The message of the book is like a supper open to the community, providing nourishment for the guests, drink for the thirsty and sustenance for famished spirits.

---

[30] To my knowledge there has been no detailed research into this subject. There is some information in E. R. Curtius, *European Literature and the Latin Middle Ages*, pp. 134–6. Little consideration is given in the following pages to the biblical tradition, the alimentary imagery of which was certainly known to, but rarely exploited by, the authors studied here (see chapter 1, The feast of the gods).

[31] See chapter 6, Satire and its cooking.

[32] The culinary metaphor was little used in France, but flourished particularly in Italy, perhaps due to the influence of Dante's *Convivio* (*The Banquet*). See S. Longhi-Gorni, *Lusus. Il Capitolo burlesco nel Cinquecento*, and chapter 8.

[33] The same metaphor is used in the introductory poem in *Les Regrets*.

Since the time of the Fathers of the Church, the religious tradition has used many such metaphors generated by the Eucharist – 'take, eat, this is my body . . .' and by the Incarnation – 'And the word was made flesh and dwelt among us'. One must also recognize in these metaphors the decisive influence of Jewish tradition. Christian memory only retains traces of it: the forbidden fruit, which when ingested, according to Genesis, gives knowledge, or the book of the prophet Ezekiel, which God makes its interpreter eat. But the Cabbala and Jewish ritual are full of this sort of metaphor. The Hebrew word *seder* can mean both a liturgical meal or a book, the Talmud. In religious ceremonies there are many variations on the association of word and food, the assimilation of a dish to a term, a letter or a scripture, and the interaction between speaking and eating.[34] The Humanists doubtless only had fragmentary knowledge of this field and their empathy with the Jewish culture was far from strong; but some resonances from it must have been present. When Jean Thenaud, a protégé of Francis I and an author whose work was probably read by Rabelais, writes his *Traité de la Cabale*, he echoes metaphors that are far from being isolated ones:

Holy Scripture is like a dish of all kinds of foods into which the sovereign king who makes a banquet for all spirits has put all kinds of meats . . . The main thing is to know how to slice it up and dress it up so as to live spiritually by it in great happiness. For he who chews it correctly . . . will find in it much sweet happiness. (Quoted by M. Holban, 'Autour de Jean Thenaud et de Frère Jean des Entonneurs', p. 57)

The contribution of the Cabbala is paralleled by that of Greek poetry. Following Pindar, Ronsard figuratively offers his text to be eaten; he invites the reader to taste his poems which, he says, rival the sweetness of honey and the savour of nectar and ambrosia. The first collection he published, the *Odes*, opens for example with the following comparison, which is shot through with convivial generosity:

Like one who takes a goblet,
The only honour of his treasure,

[34] See G. Haddad, *Manger le livre. Rites alimentaires et fonction paternelle.*

And gives to the company wine
Which laughs inside the gold:
Thus pouring the dew,
With which my tongue is stimulated,
To the family of the Valois,
I offer my fine Nectar
To the greatest King there has ever been,
Either in arms or in laws.
                    (Ronsard, *Oeuvres complètes*,
                                        vol. I, p. 61)

Although the Pindaric *topos* is not new, it recurs persistently throughout the *Odes* to put the joys of consuming poetry firmly in the realm of the mouth and the tongue. My song, suggests Ronsard – perhaps punning on the Greek *melos*, melody – flows like honey (*'miel'*), and I give it to you to savour. I am the lord of the feast and I lavish on you words which are food.[35] Elsewhere he writes: 'My book is like those splendid tables/That a Prince has covered in various dishes' (ibid., vol. X, p. 363): it is a 'banquet' with a varied menu, where the reader may help himself to whatever he likes. Once more, parallels with food tend to concretize and naturalize the text, restoring the diction – the timbre of the voice and the swing of the rhythm – to the register of organic expression. Bringing forth words is a physical act which calls into play one's whole being; verbs like 'disgorge', 'vomit', 'belch' and 'chew' are all applied to the production of lyrical language.[36] It is possible that this re-evaluation of the oral, this relocation of poetic activity into the mouth which shapes and savours words, is associated with the defence of the native language, a living, nurturing language, the language of the mother country which as Du Bellay says 'has

[35] N. Zemon Davis notes in 'Beyond the Market' that in the sixteenth century books were still occasionally given as gifts or bartered, in the same way as clothes, foods and other goods. It is not impossible that Ronsard is seeking, through his use of food imagery, to remove his book from commercial exchange and place it in an older and more prestigious economic system. I would add that the contiguous relationship between books and consumption is reinforced by the fact that merchants habitually carried books about in barrels.

[36] 'Disgorge' (*dégorger*): *Oeuvres complètes*, vol. I, pp. 65 and 92; vol. II, p. 85; vol. X, p. 37. 'Vomit' (*vomir*): vol. II, p. 49; vol. V, p. 171. 'Belch' (*roter*): vol. II, p. 49. 'Chew' (*mâcher*): vol. III, p. 154.

nourished [*nourry*] me for a long time with the milk of [its] breast' (*Les Regrets*, sonnet 9, line 2).

This verb *nourrir*, to nourish, is interesting because of its ambiguity, with its connotations of both the physiological and the intellectual. In Latin, *nutrire* and *alere* already combine the meanings of to feed and to educate. The expression *alma mater* and the image of poets as nurslings of the Muses are survivals of this. In sixteenth-century French, the same is true of *nourrir* and *nourriture* ('to nourish', 'nourishment'), whose double meaning is frequently exploited by writers: 'Gargantua was brought up and disciplined [*nourry et institué*] in all necessary ways . . . and he spent that time in the same manner as the other little children of that country: that is to say in drinking, eating, and sleeping (*Gargantua*, p. 62). In *nourry et institué*, which is a common phrase which would usually be tautological, Rabelais reintroduces the notion of food through a play on words. In the giant's education, food for the mind and food for the body are one and the same. When Montaigne, in his essay 'On the education of children', uses turns of phrase like 'training them and bringing them up [*nourrir*]' (*Essays*, I, 26; p. 53) and 'which his mind should be made to absorb' (ibid., p. 65), or when he calls the pupil an 'unweaned infant' (*nourrisson*) who must 'bite and feed on' knowledge as on a 'fruit' (p. 66), or when he recommends that the child, when reading the great authors, 'must imbibe their ways of thought, not learn their precepts' (p. 56), he too is giving new life to well-worn metaphors. Not only does he refuse to dissociate the psychological from the physical, he also explicitly associates the body and nutrition with the acquisition of knowledge. Learning about life lies in 'relishing books' (p. 82), absorbing them, and making them flesh and blood, engaging oneself in a transformation which involves the whole person.

Montaigne's notion of a complete education is of the same order as the reciprocal relationship of the two registers in the theory of *imitatio*, where the interdependence of words and food and the devouring of the book is most developed, at the boundary between the metaphorical and the literal. Quintilian had recommended that we should assimilate what we read in the same way that we chew and digest food (*Institutio oratoria*, X, 1, 19); thereafter variations on this theme are numerous.[37] In a famous passage, Du Bellay explains that in order to defend and illustrate their language, the French should do as the Romans did when they ransacked Greek literature:

> Imitating the best Greek authors, transforming themselves into them, devouring them; and, after having well digested them, converting them into blood and nourishment, taking for themselves, each according to his nature, and the argument he wished to choose, the best author of whom they observed diligently all the most rare and exquisite virtues, and these like shoots . . . they grafted and applied to their own tongue. (*The Defence and Illustration of the French Language*, I, 7; p. 37)

Analogies with food and gardening combine here to make the *translatio studii* seem natural and more authentic. The verb to digest, which is frequently used in discourse on *imitatio*, is also typically ambivalent. In sixteenth-century French and in the Latin *digerere*, the physiological meaning is combined with the more general sense of to separate, sort out, order or classify. In Cicero and Quintilian, *digestio* is defined as a figure of rhetoric whereby a general idea is divided into particular points, hence the sense of classifying and setting out;[38] similarly *digesta*, like the French *digeste*, means any sort of book divided into chapters (cf. 'digest' in English). To digest, in these languages, is to separate and then deal with elements of food or fragments of a text; Du Bellay, and Quintilian before him,[39] made the most of this ambiguity of meaning.

Another archetypal reference in this area is provided by Seneca who, in one of the *Letters to Lucilius*, uses all the elements of the alimentary theme to describe literary creation. To illustrate the idea that reading nourishes (*alit*) the mind, he first uses the metaphor of the bee: 'we should follow . . . the bees, who flit about and cull the flowers that are suitable for producing honey, and then

[37] See also T. M. Greene, *The Light in Troy. Imitation and Discovery in Renaissance Poetry*, and T. Cave, *The Cornucopian Text. Problems of Writing in the French Renaissance*.

[38] Cicero, *De oratore*, I, 186 and 190; III, 205; Quintilian, *Institutio oratoria*, IX, 2, 2; X, 4, 1; XI, 2, 37.

[39] *Institutio oratoria*, X, 1, 19 and XI, 2, 35.

arrange and assort [*digerunt*] in their cells all that they have
brought in' (*Ad Lucilium: Epistulae Morales*, 84). This comparison
also has imitators: Ronsard uses it to give a kind of natural
legitimacy to his tendency towards abundance and variety.[40] Like
the bee who makes its honey out of all the wealth of the fields, the
writer gathers his material from his favourite books. *Imitatio*,
henceforth, is no longer mere absorption, but a stroll among the
plants of a library which is like a garden. But the stroll has a
purpose. The various sources are transformed into a homogeneous
product: 'we should . . . blend those several flavours into one
delicious compound [*sapor*]', says Seneca (ibid.). The word *sapor* is
again ambivalent: like *sapientia* (savour and wisdom),[41] it is close
to the verb *sapere*: meaning both to have flavour and to have
intelligence and knowledge. The wise man and the knowledgeable
one are also greedy; intellectual activity is combined with an
olfactory and gustatory appreciation of the object and forms part
of the pleasure of eating. Judging by etymology, *Homo sapiens* is
more than a man of intellect: he has a good nose and well-
developed senses.

Seneca immediately builds a metaphor of digestion on his
metaphor of the bee: as in the making of honey, the body
transforms food into energy and blood. 'So it is with the food
which nourishes our higher nature, – we should see to it that
whatever we have absorbed should not be allowed to remain
unchanged . . . We must digest it [*concoquere*]: otherwise it will
merely enter the memory and not the reasoning power' (ibid.).
Seneca uses two other analogies to describe this process of
impregnation and integration: the resemblance of a son to his
father and the voices that merge together in a choir. Herein lies the
whole problematic of writing in the age of *imitatio*.[42] A process of
osmosis between the self and the other, the present and the past, is
necessary to carry on the work of the Ancients without copying
them, in order for memory, instead of mechanically reproducing

[40] *Oeuvres complètes*, vol. XI, pp. 160–1 and vol. XV, p. 252.

[41] See L. Quicherat, *Thesaurus poeticus linguae latinae*.

[42] Among the many authors who refer to the text of the letter to Lucilius,
Macrobius quotes almost word for word Seneca's comparisons with the bee and
with digestion (*Saturnalia*, Preface, 5–7). The wide circulation of Macrobius's
works in the Middle Ages and in the Renaissance makes this particularly
important.

what has already been said, to contribute to the creation of a new work. Where theory is lacking to explain this symbiosis, metaphors come into play and the metaphor of digestion is very significant among these. Monks of the Middle Ages had invented an even more expressive figure for this process of internal assimilation: *ruminatio*. Petrarch adopts it to stress the need for complete fusion between the eater and eaten, the reader and the read. He says that he has devoured the classical Latin texts:

> I ate in the morning what I would digest in the evening; I swallowed as a boy what I would ruminate upon as a man. These writings I have so thoroughly absorbed and fixed, not only in my memory but in my very marrow, these have become so much a part of myself that even though I should never read them again they would cling in my spirit, deep-rooted in its inmost recesses. (*Lettere*, XXII, 2)[43]

Without denying the necessity of omnivorous reading, nor challenging the need to internalize classical models, the Humanists insisted on the emergence of a new type of consciousness, imbued with culture but aware of its own identity and concerned to prove its originality. Against the dangers of mindless copying, Erasmus insists on the importance of a writing which reflects the self and expresses a distinctive personality to counter the dangers of a distancing imitation. Again, alimentary imagery is used to mark this essential affirmation of the individual voice in and through dialogue with other writers. One must devour authors, transform and assimilate them so that one can become oneself:

> You must digest what you have consumed in varied and prolonged reading, and transfer it by reflection into the veins of the mind, rather than into your memory or your notebook. Thus your natural talent [*ingenium*], gorged on all kinds of foods, will of itself beget a discourse which will be redolent, not of any particular flower, leaf or herb, but of the character and feelings of your own heart, so that whoever reads your work will not recognize fragments of Cicero, but the image of a mind replete with every kind of learning. (*Dialogus Ciceronianus*, p. 652)[44]

---

[43] F. Petrarca, *Lettere*, ed. Giuseppe Fracassetti (5 vols, Firenze, Le Monnier, 1863–7), vol. V, p. 422; quoted by T. M. Greene, *The Light in Troy*, p. 99.
[44] Quoted by Cave, *The Cornucopian Text*, p. 45.

When Montaigne, later, calls his essays 'the excretions of an old mind, sometimes hard, sometimes loose and always undigested' (*Essais*, III, 9; p. 946), he is giving a deliberately grotesque twist to a traditional metaphor. But it is always, for the reader, a question of eating the book: and that is the point of Montaigne's reversal.

6

Classical banquets

The banquets of classical literature, like those of Renaissance literature, cannot be reduced to the thematic, structural or stylistic constraints of a single genre: what makes them distinctive is their variety and polyphony. They are too heterogeneous to adhere to a unique model, and also do not have a clear evolution, their genealogy remaining uncertain.[1] There are however some constant features: the table is seen as an appropriate place for linguistic experiment and exuberance; the description of a meal forms a text which is composite, rhapsodic and suited to literary *bricolage*. In the following pages I shall not attempt a systematic study but rather consider Greek *symposia* and Latin *convivia* with a view to isolating those tendencies which do after all give the corpus a certain unity, and which moreover we rediscover in sixteenth-century banquets. I shall not be trying to establish that these were influenced by classical banquets, even though the texts examined here were available in the Renaissance,[2] but rather that the features of the symposiac theme remain the same from one era to another.

---

[1] J. Martin's developmental study, *Symposion. Die Geschichte einer literarischen Form*, is useful, but the continuity it seeks to establish is not convincing. F. Dupont's book, *Le Plaisir et la loi*, centred around the *Satyricon*, is more useful; see also M. D. Gallardo, 'Estado actual de los Estudios sobre los Simposios de Platón, Jenofonte y Plutarco' and 'Los Simposios de Luciano, Ateneo, Metodio y Juliano'.

[2] Except for the *Cena Trimalchionis* in Petronius's *Satyricon* (see chapter 3, note 9).

Philosophy at meal time

When in Xenophon's *Symposium* Socrates goes to supper at Callias's, it is not to indulge in dialectics or to help others give birth to ideas at table. Nonplussed modern supporters of Socrates protest: 'Xenophon's Socrates . . . is doubtless a fine man, but mean-minded and fond of scoffing' (L. Robin, Introduction to Plato, *Le Banquet*, p. cxii), but this reaction does not allow for the particular atmosphere of the *symposion*. In Athens, celebrations of the Great Panathenaea are being held and Callias gives a feast in honour of the young Autolycos, the victor at the pancratium, and with whom he is in love. The food is soon cleared away; improvised conversation and entertainments can then begin. The text reflects the disjointed nature of the revels. It is constructed like a narrative, with snatches of dialogue alternating with descriptions of the different scenes which take place throughout the evening. Events, unforeseen circumstances and digressions intervene; there is great variety.

The conversation is well furnished, but has no unity or direction; it wanders, as is inevitable around a table where the talk is desultory. The guests are educated people, and there is no shortage of serious subject matter: virtue, courage, dancing, and, towards the end, a long speech by Socrates on love. But centrifugal impulses and ideas which are cut short ensure that the dialogue as a whole has a colourful and varied character and make its progression erratic. Above all, after a serious passage, the guests are always keen to digress on to more light-hearted topics to keep the conversation moving and to maintain its jocose tone. The most structured debate in this motley proceeding is a significant one: everyone has to say what he is most proud of, and then explain why (Xenophon, *Symposium*, III–IV). There follow the most unexpected arguments: one boasts of being poor, another of knowing by heart the verse of Homer, Socrates of being a pimp; and everyone defends his choice by arguments of a fair degree of sophistry. The taste for riddles and for paradoxical *encomia*, which is characteristic of table talk,[3] is evident here; the conversation is

---

[3] See chapter 4, Convivial speech.

organized but, as later in the game of caricature comparisons (ibid., VI, 8–10), its aim is to entertain or to surprise, even at the expense of morality and realism. Most commentators try to find a single cohesive theme to overcome this fragmentation;[4] but the idea that there is one is all the more dubious since the guests have very different views, characters and tones, and all have their say in the matter. No doubt Socrates is more prominent than the others, but he lets the others speak; barely has he a role in directing the free flow of the conversation. No criteria of truth or relevance, and no methodology are ever adduced to disallow anything that is said.

The role of spectacle increases the lawlessness of the banquet. The host has hired a troupe of players under a Syracusan impresario: a flautist, an acrobatic dancer and a boy who plays the cithara and dances. The guests frequently suspend their discussions to watch or even participate in displays of skill, musical interludes, dances and mime – genuine cabaret turns which the narrator sometimes describes in detail. There is also a kind of clown, Philippe, who arrives to liven up the festivities. He is a parasite who has not been invited and earns his pittance through his practical jokes, gesticulations and facial expressions; he seems to have stepped out of a farce and, as a comic player, makes the atmosphere of the feast even more theatrical. The guests in Plato's *Symposium* show the flautist the door. Those at Xenophon's *Symposium*, on the other hand, do not object to any form of pleasure. Socrates only interrupts the juggling once to suggest an alternative entertainment (ibid., VII, 5); he voices his approval of these *divertissements* and, in passing, gives a speech strongly praising dance (II, 15–20). When the discussion on virtue appears to drag on, he diverts the attention of the guests: 'Let us reserve it for another time; for the present let us finish what we have on hand. For I see that the dancing girl here is standing ready, and that some one is bringing her some hoops' (II, 7).

This shift is significant; from elevated ideas one moves on to the observation of the body. Physiological elements recur throughout the narrative and continually challenge the philosophical ones. At the end of the banquet, sensuality reaches its peak: scarcely has

---

[4] In his edition of the *Symposium* (*Le Banquet*), F. Ollier suggests the *kalokagathia*; R. Flacelière replies with *eros*, 'A propos du *Banquet* de Xénophon'.

Socrates finished his edifying discourse on love when mountebanks come on stage and act out the embrace of Ariadne and Dionysos; this is such a lascivious scene that the audience, seized with desire, rush home to embrace their wives! The shock of this transition from speculation about love to the act of love has an unbelievable force. There is a total contrast which no system can do away with between the wise man's speech on spiritual love and the sensual ardour of men attracted to sex. Earlier on, physical representation had already revealed a tendency towards the grotesque; far from sublimating heavy physicality, the narrative emphasizes its characteristics. Philippe the clown's postures when he is imitating the artistes' dance reveal his clumsiness and indecency (II, 22); the gods at their feast in the *Iliad* had also laughed at the lame Hephaistos (Homer, *Iliad*, I, 599–600). Socrates himself parades his ugliness; as well as portraying himself as a pimp, he paints a deliberately unflattering portrait of himself: bulging eyes, a snub nose and thick lips, everything that makes him look like Silenus, without there being any question here of inversing the comparison by the revelation of hidden beauty, as in Plato. Flesh occupies centre stage, accepted, exaggerated and unabashed.

Socrates's position seems ambiguous: his superiority is recognized and he dominates the conversation, but at the same time he humiliates himself, exposing himself to mockery and agreeing to talk about trivia. In other words he plays along with the fundamentally heterogeneous nature of the banquet. Other sources reveal that he is a man who can cope with all situations, who can fit in with any group of people, who can adapt to the most elevated and the most base things, but perhaps it takes the freedom of the symposiac device to display this fully. Philosophy, when it takes its place at table, agrees to be interrogated by the non-philosophical, it exposes itself to the challenge of pleasure, of chance and of multiplicity; confronted by the irreducible nature of everyday life, its morality becomes immanent, and it simply takes a holiday from elevated ideas. The thematic extension of the narrative, its variety of tone, and its digressive nature are all linked to this, as is the astonishing realism of the descriptions.

The writer's freedom is expressed through that of the guests; it is as if the banquet scene gives his imagination virtually unlimited room for manoeuvre. Voices and ideas mingle; they are not ranked or integrated. Contradictions remain unresolved, loose ends are left. Philosophical, narrative, dramatic, serious and comic elements exist side by side for better or for worse in a text which is fundamentally pluralistic in nature, and where generic rigour is non-existent; it could be described as a foretaste of the Menippean satire.[5] Dialogism and heterogeneity[6] enter the history of the literary banquet with Xenophon and remain part of it from then on.

Normally readers judge Xenophon's *Symposium* in relation to Plato's and find it lamentable or irritating. Perhaps they are using the wrong yardstick; perhaps it would be better to look at things the other way round.[7] For Xenophon's text illuminates the truly symposiac nature of Plato's and allows it to shed the philosophical straitjacket in which it is most often placed.

Of course, there are considerable differences between the texts. In Plato the centrifugal forces and the latent disorder of the convivial scene are largely controlled. The decor and the occasion are briefly described, the meal is quickly dealt with (this is the rule of the *symposion*) and entertainments are non-existent – the flautist is sent away and with her goes erotic temptation. In other words, description and narration occupy a very limited space. The field is left free for the discussions which follow one on the other while the wine is passed around. The pleasure of speaking needs no adjunct, and the conversation provides another element of cohesion by being all (or nearly all) on the single theme of love. It is no surprise if readers searching for order and unity are more at ease with this text than with Xenophon.

But there is room for play. The procedure of the evening and the distribution of speeches are carefully ordered, but do leave room for some surprises. The guests have come to celebrate with Agathon and to have a good time together. The usual rules of pleasure impose some precautions: drunkenness will be avoided because it dulls the senses, but, in praising Eros, the guests must also not succumb to pedantry; rigour of method and the pursuit of

---

[5] See Satire and its cooking, below.
[6] See chapter 7, The copious and the varied.
[7] I am not making a value judgement or a chronological argument (we do not know in what order the two *Symposia* were written), but rather trying to find the most appropriate point of view.

truth are less important than the quality of the conversation. Wine will loosen tongues and tongues will control the intake of wine. Nevertheless the feast is under the sign of Dionysos: imagination is on the agenda, and freedom of behaviour and ideas, as long as they do not spoil everyone's enjoyment, will provide the entertainment, which in fact is not lacking. A few judiciously placed episodes suffice to produce the unexpected and to maintain the atmosphere of gaiety. At the beginning, Socrates brings a guest who was not invited, but he himself is late and arrives in the middle of the supper. After the first two speeches, a comic interlude provides a diversion: Aristophanes has hiccups and, while he tries to cure them by holding his breath, gargling and sneezing (Plato, *Symposium*, 185c–e), he misses his turn to speak. But these convulsions are just a prelude to his speech, which introduces into the discussion, along with the image of the grotesque body we have already noted in Xenophon, the hermaphrodite myth; there is a great resemblance between the comic Aristophanes and the clown, Philippe. There follow two serious expositions which are interrupted by another burlesque episode: Alcibiades arrives, drunk and surrounded by revellers. He spreads disorder and starts to speak, but goes off at a tangent, praising not Eros but Socrates. His portrait of Socrates combines extremes: the sublime and the trivial, the height of wisdom and the height of sensuality, with, once again, the overwhelming presence of the physiological alongside the highest ideas.

Many people in the sixteenth century would have recognized this: Bouchet comments, for example: 'so we see that Plato's *Symposium* is stuffed full of madmen and jokers who jibe and mock each other' (*Les Sérées*, vol. I, p. xiv). Herein lies the beauty of this text: it confronts major philosophical themes (as the continuing tradition of commentaries on it shows) without avoiding the questions posed by pleasure and fiction. When philosophy is invited to sit down at the banquet it is heckled and jostled. Other rules are imposed on it, and it is worth outlining how these operate.

The main point can be demonstrated quite quickly. Socrates is present, but there is no Socratic dialogue nor, in fact, dialogue of any kind. The Socratic method is well known: through reasoning and through irony, through the dialectical sequence of questions and answers, he leads his interlocutor to discover a certain truth; although it has the appearance of a spontaneous conversation, the course of the dialogue is clearly marked out and orientated towards its conclusion. At Agathon's table this is not at all the case. Each of the friends in turn pronounces a eulogy, perhaps referring to a previous speech but without there being any communication or convergence between them. As in Xenophon, but in a compartmentalized way, everyone democratically has the right to speak. Socrates by no means approves of the speeches, but only criticizes them later on; he lets others have their say and does not have a dominant role. It is true that when he does intervene he raises the debate to a much higher level, but although his contribution is qualitatively different from the earlier speeches, it does not mark a logical conclusion to them. The speeches do not cancel each other out, nor are they co-ordinated: they develop according to the whim of each speaker. Convivial polyphony is at its height here: opinions, methodologies, points of view and manners are freely expressed without being subject to any overall system; no voice is authoritative and there is no impulse towards the synthesis of the diverse viewpoints. Socrates's strategy in his speech shows the strangeness of the situation from the philosophical point of view. First he addresses Agathon and hounds him with questions, as the dialectical habit reasserts itself. But the others are not equal to the challenge; moreover this interrogation would upset the harmony of the banquet. So Socrates plays the game; he too makes a speech, but it is a speech in which he maliciously introduces dialogue: he relates the conversation in which Diotima once upon a time had enlightened him as to the true nature of love. Diotima asks the questions and Socrates replies, putting himself into the position of a disciple. The trick is significant: in order to exorcize the dogmatism of the monologue, Socrates resorts to the technique of interrogation after all. The dialectic comes back in through the back door – underlining its absence from the rest of the text.

Besides, the other friends do not claim to be making philosophy. Their aim is different: they are praising love. When he sets out this plan, Eryximachus quotes the example of poets and sophists (ibid., 177a–c): they are the specialists in this matter, and it is their failure which must be made good by celebrating and praising Eros. Above all, the art of paying homage is a part of rhetoric; the terms used –

encomion, epainos – are precise technical· categories, with clear rules;[8] the speeches are scholastic exercises, eloquent pieces where fine language is more important than the search for truth. In Agathon's ceremonious, solemn and flowery speech, Socrates himself recognizes the influence of Gorgias (198c). Critics have had no difficulty in isolating in the other eulogies elements of style which belong to a certain school or author; intertextual references, whether parodic or not, seem numerous. I am not sufficiently expert to define the style of each speaker, but some general tendencies can be seen in the speeches which precede that of Socrates. Laudatory hyperbole, structuring techniques and gradations show that some speakers have studied rhetoric; there are specious arguments, subtle distinctions and erudite references which smell of sophistry; and there is a taste for mythological narrative which is reminiscent of poetry. Louis Le Roy, who translated the *Symposium* with a critical commentary in the sixteenth century, saw this clearly:

> There is nothing more rhetorical or more ornate in language than this book, nor anything more poetic on account of the fine stories and descriptions which occur throughout... Here he does not make use of long and specious questions or violent demonstrations to persuade, as he does in his other dialogues, nor does he use words that cannot be understood . . . instead there are graceful arguments, friendly questions, pleasant examples and gay tales, as is suitable for such a feast and in such company. (*Le Sympose de Platon . . .* , pp. iii–iv)[9]

The friends are philologists rather than philosophers, and they show off their eloquence; the pleasure of fine speech is for them a major part of symposiac enjoyment. Rhetoric and poetics parade their charms at the expense of intellectual rigour: philosophy at table finds itself overcome by literature.

Socrates owes it to truth to correct this drift. He has been in a convivial frame of mind, and has let the company revel in words. But when it is his turn to speak, he makes an uncompromising appraisal of the preceding table talk. He ironically congratulates

---

[8] See Robin, Introduction to Plato, *Le Banquet*, p. xxxii.
[9] *Le Sympose de Platon . . . traduit de grec en françois, avec trois livres de commentaires . . .*

the previous orator, Agathon: ' "The beauty of the words and phrases . . . would have taken anyone's breath away" ' (Plato, *Symposium*, 198b). Agathon is a disciple of the orator Gorgias, and an author of tragedies; he is certainly a fine speaker and clever persuader. But his flowing words are hollow. After suffering a few minutes of dialectical questioning from Socrates, he admits: ' "It looks, Socrates, as if I don't know what I was talking about" ' (ibid., 201b). The orators are carried away by their love of language, and would say anything, and defend any cause. Socrates charges that the panegyrics about love which we have just heard are all hot air, elegant but futile words; he regrets now that he got involved in the game:

> I was stupid enough to suppose that the right thing was to speak the truth about the subject proposed for panegyric, whatever it might be . . . But now it appears that this is not the right way to set about praising anything, and that the proper method is to ascribe to the subject of the panegyric all the loftiest and loveliest qualities, whether it actually possesses them or not; if the ascription is false, it is after all a matter of no consequence. In fact, what was proposed to us was that each of us should give the appearance of praising Love, rather than that we should actually do so. (Ibid., 198d–e)

Socrates substitutes words of truth for these words of theatre and fiction, words given over only to circumstance and effect. Two ways of thinking and two ways of speaking confront each other: it is, as some have suggested, a battle (*agôn*) between rhetoric and philosophy. On the superficial level, Socrates wins the day. Alcibiades says he is always far superior (215e). But the fact remains that the speeches of the friends (178a–197e) outweigh those of the philosopher (198a–212c) by a ratio of three to two; was so much eloquence necessary to discredit eloquence? The banquet has a different scale of values: from a philosophical point of view, Socrates is right; from a literary and symposiac point of view, the result is less clear.

Whatever the rights and wrongs, the law of polyphony is respected. The philosopher's voice follows the sequence of orators, which itself is varied; Socrates replies to the genre of eulogy by using dialogue. The noisy entrance of Alcibiades, coming just after the transcendental revelations of Diotima, is brutally bathetic and provides further evidence of the composite nature of the text. He changes the subject (apparently at least), he changes the tone and, with the freedom of the drunkard, uses outrageous comparisons, comes out with daring revelations, and alternates strangely between the basest kind of desire and the highest virtue. Within this speech, as with the text as a whole, the contrasts are sharp; once more, but in another mode, the exuberance of the word puts philosophy to the test. Louis Le Roy's translation ends after Diotima's sublime words: therein lies, he says, the *telos* of the banquet; the rest is mere debauchery, impropriety and weakness on the part of Plato, who 'added it only for pleasure, responding to the taste of his time and the licentious life of his country' (*Le Sympose de Platon*, p. 174). The sixteenth century however was not as prudish as this might imply, and Le Roy's condemnation is therefore all the more significant: he reluctantly recognizes the essential role of pleasure and variety but condemns the ending as incongruous and incoherent. His reading has systematically ignored the symposiac setting, and his conclusion is therefore logical.

History teaches us that from the dawn of Greek civilization the banquet has an essential role as a social institution; it is a meeting place where the ties of the community are strengthened.[10] Documentary evidence also proves that in the context of the *symposion* wine and the poetic word are closely linked.[11] In the megaron of Homeric princes, bards recite their epics while *kraters* of wine are being emptied. Elsewhere in the archaic period shorter forms of poetry are specially designed to be sung at meal times and to accompany drinking. The birth and development of the elegy, of iambic poetry and of the epigram, not to mention the *skolia* and other minor genres, are all connected to the symposiac setting. Poems by Alcaeus, Sappho, Solon and Anacreon and his followers[12] only make sense against a background of conviviality where wine

---

[10] On the relationship between the banquet and communal life, see the beginning of Plato's *Laws* (and my chapter 3, An archaeology of the table).

[11] See Dupont, *Le Plaisir et la loi*, and O. Murray, 'The Greek Symposion in History'.

[12] See the texts brought together by A. Delbouille: *Anacréon et les poèmes anacréontiques.*

and words come together. Agathon's guests, of course, had other plans; they had better things to do than to sing songs. But their aim still formed part of this tradition and respects its laws: they were seeking pleasure and, with the help of Dionysos, they find it, through the beauty of inspired words.

Satire and its cooking

In Greece and Rome many other banquets were based on Plato's model, but these have been lost or reduced to fragments. Judging by the texts that have survived, one can distinguish two trends in the first centuries after Christ: satirical banquets and encyclopaedic banquets, in which conversation, still plentiful, takes on new forms.

Lucian of Samosata, the satirist and sceptic, has a bone to pick with all the great authors. His banquet, *The Lapiths*, is full of allusions to the models of Plato and Xenophon: he uses the same narrative device and the same gathering of philosophers interspersed with episodes, recalling those of the standard texts. But the model is systematically reversed: the feast degenerates into an orgy, the conversation takes place *during* the meal, and it ends in a fight – war taking the place of love. The parodic intention is obvious, and burlesque debasement predominates. And yet Lucian is merely liberating the centrifugal forces which are always latent in the symposiac scenario. The colourful variety and the grotesque aspects which are controlled in Plato and only partially released in Xenophon are here given free rein.

In *The Lapiths*, philosophers of all persuasions have been invited to a wedding feast. Following contemporary (second century AD) eclecticism, the host has not forgotten any of the rival Schools: there is a Stoic, an Epicurean, an Aristotelian, a Platonist, a rhetorician and a grammarian; counting the Cynic who was not invited, the whole cultural elite is represented and the pluralist nature of the banquet is taken to the limit. Helped along by drink, quarrels soon develop. In line with the rules of comedy, the hatred and jealousy is immoderate: the conversation (sometimes in reported, sometimes in direct speech) is invaded by arguments, challenges and insults, and turns into logomachy. Differences of opinion are irreconcilable, and there is no real dialogue. The conflict of ideas exacerbates the crises of a culture in which syncretism leads to the destruction of all philosophies. In Lucian's burlesque style convivial polyphony becomes a cacophony which is as lamentable for the history of thought as it is fertile for the writer.

The linguistic jousting is soon followed by actual blows; the feast frequently degenerates into fisticuffs and ends in a general free-for-all. This explains the title of the book: 'You would have said they were Lapiths and Centaurs, to see tables going over, blood flowing and cups flying' (*The Lapiths*, 45). After filling their stomachs, the philosophers exercise their muscles; the antagonism which Plato's *symposion* controlled through the *logos* is resolved here by force. The civilizing influence of the meal is lost as passions overflow; unsublimated Dionysian fury is expressed through the wild language of the body. The comic vision reveals the hidden side of the banquet, namely the orgy; it releases the converse aspect of reasonable words, namely violence. The so-called thinkers are incapable of controlling their natural instincts and show the emptiness of their fine doctrines; and Lucian, who does not have any strong beliefs, denounces them all as so many impostors.

But there is more to it than a circumstantial criticism of contemporary philosophers. Lucian is exploring the potential of the symposiac device on two levels. In Plato's model the potentially composite convivial setting had overcome the fragmentation of voices and had maintained the possibility of harmonious polyphony. But in Lucian neither reason nor politeness can stifle the disseminative forces. In this sense, his banquet is a failure – the first in a long line which, far from reducing the plurality of opinions at table, exploit their subversive value in order to reveal the divisive factors at work in a particular society or system. We shall see that the 'exploded' banquet is frequently used as a weapon against universalizing orthodoxy and as an allegory of sceptical or relativist ideas.[13]

However the message is not only ideological; it is also a literary one. For the tensions inherent in the symposiac scene are also a

---

[13] See Greedy grammarians, below; chapter 7, The copious and the varied, Guillaume Bouchet: stuffings, and Giordano Bruno: the failed banquet; and chapter 9, 'Monarch of ecumenical symposia', and 'You only talk about sex'.

result of the multiplicity of styles and the latent disintegration of a genre in which so many kinds of discourse are involved. With no regard for unity of tone, Lucian and many others after him[14] actualize the capacity for mixing different voices and the tendency towards parodic *bricolage* which are inherent in the description of banquets. The battle in *The Lapiths* is also scriptural; heterogeneous gobbets of texts, literary reminiscences and samples from all genres are juxtaposed without any hope of integration. Whether they are speaking or reading from their works, the scholars all more or less have their own style; a letter or a poem is transcribed; Homeric epic and mythology are mentioned; allusions to Plato and Xenophon are included; and so on. The narrative, like a literary montage, is an unstable mixture, a text which, like the company of diners, threatens to disintegrate at any moment.

In his banquet Lucian uses humour to criticize the manners of the time; and he combines a variety of styles: two devices corresponding exactly to the two definitions of satire which were current in the Latin world. Satire is a form which is highly relevant to my study, and it is worth dwelling on this in order to place *The Lapiths* in its generic context, to bring in Petronius's *Satyricon* and to examine in a new light the relationship between feasts and words.

In spite of its other derivations and meanings,[15] satire seems to have been considered metaphorically as a culinary object: the copious product of a mixture of ingredients. Among the various etymologies suggested by classical writers (who, as we know, attached great significance to this sort of relationship) two are relevant here, and these are also the most likely derivations. The first belongs to the field of religion: 'Many say that satire acquired its name from the dish (*lanx satura*) which, filled with different fruits, was carried into the temple of Ceres. And therefore they named this type of poetry satire because it is so stuffed with different things that it satisfies the hearers' (Acron, c. fifth century

---

[14] Apart from Petronius, *Satyricon*, see Greedy grammarians, below; chapters 7, 8 and 9. By Lucian, see also *Lexiphanes*, a pastiche on pedantic and archaic jargon in the form of a banquet.

[15] See U. Knoche, *Roman Satire*, and J. W. Jolliffe, 'Satyre: Satura: *satyros*. A Study in Confusion'.

AD).[16] The second derivation is directly related to cookery: '*satura* is derived *a quondam genere farciminis* ("from a certain kind of stuffing") which was filled with many things and called *satura*, according to the evidence of Varro', (Diodemus the Grammarian, fifth century AD).[17] These two solutions are complementary: they both associate with the word 'satire' ideas of abundance and of the mixture of foods. Juvenal, when he compares the themes of his satires to a *farrago* (a medley, a hotch-potch or a pot-pourri), confirms the analogy (*Satires*, I, line 86).

The satire then owes its name to 'the variety of metre or . . . the abundance of subjects which are treated in it' (Robert Estienne, *Thesaurus Latinae Linguae*, 1531).[18] As far as we can deduce from surviving fragments (especially those by Ennius, Pacuvius and Lucilius), the word 'satire', in the first centuries of its existence, did denote a collection of various kinds of poetry with differing metres, themes and styles: a collection of texts with no apparent unity, a disparate grouping or a miscellany. The polemical nature of the satire was absent to begin with, but gradually became more important. The word came to mean a single poem, and the connotations of food, as well as the idea of a mixture, gradually disappeared.

It is the sense of experimentation, common to both the notion of cooking and that of a literary hotch-potch, which interests me here: it implies that authors and cooks are chemists who produce a clever mixture of ingredients out of a love of words or food. Thus we return, in a different way, to the association between food and verbal inventiveness which we have already seen in table talk.

This association becomes even clearer in one particular branch of the genre: the Menippean satire.[19] Nothing survives by its founder, the Cynic Menippus of Gadara (third century BC). The works of Lucian and texts like Seneca's *Apocolocyntosis* and Petronius's

---

[16] Acron, a commentator on Horace, quoted by Jolliffe, ibid., p. 88. This religious derivation was known in the sixteenth century: see Isaac Casaubon, *De satyrica Graecorum poesi, et Romanorum satira libri duo*, pp. 318–19.

[17] Quoted by Knoche, *Roman Satire*, p. 13.

[18] The entry on *Satyra*, quoted by Jolliffe, 'Satyre: Satura: *satyros*', p. 91.

[19] Apart from Knoche, *Roman Satire*, and works mentioned in his bibliography, see Bakhtin, *Problems of Dostoevsky's Poetics*, chapter 4.

Satyricon allow us by extension to reconstruct the genre;[20] but the most likely approximation to it is no doubt provided by Varro (first century BC), who popularized the Menippean satire in the Latin world. From the few surviving fragments we can deduce that satire's taste for the motley jumble of composite elements was taken to its extreme here. The general theme (the critique of manners) seems to have left the field open for a broad range of subject matter: but the freedom of composition is mainly seen in the different forms of writing used – a characteristic mixture of prose and poetry, with the latter involving a diversity of metre. The language used also contains all kinds of experiments which are normally absent from literary texts, such as the coining of neologisms, etymological figures, puns and other paronymic effects and the inclusion of Greek terms: the whole gamut of creativity afforded by words seems to have been covered. The Menippean satire, in Varro and its other exponents, does not have a single style or a single tone, but many deliberately contrasting types of each: the sublime and the vulgar, the didactic and the playful, academic terminology and the words of the people all interact without sacrificing their own identity. Different types of discourse, which are normally reserved for specific genres, also contribute to the composite nature of the works; we saw that Lucian included a letter and a poem in his narrative, and this is a typical combination. Elsewhere, the pattern is made up of maxims, proverbs, quotations and pastiches; all the resources of parody and intertextuality are used. Menippean satire is basically open and unfinished, in that it carries on a continuous dialogue with other works and other linguistic systems; beyond the porous boundaries of a given text, other texts can be glimpsed, stimulating the memory, taking the reader off at tangents and constantly upsetting the balance of the discourse. The work seems to make itself up as it goes along and all kinds of fantasy seem to be permissible. This sense of liberty has a particular effect: it may or may not be genuine, but it highlights the problematic function of writing and reveals language and literary forms at work. The Menippean satire

---

[20] The Emperor Julian's (also called Julian the Apostate) *Banquet* could be added to this list, but I shall not refer to this text, which does not exploit the convivial situation and the essentially polemic and political aim of which compromises the literary interest of the book.

draws attention less to the story being narrated than to itself as a product of artifice and knowledge. It sharpens the linguistic and stylistic consciousness of the reader.

As if by chance, the meal scene seems to provide a favourite setting for these verbal and textual manipulations. Lucian is not an innovator in this; a *Symposion* has been attributed to Menippus and some fragments survive of a banquet by Varro (*Agatho*, in *Satires ménippées*); soon Petronius was to exploit extensively the affinity between the Menippean pot-pourri and the convivial theme. Of course, conviviality does not have an exclusive claim to this relationship: that would run counter to the diverse nature of the genre. However the homology is evident in the way in which the flow of table talk reflects a whole range of themes and voices. Uninhibited conversation, and the frankness of the narrator who makes the most of the freedom his subject matter allows, result in satire being a real testing ground: as a writer/cook, the Menippean satirist logically chooses as his characters philological diners!

Apart from the well-documented influence of Lucian, it is difficult to gauge what the direct effect of the Menippean satire was in the Renaissance. Whatever it was, as Bakhtin has shown (*Problems of Dostoevsky's Poetics*)[21] Menippean satire provides a particularly appropriate model of the rhapsodic, polyphonic and parodistic nature of so many sixteenth-century works. Before the new broom of Classicism swept clean, narrative literature enjoyed almost total freedom of structure and tone, as Erasmus's *In Praise of Folly*, Rabelais and *Don Quixote* all show. One of the best satires of the time was in fact called *La Satyre ménippée* (1594). It proves that the paradigm was active and, in order to present itself as a 'saturated' text, it does not omit the traditional metaphors:

The word *satyre* does not only mean a slandering poem which criticizes public or individual vice . . . but also any sort of writing full of various things and various arguments, sandwiching prose and poetry together, like a dish of salt beef tongue. Varro says that formerly *satyre* was a kind of pasty or stuffing in which there were several sorts of vegetables and meats. (*La Satyre ménippée*, pp. 11–12)

---

[21] See also Northrop Frye, *Anatomy of Criticism*, pp. 308–11.

La Satyre ménippée is a composite collection of scenes, descriptions, and speeches in which several languages and styles mingle and short-circuit each other, thus fulfilling the programme set out in its title: but it does not contain a meal scene. Other texts do resolutely link the disparate nature of the form to the setting of a meal: Rabelais, of course, but also Erasmus, Béroalde de Verville and another Protestant satire called *Satyres chrestiennes de la cuisine papale* (1560), to which I shall return later.[22]

Although Trimalchio's feast (*Cena Trimalchionis*) – the longest fragment remaining of Petronius's *Satyricon* – was only discovered in the seventeenth century, it is of particular importance in my examination of the relationship between table and fable. Although the novel escapes from the form of the Menippean satire because of its size and essentially narrative character, it derives from it its variety and the dissonance of its material. Once more, the point of utterance is unfocused and the message is disseminated by a multiplicity of heterogeneous voices. There is a great medley of genres: prose mixes here and there with poetry; erudite dissertations and poetic reminiscences are found alongside old wives' tales and empty chatter. Literature is now more than ever parading its literarity, as it cuts up and sticks together commonplaces. Everything borders on parody, to such an extent that in almost every page a reworking of some earlier text is recognizable or hinted at. Above all intertextuality with Greek literature is plentiful. Epic sequences and vestiges of elegy or mythology introduce alien voices as they are stuffed into the narrative. The Hellenistic love story seems to provide a more systematic counterpoint to and incongruous parallels with the outrageous adventures of the characters. But burlesque inversion also operates at the expense of the philosophical banquet. As with Lucian, the memory of the ideal yet unattainable Platonic prototype looms over the narrative.[23] The *Cena Trimalchionis* is a lavish meal rather than a *symposion*, with ignorant guests rather than refined and educated ones. It is a vulgar and trivial version of the meeting at

---

[22] On Rabelais, see chapter 4, A mouth full of words, and chapter 5, 'Our after-dinner entertainments', and The marrow bone; on Erasmus, see chapter 7, Erasmus: feasting on words; on Béroalde, see chapter 9; on the *Satyres chrestiennes*, see chapter 8, Dog Latin, cooks' talk and gibberish.

[23] See the detailed proof of this by Dupont: *Le Plaisir et la loi*.

Agathon's, with more brawn than brain; the weight of the bodies, the opacity of the objects and the mediocrity of the setting upset the original balance of the pleasure. In the development of the banquet, this is more of a degeneration than an explosion. But morality's loss is writing's gain; words have a field day at this feast. The tricks of parody and the faking of an inept conversation inject new energy into table talk.

Except for the narrator and his friends, who are orators and parasites, the diners are boorish freedmen, wrapped up in the trivia of everyday life, such as the management of their money, items of news, gossip about their neighbours or social rivalry. This is the nonsense which makes up the conversation of Trimalchio and his guests. There are pages and pages of truisms, trivial tales and stupidity: this in itself is quite a literary performance. Under cover of the freedom of the table, Petronius rids himself of the conventions which govern dialogue in the Greek novel and theatre in order to explore language which is so commonplace and so obvious that normally it has no place in books. Occasionally, it is true, a story intervenes to alleviate the boredom and make the company come alive: examples of this are the two fantastic tales about werewolves (*Satyricon*, 61–2), and the ones about vampires and the evil eye (ibid., 63). In their naïveté, the audience delights in these tall stories, 'like a donkey on the tiles' (63, 2). It is also a way for them to enliven the conversation, which is usually limited to anecdotes and tittle-tattle. They speak disjointedly about nothing in particular as if to kill time: about someone who is ill, someone else who has just been buried, about prices going up, about the next gladiator fight. But it is not enough to talk about local news, one must also (like philosophers) rise above them. And so the conversation is laden with aphorisms, and pompous platitudes; when the guests try to think, they invariably end up mouthing clichés. They invoke the wisdom of nations, they babble on and repeat the same things over and over again: it is as banal as can be, but also, from a literary point of view, a great challenge to accepted values.

The characters have more pretensions than brains. ' "One must not forget one's culture [*philologiam nosse*] even at table" ', says Trimalchio (39, 4). Former slaves, eager for social recognition, they would like to imitate educated people and take advantage of the liberation culture provides: this would be to model themselves on philosophers who, from Plato to Plutarch, and at the tables of the Roman elite, combined high literature with their meals. For Trimalchio, ostentatious knowledge of the classics is a sign of power and a way of getting on in life. He quotes authors and airs literary questions, holds forth on mythology and astrology and even reads some of his own poetry (55, 3), but always gets things wrong. He and his portly friends dream of sublimating their appetite through the proper use of knowledge. In their own way, they too are philologists who want to associate food and culture. But lack of education and the awareness that something is wrong dominate the meal. It is no coincidence that the *Cena* is narrated by Encolpe, the orator, who speaks ironically of the pretentious ignorance of the host and his guests. The educated observers listen and sneer; in fact one of the guests feels watched and admits: ' "I am afraid your clever friends will laugh at me" ' (61, 4).

He has another, more pressing reason for being wary. The freedmen not only think and quote badly, they also do not speak correctly. They do not really know what to say, still less how to say it. For them, language and style are problematic, and thus once more become one of the major themes of the narrative. Their vocabulary comes from the street, from shops or kitchens, and it is concrete and highly coloured, but with no literary merit. It reflects another feature of popular language in that metaphors abound, establishing vivid, debasing and preposterous analogies with the basic things of everyday life. Syntax, in most cases, is poor, with short groups of words, peremptory and poorly articulated clauses and no suppleness in sentence structure. Furthermore, one notes numerous set phrases: maxims, proverbs and ready-made and anonymous turns of phrase which are hallowed by common usage and seem to wrap up expression and thought in worn out clichés.

But it is difficult to generalize because Petronius, while remaining within the register of spoken Latin, gives each of his characters his own style.[24] Moreover, it is through what they say, what they recount and how, that the characters achieve their individuality. The construction of their discourse, its logic, rhythm and figures and the breadth of its vocabulary all add to the

---

[24] See Knoche, *Roman Satire*, chapter 8.

depiction of each of them. The novel, because it is interested above all in language as a social and psychological index, functions as a play during the long sequence of table talk. It analyses a milieu and the individuals in it through the expressive power of words. As is usual in a dialogue (but is surprising in a narrative), all the information is mediated by the speakers and determined by their linguistic competence. This experiment gives the *Cena Trimalchionis* a unique documentary value which has been recognized by historians of language. Vulgar Latin only spread much later, and the *Cena* is the most complete source in respect of spoken Latin at the beginning of the Empire. No other author of the classical period dared to record language at this level (popular parlance and working-class jargon) in a written text, at least on this scale. This would have been impossible without the model of the Menippean satire: I am tempted to suggest that it would also have been impossible without the experimental freedom provided by table talk.

That language occupies centre stage during the meal is again confirmed by various games played by Trimalchio, who likes words just as much as food. Because expressing himself does not come naturally to him, he has a sharp awareness of language which inspires all sorts of verbal manipulations. He listens to signifiers, dusts them down, revitalizes them and discovers in them hidden depths of meaning which shift the normal mechanisms of language. Most of his wordplay is based on homonymy, paronymy and semantic ambiguity. Some of his puns are so recherché and given so much importance that they can determine what happens next. Of course, his linguistic discoveries are untranslatable: for example in the lottery scene (56), when the guests play charades which reveal hidden words in well-known ones. The episode with the master carver Carpus (36) is typical: by repeating *Carpe*, his master kills two birds with one stone: he calls his servant (*Carpus* in the vocative case) and at the same time orders him to carve (the imperative of *carpere*), providing a fine example of verbal economy and of popular mimologism. Another scene (41) is worth analyzing because it consists of a cascade of puns. First, a boar is brought on wearing a freedman's cap. A guest explains that there is a simple reason for this: the animal was served yesterday at the last sitting but was sent back (*dimissus*) by the guests; it therefore appears today liberated, that is, as a freedman (*libertus*). The ambiguity here is at the level of the signified. Next, a slave serves grapes while acting out various incarnations of Bacchus. Trimalchio says: ' "*Dionyse, liber esto*" ' ('Dionysos, rise and be liberated'). There are three meanings here: the slave is called Dionysos and his master is freeing him, as the boar was freed earlier; but *Liber* is also a Latin name for Dionysos, hence the two other possible interpretations: the master is asking the slave Dionysos to play the part of the god, which he is in the process of doing; or the Greek god Dionysos is being asked to become the Latin god *Liber*. Finally, Trimalchio adds: ' "I am sure you will agree that the god of liberation is my father" ' ('*habere Liberum patrem*'), that is to say, my father is free (so I am a Roman citizen) or I possess the divine (*pater*) Liber.

Notice that Trimalchio simultaneously exploits two systems of signs, namely words and images. Linguistic tricks and visual riddles are often combined, the pun producing the scene and the scene sanctioning the pun. Other artificially prepared spectacles, like the famously constructed dishes which transform natural food into a cultural feat, have a commentary in which verbal acrobatics often parallel this theatricality. But there is more to it than that: cooking and the meal-time ritual constitute for Trimalchio a second, compensatory language, an alternative means of communication revealing a form of knowledge which is absent elsewhere. In this world which is saturated with the material and devoted to consumption, linguistic finesse is found everywhere. Whether they are educated or ignorant, the narrator and the characters treat words as things; speech for them is not only an instrument, it is full of substance. It is no coincidence that language realizes its full potential at table; it simmers away like a stew and is savoured like a fine dish.

Greedy grammarians

In late antiquity the development of banquets culminated in the work of three compilers or grammarians – specialists in literature or philologists, guardians of ancient language and knowledge. Plutarch (first century AD) uses the convivial scene twice, in the *Symposiaka* or *Table Talk* and in *The Dinner of the Seven Wise*

Men; Athenaeus (third century AD) uses the device of the banquet in *The Deipnosophists*, as does Macrobius (fifth century AD) in the *Saturnalia*. Each claims to belong to the symposiac tradition:[25] they quote their models and unanimously claim that Plato is their authority. But in fact they are vastly different from Plato. Instead of philosophical entertainment, they invite their reader to an orgy of erudition. Their books aim for quantity and are vast collections containing all kinds of knowledge. Decor and dialogue are blurred behind the mass of documentation; comic impromptus and playfulness are simply banished, and with them the pretence that any character is really speaking. In these mausoleums, all that remains are quotations, information, and archives, a collective memory in written form. Mimetic illusion is removed, but some factors common to earlier works remain: a taste for words, the association of gastronomy and philology and, as in the satire, the uninhibited combination of heterogeneous material, an unfocused and unending diversity of texts. These grammarians deserve better than being treated, as they generally are, as encyclopaedists. Their knowledge is still bound up with reflection on language and narrative forms. They seat their characters at a banquet because they are themselves greedy for words and literature; they choose this experimental structure because it can cope with their bulimia.

These authors have already been referred to[26] because of their documentary value in respect of table manners. I will now examine them from a literary point of view, in terms of the relationship between their style and the theme of food. In an attempt to isolate some of the main features, my approach will be a general one, at the expense of some nuance and detail.

Athenaeus's ancient editor announces that: 'The economy of discourse [*hè tou logou oikonomia*] is the imitation [*mimèma*] of the magnificence of the meal' (*Deipnosophists*, I, 1). And to introduce the book, he invents the compound noun *logodeipnon*, a meal of words. In all four texts under consideration, the diners

---

[25] I shall not deal with the Greek *Banquet* by Bishop Methodius of Olympia (third century AD), which is also heterogeneous and full of literary material. It is a *summula theologiae* which discusses various points of doctrine and is an apologia for chastity. The convivial device, which is outlined at the beginning, is merely an allegory of the feast at the wedding between God and the Church.

[26] See chapter 3, An archaeology of the table.

absorb as many words as foods. The economic metaphor and the claim to mimesis, on the other hand, seem groundless. It is true that each of the works opens with the description of a banquet, and from time to time reminds us that the speakers are also eating. Plutarch finds the best formula for this: of the eighty-four discussions of *Table Talk* that have survived, most take place at a particular meal, and the occasion for the conversation is often specific. All of the action in the 400 pages or so of Macrobius's work takes place on three days during the feast of the Saturnalia, and the alimentary fiction rarely surfaces. It is even more scanty in Athenaeus, where the first meal lasts through ten books or four volumes, although thereafter the pace tends to speed up[27] and conversation constantly refers to one aspect or another of the banquet. As for the guests, in all four texts they merit the name that Athenaeus gave to his characters – deipnosophists. All are wise or educated men who represent the great disciplines of knowledge: historical characters, contemporaries in the case of Athenaeus and Macrobius, but more spread out through time and space in Plutarch. Their identities and specialities are taken into account, although the mass of documentation and the priority of the said over the saying often obscures personal details. The grammarians are not very interested in description or psychology, and realistic effects are not their forte.

The list of themes is virtually unlimited. Plutarch nevertheless makes a useful distinction between *sympotika* (questions about meals or other aspects of food) and *symposiaka* (questions of whatever kind suitable for discussion at table), and he adds: 'the conversations which follow have been written in a haphazard manner, not systematically but as each came to mind (*Table Talk*, vol. VIII, p. 109). To talk about food when one is eating is an almost universal element of table talk and none of our authors is an exception to this rule. This mirroring device has two advantages: discussion is rooted in the situation of the meal and revitalizes the description of the setting; and, conversely, the sequence of the dishes and the ceremony conveniently underpin the disjointed treatment of all possible aspects of the meal. Athenaeus is the only

---

[27] The second meal takes up books 11–14; the third meal starts at the beginning of the fifteenth and last book (but the original text did continue beyond this).

one who limits himself to *sympotika*, but this is not really a sacrifice. The subject of food is so vast that it leads on to everything else and easily fills the 1700 pages of *The Deipnosophists*, which themselves are only a summary or an incomplete series of extracts compiled by a later editor; it is hard to imagine what the size of the original was. Everything is included, from the production to the tasting of the food: hundreds of dishes known to man, and an inexhaustible variety of drinks: their origin, their composition, their preparation; advice on hygiene and diet; chefs and their art; the crockery, goblets, and all the serving dishes; manners and conduct; entertainments, the whole range of attendant pleasures, the luxury and extravagance of legendary banquets; all accompanied by historical, geographical and moral comments. Even if it is highly specialized, the enquiry is none the less on a grand scale.

There is something to get your teeth into in Plutarch too, and without thematic restriction. In both of his treatises, the proportion of matters concerning the banquet as opposed to other hetero-geneous discourse is approximately equal. Put together, the *sympotika* lay down the foundations of an ethical system of table manners and recommend moderation of appetite in the name of a very strict spiritual hierarchy. This is probably why Plutarch mixes his themes: it is important that the guests remain in control of their senses and ready to face all kinds of subjects. Knowing how to speak lucidly about this and that is to defeat the imperialism of the stomach. Food itself inspires meditation and leads to thoughts which prove that the mind is still vigilant. Macrobius has no such edifying intention, but also jumbles together different subject matter. He is interested in the codification of the banquet: book VII of the *Saturnalia* is in fact a compilation of Plutarch's rules on good conduct at table, and book II contains a list of jokes to amuse guests. This does not stop him introducing between the two, like a compact mass, his commentary on Virgil: Virgil on religious institutions, Virgil's use of rhetoric, his relation to Homer and other poets, etc.

The convivial scene therefore provides the encyclopaedic pro-gramme of the grammarians with a context which is sufficiently flexible to take in everything. Mimetic effects are just a means to an end, and are subordinated to an aesthetic of abundance (*copia*) and variety (*varietas*). The meal is a *topos* which justifies the disparity of the texts, as if table talk, which is improvised and resists systematization, can give a decidedly artificial compilation a sense of authenticity and humanity and the appearance of a society game. Jumping from cosmology to grammar, mixing bits of metaphysics with fragments of history (as Macrobius does, for example), is merely to follow the common practice of entertaining and informative conversation between decent people. This attempt at naturalization is obvious in Plutarch:

> What is undiluted is everywhere surfeiting and often harmful . . . therefore, it is clear that the gentleman who presides will provide for the drinkers a mixed programme of entertainment. (*Table Talk*, vol. VIII, pp. 57–9)

Variety is quoted as a universal law, and is therefore a necessary condition for the success of a meal; Plutarch and Athenaeus add that it must also apply to the organization of the menu and the composition of the dishes, for pleasure is a function of novelty, whereas uniformity dulls the appetite. Athenaeus uses the same word, *poikilia*, in the sense of desirable variety in cooking, in the menu and in discourse.[28] The palate must be tickled just as the reader's curiosity must be aroused. Thematic diversity creates surprise and maintains interest. It does not arise from faulty composition, but is deliberately based on a poetics of the fragment, to which desultory conversation brings some kind of legitimacy. It therefore seems futile to search for principles of classification and unifying themes in these grammarians' collections. Of course, coherent sequences and semantic similarities help stabilize the discourse from time to time; capricious organization does not exclude some kind of order. But there is no need to hide discordances and correct tangents in texts which deliberately practise *varietas*. Encyclopaedic banquets are not meant to be systematically analysed; the rejection of linearity makes a logical reading impossible. Table talk guarantees that literature can have an exploded structure, proliferating according to no other principle than that of improvisation.

It is true that this mixture of various elements was common in

---

[28] See also Plutarch, *Table Talk*, vol. VIII, pp. 294–317.

antiquity and is not necessarily associated with the convivial theme. In an age when books were rare and people read with pen in hand, the genre of learned compilation or literary anthology played an essential conservational role. Aulus Gellius, in his *Attic Nights*, gathered together in no particular order and without method a mass of notes on his reading – extracts (*excerpta*) and commentaries (*commentarii*) on grammar, history, law, literary criticism, etc., which act as a catalogue or an *aide-mémoire*. In his preface, he himself explains that the publication of erudite miscellanies, whether thrown together at random or classified, was common practice among the Greeks and Romans. Scholars, he says, set down 'varied, manifold, and as it were indiscriminate learning' for its documentary value (Preface to *Attic Nights*, 5): this gave a respectable status to the aesthetic of variety.

This is the generic framework in which our grammarians belong. They too serve up notes on their reading. Their diners are passionate antiquarians or greedy collectors who set themselves up as preservers of culture. They gather together all that is worth remembering: fragments of archives from the most ancient history, as in Macrobius; anecdotes and curiosities, exemplary illustrations, axioms and notable formulae, as in Plutarch's *The Dinner of the Seven Wise Men*, and in many other works besides. The textual origins of these treasures are not hidden. The compilers either quote an author directly or they report a thought in indirect speech; systems of reference and transcription vary, methods of preservation and redistribution can change, but the material almost always originates in books. It is usually impossible to tell whether the compilers go straight to the primary sources in the classical authors or quote them at second hand from other anthologies, but in any event the information they communicate has already been mediated through a text or a series of texts. It is never claimed that the material is guaranteed by direct experience. The writer is merely an intermediary – he does not claim to have the status of an author – and he manipulates data which are already cultural objects, filtered through writing and the authority of tradition. It would be otiose to speculate on whether Athenaeus was a gourmet. He was an insatiable reader, an extraordinarily effective bookworm.[29]

[29] See chapter 3, An archaeology of the table.

In such an orgy of erudition, narrative realism in the banquet, and even the referential value of the documentation (from say a historical or anthropological point of view) count less than the purely literary goals of quotation and conservation of textual material for its own sake.

For this was the purpose of encyclopaedic banquets. As collections of facts, thoughts, or remarkable formulae, they were to be used for many years like those handbooks of commonplaces one can dip into to embellish a speech, a letter or a conversation. As long as the authority of the past and the sanction of tradition remain essential parts of culture, anthologies like these will help men of letters to remember things: they are stores of words and of other things from which, if they cannot consult original texts, imitators can take nourishment to digest in order to feed their own works. Compilers are purveyors of knowledge, eating the texts of the past in order to communicate them better to others. And this is certainly how they were seen in the Renaissance. The Humanists were very eager for information on antiquity and stocked up with plenty of material from these compilations. Scholars consulted them, writers referred to them. Plutarch, Athenaeus and Macrobius were reprinted several times;[30] the first two, in spite of their length, were translated into Latin[31] and Plutarch into French[32]; a lengthy commentary was also published on Athenaeus.[33] The form of the encyclopaedic banquet and the traditional symbolism of food would doubtless not have had the same resonance in the sixteenth century without the benefit of these vast repositories of Greek and Latin culture.

In the mind of the compiler, it is less a question of choosing than of amassing. With no set criteria, the grammarians record an immense variety of opinions. Their curiosity and openness exclude

[30] The first edition of Plutarch's *Moralia* was published by Alde in 1509; that of *The Deipnosophists*, published by Alde in 1514; and that of the *Saturnalia* in Venice by Gallici in 1472.

[31] The first Latin translation of the *Table Talk* was by Melanchton and was published between 1517 and 1521; the first Latin translations of *The Dinner of the Seven Wise Men* and of *The Deipnosophists* were published in 1551 and 1556 respectively.

[32] Fragments of the *Moralia* were translated into French before the sixteenth century; Aymot's complete translation dates from 1572.

[33] By Casaubon in 1597.

any kind of system; they collect conjectures and mix together diverse voices without trying to unify them. What is often said about Plutarch is also true of the others: they are basically eclectic. They neither judge nor criticize, but rather put things on show. Such tolerance fits in very well with the device of table talk, where each guest has an equal right to speak and where no one is proved wrong, violent dogmatism being contrary to the festive spirit. Plutarch's technique is significant: two speakers defend opposing views, but neither wins the argument and no authority intervenes to settle the dispute. As opposed to philosophical dialogue, which tries to reconcile opposites, it has the same form as the scholastic dispute in which thesis and antithesis confront each other without resolving themselves in a synthesis. It is also what Macrobius calls the *palinody*, 'the practice of the schools of rhetoric, in treating their stock themes, to present in turn the points to be made for and against the subject in issue' (*Saturnalia*, VII, 5; p. 462). In a riddle which is typical of table talk, the guests in Plutarch and Macrobius discuss which came first, the chicken or the egg (*Table Talk*, vol. II; *Saturnalia*, VII, 16),[34] a question which must of course remain open. The argumentation is more important than the conclusion; conversation is not designed to establish the truth, but to set out theses and to loosen tongues. It is not a matter of sorting out the true from the false, and even less the real from the unreal. Eclecticism appears to be credulous, because it suspends judgement and does not reject anything; the diners promote illusions and report fantastic stories in the same half-serious and half-joking way in which they deal with more sensible questions. Once preserved in writing, facts seem to have intrinsic value. The author melts into an anonymous collector and mediator; he lets the books, of which he is a mere interpreter, speak for themselves. In the polyphony of the banquet, questions of authority and origin are always deferred, a point to which I shall return later.[35]

Our authors are also eclectic in their methodology, since they are as interested in words as they are in things. They merit the title of grammarian, as their sensitivity to language surfaces throughout.

[34] Book VII of *Saturnalia*, as I said earlier, borrows extensively from the *Table Talk*.
[35] See chapter 7, Guillaume Bouchet: stuffings, and Giordano Bruno: the failed banquet; chapter 9, 'Monarch of ecumenical symposia'; and my Conclusion.

They readily accumulate well-turned phrases and memorable expressions, such as witty remarks, aphorisms, and paradoxes. The catalogue of jibes and jokes (*dicteria*) compiled by Macrobius (*Saturnalia*, II) shows the hedonism of which language is capable: there is pleasure in manipulating the signifier, since laughter often comes from puns; pleasure in enriching the lexicon, when a rare word has to be explained; and pleasure in quotation, because witticisms hallowed by time go back to a particular classical author or a particular tradition. Literary references are not only omnipresent because of a concern for erudition; they also provide the opportunity to listen to a fine text and an example of good style. The diners in the *Saturnalia* devote themselves, as they say, to the 'study of literature' (*studium litterarum*) (ibid., I, 7; p. 56). This is proved by their glosses on Virgil, which are full of technical observations, as if it was not only a matter of understanding the function of rhetoric or poetics, but of being able to appropriate its qualities. The concern for linguistic correctness and the problematics of language are present throughout Macrobius's text: he was probably a foreigner, writing in clumsy Latin, full of Hellenisms and dotted with many Greek quotations; but his meticulousness as a grammarian is no less acute for all that.

With an aim which is obvious in Athenaeus and Macrobius but more diffuse in Plutarch, the study of documents is accompanied by research into words, and from time to time the latter takes over completely, as if the referential value of the *res* could not be fully appreciated without a detailed study of the *verba*. One paradigmatic scene recurs systematically throughout *The Deipnosophists* and is also present less regularly in the *Saturnalia*: it only needs a dish to be brought in, an event to happen or an object to attract attention, for the focus to shift immediately away from the thing towards the word, leading on to a learned discourse on the linguistic status of the term, its usage in the texts, and so on. One learns by expanding one's vocabulary, alimentary history is superimposed on to literary history, anthropology on to grammar and gastronomic pleasure on to philological pleasure. Two characters play an important role in this regard: Ulpien, in Athenaeus, cannot hear any word which sounds new without asking whether it has been sanctioned by a quotation from a classical author; and then the quotation in turn is commented on, and so forth. Servius the grammarian in Macrobius is constantly called upon to explain a difficult turn of phrase, to give a precise definition or to correct a barbarism. The contribution of *The Deipnosophists* to Greek lexicography and (to a lesser extent) of the *Saturnalia* to Latin linguistics is well established. Rare words are explained, set alongside their synonyms, distinguished from their homonyms and even sometimes translated from Greek into Latin or vice versa. Etymology is regularly used, according to the poetic method of Latin grammarians, to reveal the nature of the object or to bring out a hidden meaning. The Greek texts referred to in Athenaeus sometimes lead to remarks on dialectical forms, on the evolution of a term or on the accidents of morphology and of pronunciation. It is a question both of understanding vocabulary better and of ensuring precision and elegance of usage; an air of Atticism is discernible among the company of deipnosophists. As in Rabelais, but in a more serious vein, the dialogue is also sometimes interrupted by lists of words: a catalogue of the names of fish (*Deipnosophists*, VII), an enumeration of drinking vessels (XI), and other collections of terms which, when arranged alphabetically and accompanied by definitions, for a few pages give the book the appearance of a dictionary.

Let us recall the ambiguity of the verb, *nourrir*, meaning to feed and to instruct.[36] This sums up the scope of the encyclopaedic banquet, at which the guests are hungry above all for knowledge, and do not really absorb dishes but the names of these dishes. What they learn about food owes less to their meal than to their philology. They see foods as matter transformed by culture – as linguistic signs or literary motifs – and use them as an index of their erudition. Their gastronomy is logophagy, from which it follows that the banquet which we thought we were reading about is more like a book of grammar.

Athenaeus is well aware of this shift and makes oblique comments on it through various reflexive metaphors. For example, the disquisition dwells on gluttons and their unbelievable menus, providing many picturesque details (ibid., X); then, still fascinated by excess, it moves on to describe all kinds of banquets renowned for their luxury, such as those given by extravagant Persian despots, or sensual Sybarites, etc. (XII). But it is impossible to

[36] See chapter 5, Metaphors of bibliophagy.

avoid associating with these images of greed and excess the deipnosophists themselves, who, in their hunger for knowledge, also come together around extraordinarily overladen tables. In a further mirror effect, they also resemble the cooks whose exploits they praise as great art. One, for example, slices a turnip, boils it up with oil, salt and black poppy seeds, and succeeds in passing it off as anchovy, giving rise to an oft-repeated parallel: 'the cook and the poet are just alike: the art of each lies in his brain' (I, 7).[37] Moreover, cooks occasionally leave their saucepans to come and talk on equal terms with the sages.[38] They move naturally from concocting dishes to philological discussion, for their culinary practice, as they themselves say or show, relies on all kinds of knowledge – medical, geographical, historical and religious. As repositories of art (*technè*) and wisdom (*sophia*), they claim the status of intellectuals, which is willingly granted by the guests who, for their part, also work with their head and their stomach at the same time. The makers of learned sauces, the consumers of words and the producers of texts get on so well that the distinctions between them are lost. They have in common an elaborate technique based on variety, which presupposes a whole science of mixtures and proportions; an oral sensitivity and a refinement of tongue which savours fine words and fine foods. The diners recognize it was through cooking that people emerged from cannibalism, acquired culture and organized themselves into communities (XIV, 660 ff). As at Trimalchio's table, the skilful chemistry of the cooks is one of the languages through which culture expresses its control of nature: changing primary material and transforming the raw into the cooked is a fundamental act of civilization, an authentically artistic gesture. With this argument (which is also a self-interested defence), the deipnosophists shrug off the condemnation of Plato, who had discredited cookery, like rhetoric and sophistry, as an art of flattery and a superficial technique (*Gorgias*, 464–5).

Among Athenaeus's guests, one cynical philosopher does not swallow this: he reproaches Ulpien by saying 'you like to feast on words' (*Deipnosophists*, VII, 275). The only things he is served at

---

[37] See also VII, 290–3; IX, 376–83 and *passim*.
[38] See, for example, IX, 403 ff; XIV, 658 ff.

supper are speeches – words, words, words (*logoi* – ibid., VI, 270) – but he stays hungry: 'I have swallowed nothing but words' (VI, 270). Of course, antique banquets are more than mere logorrhoea: their words are rooted in the world and they are full of things to say. But at table the tongue is at home and refuses to be forgotten; it involves the signifier in the philosophical message, in satirical narration and in encyclopaedic documentation. The symposiac scene is a precious ally for literature: it gives verbal substance back to ideas and restores them to the world of savour and play.

7

Something for every taste

The copious and the varied

Sixteenth-century painting, when it represents food, oscillates between two extremes: the banquet scene and the kitchen table. One image is dominated by people and festivity; it is organized, harmonious and conceived in an elevated style, expressing a refined culture. In the other, the diners have disappeared and the space has been filled with food and utensils; objects are arranged in more or less orderly heaps; the other side of the festive decor – equipment used at the feast, and the natural produce before it has been prepared – reclaims its autonomy, independent of humanity. The noble and animated version contrasts with quantity and inertia. Some art historians have seen this dissociation of the thing and the consumer as adumbrating the kind of still life painting which began in northern Europe at the start of the seventeenth century.[1]

Perhaps this polarity is similar to that seen in the convivial paradigm in classical literature, with its two extremes: Plato's *Symposium* and encyclopaedic banquets, quality and quantity, thought and information, concentration and dissemination. Be that as it may, a general rule emerges: the symposiac form tends to expand and become diffuse, as though it contained the seeds of its own extension and decentring. The rules of the game – different characters, a variety of pleasures and signs of abundance – are

[1] See A. Veca, *Simposio. Ceremonie e apparati*, who provides important iconographical material and a general study of the theme of food in painting.

fundamentally pluralistic. The centrifugal forces are sometimes channelled into a single direction, as in Plato or in pictures with a very coherent structure. More often, however, the exuberance of objects, voices and words is realized in a multiple and composite work. Form and content work hand in glove: a profuse and versatile text is the corollary of tales or dreams of opulence. As in Rabelais's famous lists, verbal extravagance reflects alimentary luxuriance; the discourse proliferates as if released from its shackles by the imaginative possibilities of food. It is no coincidence that one of the favourite emblems of textual abundance (*copia*) is a metaphor from food, the horn of plenty (*cornucopia*), which, in all the 'copious' works of the classical heritage – storehouses of material to nourish future works – indirectly denotes banquets at which food is available.[2] The symposiac setting is not only a special testing ground for profusion and diversity, it also has an open form, liberating an eccentric discourse which does not try to unify or totalize the multiplicity of its elements. This is what I shall demonstrate in this chapter, by referring to three works which are very different in aim and tone.

Despite this limited scope, I will touch on one important aspect of the mentality and literature of the sixteenth century: Rabelais, Montaigne and many authors of erudite treatises will be present indirectly in this discussion. Faced with an extraordinary diversity of phenomena, Renaissance man tended to observe and admire rather than to choose and classify. Naturalists, encyclopaedists and moralists were all compilers of a sort, driven by endless curiosity to cram their books with a multiplicity of credible or incredible marvels, gathered from their reading, from myths or from hearsay. They were less interested in analysing and ordering than in embracing the vital luxuriance and fantastic profusion of things. God and nature were seen as the focus of an infinitely varied creative activity, communicating with human beings through the inexhaustible richness of the universe. This always special and always exalting spectacle was observed rather than reduced by learned men; their openness led to an aesthetic of *varietas*, of medley and of mixture. Encyclopaedias and works of natural

---

[2] On all aspects of literary *copia* and the problem of the open text in the Renaissance, see Cave's indispensable work, *The Cornucopian Text*.

history embraced the disparate, so expressing the swarming proliferation of things.[3] It is precisely this tendency towards dispersion in Humanist discourse that banquets may help us to appreciate.

Other factors contribute to this. There were considerable ideological tensions in the Renaissance. The sources of conflict and uncertainty were innumerable – the opposition between biblical and classical tradition, contradictions between scholastic heritage and Humanist ideals, vacillation between Latin and vulgar language, the end of unity of faith, and so on. There was certainly no lack of Schools and Churches to defend dogma and to underline division. Neither was there a shortage of compromise solutions to neutralize or reconcile antagonisms. But under the pressure caused by incompatible theses, other milieux renounced all totalizing systems in favour of recording the infinite diversity of belief and knowledge. Once man no longer has access to original Truth and can only interpret or blindly speculate, there is no point defending problematic certainties. The plenitude of meaning is in the past or in the future; historical man no longer has access to the evidence of Revelation and must recognize how precarious his opinions are. Such views can crystallize into systems if they lead to the eclecticism or scepticism of an Erasmus or a Montaigne. More often they surface more diffusely, in various ways, without taking on the appearance of a genuinely organized doctrine. These unresolved thoughts are taken up by literature, with its strategies for diffraction of sense and multiplication of voice, as Terence Cave has shown.

The most significant form in this respect is the dialogue – a widespread genre in Renaissance Europe, which is polymorphous and used to many different ends, but which expresses the conceptual and experiential structure of a period full of non-uniform impulses.[4] Contrary to the dogmatism of rigid scholasticism and to exclusive and excessive ideologies, the dialogue demonstrates

---

[3] See J. Céard, *La Nature et les prodiges. L'insolite au XVIᵉ siècle, en France,* and F. Lestringant, 'Fortunes de la singularité à la Renaissance. Le genre de l'*Isolario*'.

[4] See D. Marsh, *The Quattrocento Dialogue: Classical Tradition and Humanist Innovation,* and M. K. Bénouis, *Le Dialogue philosophique dans la littérature française du XVIᵉ siècle.*

relativity of opinion and illustrates the historicity and instability of theories. It allows representatives of conflicting tendencies to have their say, without necessarily trying to resolve differences. Ideas flow freely around a given theme and contradictions come out into the open in a collective search for truth, which may or may not be achieved. The pleasure of debate and the stimulation of controversy often even seem to be ends in themselves, with no other aim than the hearing of unusual voices. Whereas other genres, such as speeches or sermons, systematically attempt to demolish contrary views and to impose a single truth, dialogue increases the number of points of view. Although sometimes an overwhelming goal leads it to reconcile dissonant factions (as with the philosophical dialogue), it sometimes also leaves differences unresolved (the rhetorical solution). Bakhtin's notion of polyphony is relevant here:[5] the author, instead of adopting a dominant position and imposing his own vision of the world, slips into the background and lets his various characters speak instead, with no sense of hierarchy. The dialogue does not speak in the name of a single subject providing an integrating focus or a psychological or ideological guarantor of the message; it speaks in many tongues and combines a number of plausible opinions. It does not efface the incoherence implicit in history or nature, nor does it conceal the disparity between systems of signification. It reads like a discontinuous, problematic and provisional montage of heterogeneous ideas or texts, whose tensions it does not reduce: this explains its popularity in the Renaissance and, by extrapolation, the popularity of the literary banquet, which is a variation of it. Even today the sense of the word 'symposium' is a collection of different perspectives on a given problem.

Another factor provides a motivation for experiments in dialogue. At a time when drama in the vulgar language had barely entered the realm of official literature, dialogue provided a promising testing ground for exploring the powers of language in a written form. It illustrated different kinds of verbal performance and set up models of discourse which were of direct relevance to linguistic practice. Thus we find examples of different aspects of

[5] See M. Bakhtin, *Problems of Dostoevsky's Poetics* and *Esthétique et théorie du roman*.

rhetoric – techniques of argumentation, means of persuasion and seductive effects – as if the dialogue was testing the effectiveness of words designed to convince by simulating the conditions of genuine debate. But dialogue can also serve to examine and represent another kind of oral potential which, although it was not formalized by schools of rhetoric, was no less topical: the qualities of improvisation and the impromptu expression of thoughts as they are being formulated. If it is accepted that the sixteenth century was an age of transition between the auditory era and the visual one and that it was slowly adapting to the consequences of the invention of printing, it follows that dialogue held a special position. It belongs to both eras: as a product of writing it methodically constructs an artefact, participates in the network of textual exchange and, through the authority of the book, has links with the past. As an imitation of the oral, it uninhibitedly uses all the devices of abundance and variety. Not that authors of dialogues were trying to create an illusion. In the Renaissance, true *mimesis* lay in putting some natural energy into the work of art; the mimetic text was not one which reproduced the detail of real life, but one which reflected the dynamism of living things and restored, in its language, the burgeoning creativity of the *natura naturans*. And it is precisely this that the dialogue, in its profusion and diversity, tries to do. Showing thoughts as they are being formulated, caught up in the emergence of heterogeneous ideas, it appropriates this aspect of the natural and this simulation of orality which literature uses to problematize itself. The position of the dialogue is ambiguous, but typical of the time: it pretends to escape from the scriptural by using scriptural means. It claims to derive from a model which perhaps does not exist outside the dialogue: it uses *varietas* and *copia* as artificial guarantees of naturalness.[6]

Erasmus: feasting on words

Erasmus's *Colloquies* instruct while they amuse. Everyday conversations, which could almost be scenes from daily life, illustrate a point of morality or a lesson on good conduct or doctrine, while also giving examples of good Latin. Among the *Colloquies*, six

---

[6] See my Conclusion.

dialogues (the *Convivia*) represent friends gathered together to eat and talk.[7] Erasmus did not group these dialogues together; they were scattered among the other *Colloquies*. But the common device they use justifies our studying them as a whole.

Generalization, it is true, is not easy because the aesthetic of *varietas* is present as if by chance throughout the conversations. Erasmus is a disciple of Plutarch, he has read Aulus Gellius and Athenaeus, and he too writes miscellanies. Although they are shorter, his banquets adopt the formula of the erudite compilation grafted, for better or for worse, on to a discussion about this and that. As often happens, the abundance and diversity of the subject matter absorb the individual voice of the author in its polyphony and comprise attempts at synthesis. Between the guests, and from one *Convivium* to another, the themes, the tone and the method of the conversation vary. However, one common feeling does overcome the differences: the friends together reach a balanced state of well-being in which the body and spirit are equally fulfilled in a climate of human warmth.

But there are different routes to this pleasure. The contrast between two of the longest and best known feasts, the *Godly* (*Convivium religiosum*) and the *Profane* (*C. profanum*), will serve as an example. In the former, the friends retreat to a country house, a *locus amoenus*, and celebrate a frugal meal in imitation of the Last Supper. The spirit of the Gospel, the concern for purity and for remaining faithful to the lesson of Christ dominate the gathering. The real food is God's word, and true pleasure lies in the interpretation of the biblical message. The natural setting and eating well are seen as mere symbols; everything culminates in communion in the divine mystery.[8] The counterpart of this composed atmosphere in *The Profane Feast* is the joyful consumption of nature's bounty; the guests drink in abundance, make jokes and chat about many things; the ethos of the meal has been turned on its head. This is shown in one significant contrast: in the one case there is lengthy praise of the benefits of Bacchus: 'Wine both

---

[7] *Convivium poeticum, C. religiosum, C. profanum, C. fabulosum, C. sobrium* and *Convivium dispar*. The last (in *Cinq Banquets*) is a dialogue which is not set at a meal, but is rather about meals. See chapter 1, note 8.

[8] For supplementary information and a more nuanced approach, see T. Cave, '*Enargeia*: Erasmus and the Rhetoric of Presence in the XVIth Century'.

arouses invention and ministers to eloquence [*facundia*], two things very suitable to a poet' (*Profane Feast*, C. *profanum*, in *Colloquies*, p. 597). In the other, the guests may quote the adage *in vino veritas*, but in the edifying atmosphere of the religious meal this is negatively marked: it is not sensible to drink, for wine 'commonly brings to the tip of a man's tongue whatever he was hiding in the heart' (*Godly Feast*, C. *religiosum*, ibid., p. 62). Wine loosens tongues, but what is positive inspiration for some seems, for others, to be inopportune chatter.

This variety, which is inherent in the convivial scene, often becomes a theme in itself. Since all tastes are accounted for in nature, and especially around a table, the menu for the meal and for the conversation are necessarily diverse. The friends at *The Profane Feast*, invoking Horace, make variety part of the art of good living:

> Though my guests are only three, they're inclined to disagree
>> About the dishes:
> One likes fowl, another ham, while the third cares not a damn
>> For others' wishes.
>
> (Profane Feast, ibid., p. 599)⁹

Better still, one colloquy (*The Disparate Feast*, C. *dispar*) is devoted to the description of a banquet which risks degenerating into chaos because of internal tensions. Spudus addresses the gastronomer, Apicius, presented here as a specialist in the art of entertaining, and asks him how to deal with guests if they are so different that they share 'neither the same language nor the same country'; it would be a real tower of Babel, remarks Apicius: 'If someone asks for cold water, give him hot' (C. *dispar*, in *Cinq Banquets*, p. 131). There is no question of reducing the plurality: Spudus's meal will be based on the unstable balance of disparate elements. Several dishes will be served at once, 'so that each can choose what he likes' (ibid., p. 132). The host will adapt to the multiplicity of the gathering: he will talk 'to each person in his own language' and will try to mix up subjects of conversation (*miscere sermones*), adapting what he says to the personality (*ingenium*) or the feelings (*affectus*) of the person he is speaking to (p. 133). Such a hotch-potch borders on chaos, and in his other banquets

---

⁹ Quoting Horace, *Epistles*, II, 2, lines 61–2.

Erasmus is more wary of the eccentric tendencies of the genre. The motley mixture of words and subjects nevertheless remains a permanent feature.

Since the diners often talk about food, several other conversations concern the organization of meals, menus and conduct. Erasmus recalls Plutarch's *Table Talk* and, sprinkling his banquets with precepts or examples of good table manners, contributes to the contemporary process whereby a code of conduct was being defined.[10] Whether it is a question of food, behaviour or conversation, the art of living is above all to do with moderation: one can be made merry by wine, on condition that one does not upset the other guests; one can eat, as long as the mind is not a slave to the stomach; one can chat, but without resorting to fatuous babbling or to pedantry. With their air of nonchalance, and in continually varying ways, the guests in Erasmus elaborate and illustrate a sophisticated art of convivial civility. Refined manners, moderate appetites and the creation of a small society of close friends who are both educated and Epicurean are all examples of an ideal of harmony and friendship often illustrated in the Italian Renaissance;[11] and to which the Sabine farm in Horace and Cicero's villa in Tusculum belong. Once more, the meal is seen as one of the most complete forms of culture, satisfying the demands of the body, of the mind and of courtesy.

In the manner of Athenaeus and Macrobius, and according to a common Renaissance reflex, the message is always mediated by a text, a *topos* or a word which draw attention to themselves as much as to the referent. The diners have the gift of the gab, linguistic sensitivity and great literary curiosity. They rarely miss the opportunity to stress the interaction between verbal and alimentary pleasure. More than ever, the mouth is having a field day and all of its activities are intermingled.

The transfer between words and food can operate by subsitution: since the host in *The Sober Feast* has nothing to offer to eat, the guests nourish themselves instead with literary quotations; each one reports a fine phrase, an edifying story read during the week

---

[10] See chapter 2, Civility.
[11] For example G. F. Poggio, *Historiae conviviales*; G. Pontano, *De Conviventia* and *Aegidius*, and F. Filelfo, *Conviviorum libri duo*. See L. V. Ryan, 'Erasmi Convivia: the Banquet Colloquies of Erasmus'.

(*'quod quisque . . . legit elegantissimum'* – *C. sobrium*, in *Cinq Banquets*, p. 139) and they go away replete, as if they had been to a feast at Apicius's. But normally there is no lack of either food or words, indeed they are so coextensive that the reversibility between them functions not through substitution but through a number of analogies in which the literal and the figurative tend to merge into each other. Thus we have the repeated metaphor of reading as seasoning: when the eggs are tasteless (*Poetic Feast, C. poeticum*, in *Colloquies*, p. 166) or the dessert insipid (*Godly Feast*, ibid., p. 71)[12] – when the fruits of the earth are poor – they are spiced up with some fine text which improves the flavour. As in college or monastery refectories, as in the dining rooms of the nobility, listening and swallowing, intellectual and sensual appetite reinforce each other, but with food of the mind here being at a premium. The traditional metaphors of *imitatio* – absorption, digestion and the transformation of texts into nature – inspire many kinds of variation. The affinity between food and words can also relate to order of consumption: the menu and works of literature are both laid out, and are there to be experienced, according to a similar rhythm: in a meal, there are to be as many courses as there are acts in a play and parts in a rhetorical discourse, namely five, 'with a soup as an exordium, and various desserts as a conclusion or epilogue' (*C. dispar*, in *Cinq Banquets*, p. 132). Elsewhere the parallel is between rhetoric and cooking – two arts of the tongue which the diners in *The Profane Feast* link together, with a preference on their part for cooking, although they are not to be outdone when it comes to chatter: they parody Cicero's maxim *concedat laurea laudi* by saying *'concedat laurea linguae'* ('let the laurel yield to praise/to the tongue', cf. *Colloquies*, p. 597). Organizing sentences and dishes, and tasting foods and words are two ways of savouring fully the world's riches. The friends talk about hares while they eat them, and discuss wine while they drink it (ibid., pp. 595–6), as if to show the reciprocal relationship between the referent and its linguistic sign, in a typical gesture which naturalizes art and 'artifies' nature (Montaigne, *Essais*, III, 5; p. 874)[13] in a never-ending circle.

---

[12] See also ibid., p. 57.
[13] See my Conclusion.

In a separate treatise, *Lingua*, Erasmus writes an extensive indictment of the abuse represented by chatty, fickle and hollow language, in a way which has nothing in common with the exuberance of the *Convivia* (the contrast suggesting that the symposiac situation is exceptional and enjoys special freedom). *Lingua* begins with a physiological description of the tongue and the neighbouring organs, emphasizing that vocalization is closely associated with the process of ingestion – tasting, chewing and swallowing (*Lingua*, pp. 243–5); the physical origin of words confirms their relationship to the process of eating. *The Profane Feast* corroborates this – knowledge and savour are the same: 'I am as knowing [*sapio*] in taste as in judgement. – You have a most instructed taste' (*Colloquies*, p. 597). The mouth is at the crossroads of the faculties: it demonstrates this without further ado by simultaneously eating, drinking and speaking with virtuosity and making witty puns about its own abilities. For it loves words, it rolls them round on its tongue and it is greedy for good Latin and fine style (*elegantarium heluo*, ibid., p. 608). When Erasmus offers his readers examples of Latin formulae to thank someone for a letter, he inevitably chooses comparisons with food: 'Your writing was more delectable than all ambrosia or nectar. Your letter was sweeter to me than any honey' (*Brevis de copia praeceptio*, ibid., p. 691). Reading which is sensuous because it is associated with tasting involves both body and mind; like classical medicine, it postulates the physical and spiritual unity of the individual.

In general the diners speak as readers or inquisitive lovers of classical texts. Their discourse is full of secondary discourse, which is there to be listened to, savoured and reproduced. *The Fabulous Feast*, in which funny and supposedly true stories are told in the manner of fables and folk tales, seems less bookish than the others; but the talk is full of learned allusions and is not as spontaneous as it seems; there is a complete literary landscape behind the jokes. This is even more obvious elsewhere in the *Convivia*, where we find a mass of quotations from earlier authors, extracts from anthologies and classical sayings, acknowledged or otherwise: a whole heritage in palimpsest that the tongue brings alive and recycles in the process of consumption. The companions at *The Poetic Feast* recite poetry, weigh up difficult terms, resolve problems of scansion and give more satisfying readings of traditional manuscripts. Those at *The Godly Feast* put extracts from the Bible under the microscope and respectfully and affectionately strive to clarify opaque texts and interpret them. The proximity of food does not disturb their exegesis. It seems rather to give words new substance, to revive their relevance and to give philological research more purpose. It also helps to make an activity which is normally more serious and reserved exciting and popular. Each guest brings notes from his reading, asks for clarification and suggests hypotheses; but the dialogue subverts any idea of a system and, like Montaigne later in his *Essays*, adopts a rambling style which reacts to interruptions or events. As in the classical grammarians, erudition at table retains its aims but takes on a happy and seemingly improvised character; it escapes from academic discipline and is integrated into everyday life, becoming more like an art of living or a personal disposition. From the sphere of having it moves to the sphere of being; just like food, it becomes flesh.

This appropriation is not limited to deciphering and interpretation. Reading is the first stage in writing. In a familiar impulse, the learned eaters open up their books or the treasure house of their memory in order to exchange knowledge and then redistribute it. The drive towards restoration and conservation dominates the enterprise. Through quotation they accumulate examples and apophthegms and collect a vast amount of documentation on facts and ideas – commonplaces whose status is ambiguous, since they reproduce classical models (an act of copying and preserving), but which also provide material for new works (a creative act). The transition is barely discernible; the diners are compilers, but also potential writers. The puns they enjoy making in *The Poetic* and *The Profane Feasts* themselves herald an active relationship with language; to play around with Latin words is of course to refine one's vocabulary, but also to track down surprising meanings behind sounds. Thus the Sorbonne sounds similar to *sorbere* (to swallow or absorb) and to *sorbum* (the sorb apple, the fruit of the sorb tree), and is therefore comically assimilated to the realm of food: 'Why not Sorbonne, where there's a lot of absorbing [*ubi bene sorbetur*]?' (*Profane Feast*, in *Colloquies*, p. 605).[14] Everything

---

[14] See also a pun on the word *gallus* on p. 602.

leads us to believe, once more, that the festive decor and imaginative power of the food incite the tongue to play with the signifier. The friends at *The Profane Feast* are so loquacious and inclined to speak for the sake of it that they do not even refute the accusation that they are lying and let each other's unlikely stories pass (ibid., pp. 599–600).

In the same passage, lying is seen as equivalent to making poetry (*poetari*), which is logical since the guests, as readers, quoters and fine speakers, are naturally led to write poems, at least in *The Poetic Feast*. After the meal, the friends go out into the garden, help themselves to fruits, and then devote themselves to a series of literary improvisations. First, everyone composes a poem in different metres on a given theme, and then they think of maxims – typical exercises in rhetoric in which they imitate or parody ancient texts, using a great many commonplaces. The agreed subject is significant: they must evoke the park and its lush vegetation, as if the texts themselves were produced by the garden and were part of this same luxuriance. The flowering of rhetoric and a garland of verse and maxims correspond to the floral abundance of the referent. The mirror effect is even more obvious since it is not wild nature that is being celebrated here, but the benefits of horticulture and its relationship with culture of the mind. In this way the insistence on the *copy* naturally ends up in the flowering of the *copia*.

For it is in the dynamic of abundance, and the volubility to which it leads, that the convivial situation reaches its full potential as regards verbal inventiveness. From now on I will concentrate on just one of the banquets, *The Profane Feast*, which is the richest from our perspective. In it the diners practise strange linguistic habits. They say the same thing in several different ways and linger over lexical variations, as if they find research into terminology more important that communication. Their speech is redundant; it is full of useless words and figures with no function. Synonymy, ranging from a simple repetition to the outpouring of interminable lists, is found more or less everywhere, disturbing the linearity of the dialogue throughout. Seven ways of saying 'it makes no difference what colour the wine is' are recorded, as are eight ways of expressing 'it costs me dearly', followed by a list of phrases for describing prices; whole pages are devoted to an enumeration of formulae for dinner invitations, with replies, and so on. More than ever, the tongue is enjoying itself; it is feasting on rare words and ingenious turns of phrase; it amuses itself by turning a signified into several signifiers; it gives free reign to a rhetoric of abundance, which seems to produce its own resources as it goes along.

It is true that such linguistic luxuriance can be explained by the genesis of the *Colloquies* which, in the first editions before they acquired their final form, were conceived as a school textbook designed to enrich Latin style and vocabulary.[15] Under the title *Familiarium colloquiorum formulae* (1518–26), scenes with dialogues on everyday subjects were intended to teach pupils ready-made sentences and new words, and to illustrate the rules of grammar. Lists of words in particular and groups of synonyms were used as practical exercises in verbal abundance (*copia*). Through play, the child thus accumulated a wide vocabulary, sufficient to be able later to find the most suitable term and the most appropriate turn of phrase to describe the nuances of his thought and to decorate his speech. In this way Erasmus associated an educational project with the philological pleasure of collecting beautiful classical formulae through love of language. This was the original nature of *The Profane Feast*: a medley of semantic variations and drafts of dialogues designed to teach children how to speak at meals or about meals. The definitive version of the collected *Colloquies* stemmed from this: the scenes became more diverse, the conversations became longer, the linguistic aim gave way to a moral one and the lists disappeared.[16] In this way *The Profane Feast* preserves traces of the language textbook, whereas the other, later *Convivia* have a less disjointed style.

Of course, the symposiac scenario does not have exclusive rights to this kind of verbal tinkering. Other themes can form the basis of exercises in style and stimulate the linguistic sensitivity of the speakers. But there is much evidence of the close relationship between lavish food and extravagant language. To make learning Latin more interesting, Erasmus did choose *inter alia* the semantic

[15] See F. Bierlaire, *Erasme et ses Colloques, le livre d'une vie.*

[16] The edition of March 1522, which marks the turning point between these two approaches, has a significant title: *Familiarium colloquiorum formulae, non solum ad linguam puerilem expoliendam utiles, verum etiam ad vitam instituendam.*

field of the meal ('come and eat with me, if I knew what you liked, I would serve it to you') as if the table was a special workshop of language. It is no coincidence that one of the clearest survivals from the first state of the *Colloquies*, a little treatise called *Brevis de copia praeceptio* ('A Short Rule for Copiousness', in *Colloquies*, pp. 615–20) is placed in later editions between *The Profane* and *The Godly Feasts*. This text is a first draft of *De duplici copia verborum ac rerum* (1512), and falls into two parts: theoretical advice on the many ways of embellishing and polishing one's Latin 'by the judicious use of the passive, the active, the synonym, the metaphor, the verb, the verbal noun, the participle, the adverb, the affirmation, the negation, the interrogation, the comparison, the opposition' (Bierlaire, *Erasme et ses Colloques*, p. 24); and a practical demonstration of this, in two catalogues of infinitely varied formulae. This is a fine example of lexical efflorescence which, through its very position, establishes a link between table talk and linguistic research.

These episodes of alimentary philology do not of course form a large part of Erasmus's considerable *oeuvre*. However they do help to give it the truly literary dimension that the moral, theological and didactic themes tend to obscure. Erasmus in Latin and Rabelais in French both have an extraordinarily vivid awareness of the resources – and pitfalls – of language (this is not the least thing they have in common). Words have a life of their own, forms have their own dynamics, and if certain types of discourse subordinate them to the transmission of an unambiguous message, other, more playful types liberate their creative and subversive powers. Whether he is exploiting the latent energy of words, testing the workings of rhetoric or examining shifts of meaning, Erasmus is a real writer who is attentive to literary play. The potential of the pairing of table and fable did not escape him: the virtuosity of the writing of his *Feasts* proves it.

Guillaume Bouchet: stuffings

With Guillaume Bouchet's 1500-page miscellany *Les Sérées* (1584–98), which is crammed with anecdotes and erudition, the paradigm of the banquet is entirely taken over by the encyclopaedia and reaches an impasse. The title refers to evenings (*soirées*) among friends during which information, stories and lessons are exchanged amid eating and drinking. This is the same scenario as in Erasmus, with the same promise of linguistic adventure. But there is a vast difference between the aim and the reality. This disjunction is the key to Bouchet, and also allows us to appreciate the aporias of the genre.

Throughout *Les Sérées* there is an ideal model of the banquet as a meeting place for the community and as a means of expression of a global culture. The long introductory *Discours* is doubtless the most elaborate social and anthropological theory of the meal in sixteenth-century French. Bouchet, a man of the soil, is addressing the bourgeois of Poitiers and refers to the ancient custom of get-togethers by the fireside, at which 'parents, friends and neighbours' (*Les Sérées*, vol. I, p. vi) gather round a table and then prolong the evening in discussing this and that. According to a ritual which goes back to the beginning of time, and which, the author assures us, still governs local life, a circle of people draws closer through convivial pleasure. The banquet among friends respects the principle of equality: 'there were some hosts at our gatherings who had round tables made' (ibid., vol. I, p. xxi). Other parameters – whether legendary or real – complete the model: the uninhibited immediacy of language which assures the clarity of the dialogue – the prestige of oral communication; the simultaneous satisfaction of the body and spirit, of the mouth that eats and the mouth that speaks; the just reward for the labours of the day in leisure and the happy company of 'hearty, lively, laughing and joyful men' (vol. IV, p. 208). The evening gathering as part of the rhythm of daily life (like holidays in the annual calendar) means that one can forget hierarchies and suspend the laws of production, the law of possession becoming the liberty of being, as vestiges of the Golden Age survive into an iron age.

Going beyond the rituals of ancient France, the banquet also perpetuates various classical institutions. Bouchet quotes many precedents: meals held alternately at each person's home to which all guests bring a share, as in Hesiod; citizens' guild meals – the *syssitia* of the Greeks and the *sodalitates* of the Romans – 'almost the same as the guilds of craftsmen in France' (vol. I, p. vii); recitations at table in the manner of Homer; political debates within communities as pacts are made or the truth sought through wine; the love feasts of the early Church. The French provinces, through their craftsmen and villagers, are unconsciously repeating an activity that is as old as the world. In a period of violence and disorder, when society seems to be in disarray, the permanence of the symposiac ceremony is reassuring.

The banquet cuts across history – and also across social class; the fraternity of voices is also part of the definition of this ideal model. Bouchet claims to seat at the same table both the erudite and the simple, both serious and light-hearted souls. The traditional eclecticism of table talk is here part of a democratic principle. The learned share their knowledge and make sure their readings are accessible to all present, whereas the ordinary people, with their stories and jokes, bring the interchange to a proper level; two cultures meet, that of the academy and that of the street, and the banquet neutralizes the received hierarchy between them and ensures there is a dialogue. Bacchus and the Muses, the grotesque and the intellectual, laughter and smiles preside jointly over the feast. Bouchet insists on the value of comedy, of 'entertaining stories and silly jokes' (vol. I, p. xi) which have nothing to learn from philosophers' theories in terms of the wisdom they contain. He claims the same sort of immunity for his *soirées* as public holidays have, with their games, their insults, their atmosphere of folly, and their expression of something fundamental which the ventriloquist text would like to capture. Eating and speaking, thinking and laughing, neither angel nor beast but both at once, man at table can attain ultimate equilibrium.

This is supposed to be the model to follow, and is set out at the beginning of the book. But in fact it merely reveals the extent of the disjunction with what follows. For the banquet in *Les Sérées* is resolutely writerly. Although it attempts some realistic effects (the long evenings, the Poitiers setting), it in fact continues the tradition of Plutarch's and Athenaeus's compilations, from which Bouchet in fact often quotes. He has the same passion for collecting, and his work is one more stage in the transmission of commonplaces, quotations and examples – a storehouse of fragments of culture in search of an author. All one needs to know about wine, fish, women, girls, dogs and chatterboxes, all that a curious amateur can hope to learn about natural, social, classical and modern questions are to be found somewhere. Each of the thirty-six evenings treats a chosen subject and compiles a thematic dossier on it: the classification stops there. As if liberated by the discontinuous and rhapsodic nature of table talk, the chapters strew their material around chaotically. The quantity of documentation overflows; it is the law of the jumble, the *ordo neglectus* which Montaigne practises in the 'fricassée' of his *Essays*, and which another contemporary writer, Tabourot des Accords, adopts in his *Bigarrures* ('Miscellany').

The ingredients of the conversation are, fittingly, quite heterogeneous: fragments of erudition, of natural history, of morality or of philology, abstract ideas and practical tips, from all origins and to please all tastes. Within each subject area, the range of sources and tone is virtually unlimited. Classical texts (doubtless only seen through the filter of anthologized fragments) make up the main course, along with some contemporary catalogues.[17] But Bouchet, faithful at least to one aspect of his programme, does not only collect parts of the academic heritage: he adds elements from popular and local culture. Things that have been read about mingle with things that have been heard of and experienced; subjects endorsed by the Schools and those which are passed on by word of mouth are all narrated without any distinction between the genres. Bouchet is more than an armchair pedant: he has the merit of being interested in folklore and of recording stories, spicy tales and jokes; academic notes are juxtaposed with naughty narratives, broad puns or scatological anecdotes. As is often the case, it is the eclecticism of table talk that makes such picturesque combinations permissible.

Les Sérées is not a book reflecting a single author, but rather the collation of a cultural heritage which belongs to everyone and to no one, and which moreover often has no stated origin. Bouchet acknowledges some of his sources, but conceals others and recognizes that he is tapping that anonymous store of collective knowledge to which nobody has sole rights:

> Anything which is available to the public, like books, cannot legitimately be said to belong to any one person . . . If I am said to be

---

[17] See M. Simonin, 'Un conteur tenté par le savoir: Guillaume Bouchet correcteur de sa IIIe *sérée*'.

free with other people's things, Seneca says that everything which is well said by whoever it may be, I can call my own. (Ibid., vol. III, p. 38)

The metaphor of digestion is not even present; the book harvests and redistributes material without transforming it. It remains the property of other people, so that ultimately, as Bouchet admits, 'if other people's words were removed, the pages would be blank and empty' (vol. I, p. xii). It is a book without identity, a book whose author is just using scissors and paste: this is the banquet as the apotheosis of the encyclopaedia. In fact it is so undifferentiated that it is indistinguishable from many other compilations which were extremely popular in France in the second half of the sixteenth century. In various forms, these catalogues, *aides-mémoire* and collections grew and grew. The fashion dates back to Plutarch (who, thanks to Amyot, his translator, was then very much in vogue), but it was its scale which was astonishing.[18] The fashion was for quantity, whether it was a matter of accumulating memorable facts, edifying examples, famous sayings, or all these things and more. This helps us understand Montaigne's concern to acquire a head well organized rather than just full, such was the fashion for big books and over-furnished memories.

The social background is important here: a new public seems to have been emerging which favoured these popularizing works. Bouchet dedicates his to the 'merchants of the town of Poitiers'; this was the upwardly mobile class which had not read the classics in the original, and therefore sought to acquire that culture through other channels. *Les Sérées* is a manual designed to give the bourgeoisie an *entrée* to traditional knowledge; it was probably to make their education easier that there is a mixture of styles, as if jokes and local tradition could domesticate readers and help make essentially academic learning less unfamiliar to them.[19] The emphasis on quantity and on the hoarding of information perhaps also indicates a merchant mentality. Printing here fulfils one of its functions, spreading knowledge, making it accessible to a growing

[18] See for example among Bouchet's contemporaries La Primaudaye, Béroalde, Boaistuau, Vigenère, the Spaniard Pedro de Mexia (Pierre de Messie), not to mention translations from Italian.

[19] See H. H. Glidden, *The Storyteller as Humanist: The 'Sérées' of Guillaume Bouchet*.

number of amateurs and encouraging its exploitation as if it were capital. To have the volumes of *Les Sérées* at home is to have a fantastic wealth of culture at one's fingertips – a sleeping fortune which the middle classes would gradually learn to turn into profit. Humanism is not only an art of living; in its relationship with knowledge it is also a passion for property and abundance. Bouchet and his readers are a fine example of this quantitative aspect.

The principle of hoarding in writing predominates in *Les Sérées* to the extent that realistic effects, although inherent in the convivial scenario, are merely inert remnants with no mimetic power. In spite of frequent but unavailing references to Rabelais, the fiction of the meal and the illusion of orality do not operate. The weight of documentation and the length of the expositions submerge the notional enunciative situation. The diners talk like books and have no presence. If their discourse is uniform and monotonous, this is because they themselves are undifferentiated, with no character or style of their own; they are like ghosts, with no name or identity. The subject matter they impart is valid in its own right: they never think to comment on it, to argue with it or to transform it. They cannot judge the information they are communicating, or that conveyed by others: there is no debate between them; commonplaces are neither criticized nor given new life. If any opinions are expressed, they are seen as objects or capital, thrown into the collection of goods to be preserved without discussion. The characters do not reflect, they recall; the author does not discriminate, he accumulates. He is merely an impersonal scribe, the faceless interpreter of the voice of nations.

The comparison with Montaigne highlights this tendency and is doubly relevant. The two men read each other's works: Montaigne had the first book of *Les Sérées* (1584) in his library, and Bouchet frequently quotes from the *Essays* or lifts material from it without acknowledging his source. Moreover, their projects have something in common, since Montaigne, at least at the outset, planned to record notes on his reading and to classify them, as Bouchet does, into thematic chapters more eclectic than personal. The craze for inventory, the fashion for compilation and the use of books to store excerpts of other books contributed to the initial idea of the *Essays*. But the comparison ends there: whereas Bouchet plagiarizes and transmits information without comment, Montaigne, using the same material, exercises his judgement. He does not amass, but rather selects, reflects and establishes a distinctive voice. The enormous wealth of knowledge acts as a basis for critical activity, through which the subject gains self-awareness. What could have been a collection becomes introspection; to have becomes a modality of being and writing an active means of questioning. But Bouchet is a copious copier, a worthy ancestor of *Bouvard and Pécuchet*.[20]

Giordano Bruno: the failed banquet

By pushing the propensity of the literary banquet to extremes of diversity and abundance, *Les Sérées* contributed to the deterioration of the genre. But the basis of this may also lie in the incompatibility of its voices: the disparate nature of the guests eventually paralyses the dialogue and destroys the unity of the scene. This recalls the philosophers' brawl in Lucian's banquet:[21] if the meal cannot reconcile antagonisms, it becomes dislocated, and the narrative with it. This same tendency to explore the limits of the paradigm is noticeable in Rabelais. *The Third* and *Fourth Books* show a marked degradation in the theme of food: greed gives rise to violence, and revels oppress the mind.[22] At the same time the symposiac device tends to go awry, and this failure affects the very structure of *The Third Book*. At the heart of the narrative (*The Third Book*, chs. 29–36), Pantagruel invites four learned men to dinner to consult them on the question of Panurge's marriage. In the text there are various allusions to Plato's *Symposium*:[23] the inclusion of this model only serves to reveal the scale of the failure and the subversion of the usual method. There are many symbols of this failure: one of the guests, Bridlegoose, does not come; another,

---

[20] I do not know whether Flaubert knew of Bouchet, but he started to work on his novel *Bouvard et Pécuchet* the year after the appearance of a new edition of *Les Sérées* (1873).

[21] See chapter 6, Satire and its cooking.

[22] See T. M. Greene, *Rabelais. A Study in Comic Courage*; and Jeanneret, 'Alimentation, digestion, réflexion dans Rabelais', and 'Quand la fable se met à table'.

[23] See especially chapter 35.

Wordspinner, evades questions and presents a mere caricature of philosophical enquiry. Worse still, Panurge is incapable of conversing and systematically torpedoes the project; in response to Pantagruel's plan of giving a banquet he had immediately said ' "That won't be any good" ' (ibid., p. 369). Although it starts off as serious, the conversation soon degenerates into farce (chs. 33–4) or insults (ch. 34). The authentic banquet which promotes the pursuit of truth is postponed until a better time in the future, and the guests stay hungry, already thinking of other feasts[24] which may perhaps be less disappointing. The plenitude of the Holy Bottle is notable here only through its absence. The failure of the symposiac model is repeated in *The Fourth Book*, which opens with a religious ceremony like the Last Supper: while the ships are being prepared, a communion supper is being held on deck in order to bless their quest (*The Fourth Book*, ch. 1). But the interminable voyage goes awry. The initial symbol of the banquet does not fulfil its promise; it is replaced by aberrant foods and monstrous menus, symbols of a world which, far from uniting people around a table, is assailed by strange and eccentric forces. Rabelais had created his world through a feast,[25] but he now subverts it in a series of anti-feasts.

The Ash Wednesday Supper (*La Cena de le ceneri*) by Giordano Bruno (1584) is the story of another failed banquet, one held significantly on the first day of Lent. Of its five dialogues, three (2, 3 and 4) revolve around the symposiac motif; but the unity of the whole is more thematic, the book explaining the Copernican system and Bruno's own cosmological theories. The episode is set during his stay in London in 1583–5, when, perhaps on a political mission for Henri III, he was received by the French ambassador. *The Ash Wednesday Supper* tells of a meal at the house of the poet Fulke Greville, to which Bruno is invited to debate natural philosophy with representatives of Oxford's Aristotelian School. The difference of opinion between the hermeticism of the Italian Catholic and the formalism of the English Protestant grammarians is historically authentic, as is the altercation reported in the book,

---

[24] The marriage feasts of Panurge (*The Third Book*, chapters 30, 31, 34) and Pantagruel (ibid., chapter 48).

[25] See chapter 1, The al fresco meal, and Conviviality; and chapter 5, 'Our after-dinner entertainments', and The marrow bone.

except that it actually took place at the house of the French diplomat.[26]

It is not necessary to analyse in detail here the theses of the *The Ash Wednesday Supper*, the very ones which led Bruno to be burnt at the stake. Inspired by Copernicus, who rejected the Aristotelian/Ptolemaic tradition and said that the centre of the universe was not the earth but the sun, Bruno constructs a less mathematical and more speculative cosmology which challenges both the ancient order and the new physics. The earth is a sensitive beast which is constantly changing and is not stationary: the stars move freely about in infinite space which has no centre nor boundaries. The universe is full of countless numbers of heavenly bodies, all of which are animate and mobile – a vision of nature in perpetual gestation which is the only one worthy of the excellence of God and the infinite perfection of creation. I shall not try to identify all the allegorical meanings that Bruno, through his introductory reference to Silenus (*Ash Wednesday Supper*, p. 72), is doubtless inviting the reader to uncover. It is probable that *The Ash Wednesday Supper* refers to the Last Supper and the religious debate on the nature of the Eucharist. As God inhabits and animates all things, He is really present in the Sacrament of Communion – this is Bruno's objection to the formal rite of the Protestant faith, void of spirituality. But the life of the cosmos can also serve as a political fable: the worlds which make up the universe, however innumerable and unstable, are nevertheless imbued with divine influence and form a unified whole; just as men, integral parts of the great Whole, should restore mystical harmony among themselves. This is the message of conciliation which Bruno based on his own philosophy and brought from the King of France to the English liberals – an appeal for religious and political tolerance in the name of the fundamental union of all things in the communion of the Spirit.

The Ash Wednesday Supper is a text full of symbols and laden with metaphysics, on which historians are still working and which has given poets endless food for thought. My approach is different: I do not intend to provide another philosophical commentary but

---

[26] On the historical circumstances of Bruno's stay in England and the probable meanings of *The Ash Wednesday Supper*, see F. A. Yates, *Giordano Bruno and the Hermetic Tradition*, and 'The Religious Policy of Giordano Bruno'.

rather a literary interpretation in terms of the convivial paradigm and the distortion it undergoes in the text.

So, at the beginning of the second dialogue, the guests arrange to meet at Fulke Greville's house to discuss cosmology in learned company. But Bruno, known as the Nolan (from Nola, where he was born), arrives at the poet's table only at the end of this section. A whole series of accidents, obstacles and misunderstandings has intervened. The journey to the feast is like a descent into Hell, a nightmarish wandering in the labyrinth of London. The Nolan thought he was expected for lunch; as no one collected him, he has gone out by the time they eventually come to look for him after sunset. To make up some time, Bruno and his guides hail ferrymen crossing the Thames; but their boat, which is like Charon's, is leaky; delayed and then abandoned, the travellers soon find themselves in a wasteland. They get lost in cul-de-sacs, trudge on in the dark, get bogged down in mud and at the end of this 'purgatory' finish up back where they started. They hesitate for a long time before setting off again. At last,

> having travelled impassable paths, passed through doubtful detours, crossed swift rivers, left behind sandy shores, forced a passage through thick slimes, overcome turbid bogs, gaped at rocky lavas, followed filthy roads, knocked against rough stones, hit against perilous cliffs (Ibid., p. 126)

they reach their goal. Tired of waiting, the guests are already at table. Bruno had said that the itinerary to the meal would be 'more poetic, and perhaps allegorical, than historical' (p. 69). What meaning(s) he attributes to these meanderings is not clear. One thing is certain though: the plenitude of the meal is deferred for a long time; the search for the banquet is balefully marked.

The narrative, for its part, is no less tortuous; it has a *topos* – the great symposiac debate – which should function as a pivot. But the text deviates from this, the journey to the heart of the problem is delayed by all sorts of digressions, so that the centre and the periphery, the essential and the accidental are often confused. The narrative device already distances and filters the object. Two dialogues run in parallel: a confidant of Bruno's tells three others about his master's debates with his opponents. The Nolan is treated as a character in the third person and his discourse is usually reported in indirect speech. But sometimes the two levels are confused; the distinction between Bruno and his mouthpiece becomes blurred and the subject of the enunciation is unstable. At other times the audience (especially the purist and the clown) interrupt, talk about trivia and go off at tangents. The symposiac speech is second hand, confused and interrupted, and loses its immediacy; another parasitic discourse reproduces it while at the same time displacing it.

Eventually, however, the main debate starts and in the third dialogue the Nolan sets out the nub of his theory. But the conversation soon deteriorates into a mere caricature of the philosophical banquet. The focus of communication becomes no less distant than was the location of the meal earlier. The fourth dialogue contains even more indications of failure. The two Oxford scholars raise inept objections; they are hidebound by outmoded physical categories and scholastic purism and incapable of challenging Bruno intellectually. They do not know the basic elements of argumentation, they do not know how to identify a problem, nor how to follow someone's reasoning: ' "You never once",' Bruno reproaches them, ' "set forth any fundamentals or proposed any reasons from which, in any way, you could draw conclusions against me or against Copernicus" ' (p. 198). The pedants are doubly impertinent because of the inadequacy of their criticisms and the rudeness of their rejoinders. They are ruled by passion; they attack the Nolan and insult him, and in his turn he accuses them of being mad: ' "questi pazzi barbareschi" ' ('these mad barbarians' – p. 186). The conflict between irreconcilable opinions, and the difference of manner and temperament, make the meeting a humiliation for the mind and a failure of *savoir-vivre*. The pedants can neither argue nor behave themselves; the refinement of civility, which is essential to the success of a banquet, has not penetrated the walls of their colleges. The London gentlemen, who have followed the argument and are receptive to European culture and aware of the rules of conversation and of politeness, disown the dons: they beg 'the Nolan not to be upset by the unkind incivility and rash ignorance of their doctors, but to pity the poverty of the country, which had been bereft of good scholarship' (p. 193). Polemics obscure the convivial device; the philosophical enquiry turns into a rat-race.

This dialogue of the deaf also has a source in the linguistic complexity of the encounter. The opponents use discordant concepts and their jargon is mismatched. To this is added the conflict of language: the Oxford academics would have preferred to speak English, but Bruno does not understand it; therefore they speak in Latin, which is in turn transcribed into Italian. Such translations smack of the tower of Babel; they feed misunderstanding and contribute to the breakdown in communication, while giving the text of *The Ash Wednesday Supper* the familiar polyphonic dimension of table talk. The stratification of languages is ambiguous: its opacity is negatively marked, but it is also part of the convivial pleasure and the oral gymnastics common to all diners. *The Ash Wednesday Supper* degenerates under the pressure of centrifugal voices which do, however, endow it with the motley character of language in celebration. The philologists accept the defeat of their colloquy while enjoying playing with words.

The narrator and his three listeners have a particular gift for mixing language, genre and tone. Their Italian is dotted with Latin; the pedant Prudenzio especially quotes from the classics and incorrectly recites numerous anthology pieces: from time to time, the dialogue becomes distinctly bilingual. The quotations are often verse fragments – sometimes in Latin and sometimes in Italian, including Pulci, Tansillo, Petrarch and Ariosto: this is another kind of mixture, of prose and poetry, recalling the freedom of the satire and confirming the composite style of the narration of the meal. There is even the mania for grammar – another constant feature of table talk – which also occasionally brings language to the fore. The first dialogue immediately sets the tone, with definitions, etymologies and purist observations – 'discorsi gram-maticali' (p. 84) enriched by expansive lexical variation, as if to whet the appetite with witticisms from the very start. The narrator's invocation to the Muses of England is firmly at one with the character of the convivial *copia*:

> Inspire me, breathe on me, warm me, ignite me, distil and resolve me into liquor, make me into juice and make me utter not a small, feeble, narrow, short and succinct epigram, but an abundant, broad vein of lengthy, fluent, grand and steady prose. (Ibid., p. 84)

This verbal opulence is discernible from the first lines of the dedicatory epistle and applies as if by coincidence to the banquet itself. But the elocutory exuberance is more complex than usual: it is not only a question of reflecting actual linguistic euphoria at table; Bruno's sentence expands to enumerate all the possibilities of the symposiac device, all the potential manifestations of a protean paradigm capable of infinite variation; it evokes what the *Cena* could have been but chose not to be: ' "Now behold, Sir, this book is not a banquet of nectar for Jove . . . not a protoplastic one . . . not the banquet of Ahasuerus . . . not that of Lucullus . . . nor that of Lycaon . . . not that of Thyestes . . . not that of Tantalus . . . not that of Plato . . . " ' (p. 67).[27] This cascade of negatives rids the object of all the specialities which it does not reflect and perhaps recalls the negative theology of Nicholas of Cusa. It removes the banquet from any possibility of being reduced to an actual pre-existing form in order to restore its powers of totalization. And it is in this vein that Bruno follows on, with a positive list which attributes to his text the power of embracing all opposites: ' "But this is a banquet so great and small, so professional and student-like, so sacriligious and religious, so joyous and choleric . . . " ' (p. 67) and so on: twenty oxymoronic pairs which go beyond eclecticism and polyphony to stake a claim for universality. It is the syncretic genre *par excellence*, able to contain an indefinite multiplicity of variables and to make difference coexist within unity. Like the Last Supper, whose name it bears, *The Ash Wednesday Supper* achieves an ideal of conciliation, reconciling the elements of an intangible whole. Above all, it resembles Bruno's universe: an infinitely diverse and unstable corpus, a composite, decentred, dynamic and yet cohesive system.

To express the fact that his banquet eludes definition, Bruno invokes two logical impossibilities: it is an object that has no individual identity, and one which reconciles the irreconcilable. This polyvalence is also seen on the literary level when a little later Bruno tries to exclude the narrative from any limitations of genre. Here too the sentence grows as a result of *expolitio*, a figure of open-ended plurality: the text can be read

[27] See chapter 1, notes 31 and 32.

like a dialogue, here a comedy, here a tragedy, here poetry, and here rhetoric, here praise, here vituperation; here demonstration and teaching; here we have now natural philosophy, now mathematics, now morals, now logic; in conclusion, there is no sort of knowledge of which there is not here some fragment. (Ibid., p. 72)

Bruno underlines the point: the banquet, like the original Latin satire, moves freely across the boundaries of genre, combining heterogeneous styles. But this mixture implies another, which relates to the level of ideas: 'So many diverse subjects must be put together that they do not appear to constitute a single topic' (p. 72). Multiplicity of discourse and discipline cannot be subordinated to a single meaning; the plurality of message challenges the reader and makes exegesis problematic. The dedicatory epistle gives, alongside its negative definitions, instructions for the interpretation of *The Ash Wednesday Supper* which seem contradictory: the sense is historic, or perhaps allegorical; it leads the reader down obscure paths – an invitation to look for the hidden meaning, without providing any clues on how to do this.

This is the privilege of the banquet: it speaks different languages and piles up or compiles all kinds of unsystematizable messages. The divergence of doctrine in the *Cena* mirrors the extreme diversity of style and meaning within the text. Like the academics who talk without communicating, *The Ash Wednesday Supper*, like many other banquets, certainly juxtaposes disjointed passages and risks exploding under the weight of its own richness. The demands of cohesion of thought, logic of exposition and equality of tone are all temporarily removed. But what the philosophical impulse loses on a dogmatic level, it gains in the dynamic of enquiry. And what literature sacrifices in terms of purity and unity is compensated for by the energy of the dialogue and the vitality of the diction.

8

⟨ornament⟩

Dog Latin and macaronic poetry

Dog Latin, cooks' talk and gibberish

Luther held open house in Wittemberg: members of the university, foreign scholars and politicians all came to chat about this and that. *Tischreden* (*Table Talk*) is a compendium of the master's memorable thoughts and expressions. Luther did not write any of this: it is a collection of extracts and anthology pieces which his disciples and friends selected from notes transcribed during actual conversations, and published posthumously. The convivial scene is not described, and no dialogue is reported; only fragments of the reformer's words survive. The improvisational quality and the flavour of the theology emerging between the fruit and cheese courses are no doubt somewhat diminished, but although these remarks are apocryphal and taken out of their verbal context, they are nevertheless worthy of attention.

Once again, the reference to the symposium (even though it is limited to the title of the anthology) provides an alibi for a vast assortment of disparate material; convivial talk authorizes variety and abundance. Like the grammarians and compilers, *Table Talk* is exempt from rules of order and unity; it is rhapsodic and touches on a wide range of subject matter. But its freedom does not stop there: a number of fragments are written in a curious lingo, a mixture of German and Latin. Polyphony and verbal drifting surface again:

> Wiclef und Hus pugnaverunt solum contra vitam papae, drumb haben sie es nicht erheben kunnen, quia ipsi tam fuerunt peccatores

quam papistae. Ego vero doctrinam ipsorum invasi; da mit hab ich
sie geschlagen, denn es ist nicht umbs leben, sed doctrinam zu thun.
(M. Luther, *Tischreden*, vol. I, p. 439)[1]

The shifts from one language to another are not arbitrary: they
correspond to the accepted division used by the literate in those
days. Luther generally deals with theology and unravels abstract
matters in Latin, but slips into the vulgar tongue for domestic
matters, or when the affective outweighs the rational: insults,
satirical sallies and outbursts against the devil come to him in
German. There is no documentary proof that these hybrid
constructions reflect Luther's actual practice, but they are present
in the text, displaying their linguistic oddities under the cover of
the symposiac genre in a new modulation of the exuberance of the
tongue that speaks while it eats. Moreover the credibility of this
bilingualism has not been challenged: the educated classes in the
Renaissance were constantly torn between the use of Latin and the
use of the vulgar language; in teaching, preaching and all oral
expression of knowledge, interference between them was much
greater than one might imagine from looking at written evidence.
The occasional crumbling of the façade allows us to glimpse the
composite character of scholarly communication, and it comes as
no surprise that the literature of table talk, accustomed as it is to
verbal manipulation, plays a role here.

The rivalry between Latin and the vulgar tongue in everyday
communication in schools, churches and the courts led to all kinds
of mutual contamination and, of course, to the bastardizing of
classical Latin. There was a wide debate throughout the Renaissance:
although the Humanists all agreed on the necessity of Latin as a
vehicle of learned exchange, some of them accepted that it had
evolved or even degenerated, whereas others defended the strict
Ciceronian orthodoxy. The quarrel of the purists and the anti-
purists in the republic of letters goes through different phases and I
cannot deal with all of them here. But it is in this context that the

---

[1] 'Wiclef and Hus only fought against the life of the pope. That is why they
achieved nothing, because they were as sinful as the papists. But I attacked their
doctrine and that is why I beat them, for it is not a matter of life but of doctrine.'
See B. Stolt, *Die Sprachmischung in Lüthers Tischreden. Studien zum Problem der
Zweisprachigkeit.*

expression 'dog' or 'kitchen' Latin (*latin de cuisine*) emerges and that the similar French words 'cuistres' (ill-educated pedants) and 'cuisiniers' (cooks) begin to be related in popular parlance.

In the middle of the *Quattrocento*, there was a quarrel between Lorenzo Valla, a strong defender of classical correctness, and Poggio, the author of the *Facetiae*, who was less concerned with philological rigour.[2] As part of the exchange of invective, Valla wrote a dialogue (in *Opera*, pp. 366–89) in which the tutor, Guarino, reads passages from Poggio to stigmatize his barbarisms. ' "I have often heard my cook and my groom speak like this",' he says. A kitchen boy is in fact present; he listens and comments: ' "This Poggio speaks worse than I do as a cook; please, master, let him do the cooking under me".' And so the writer is promoted to 'subcoquus'; it serves him right, since ' "he massacres Latin grammar like he breaks saucepans".'

The intention is obvious: Valla's comparison between Poggio's writing and cooking is humiliating and is used as a weapon to attack the bad Latin which was flourishing. The analogy spread in the sixteenth century and had many variants, such as 'coquinaria latinas', 'culinaria lingua' and 'orationes popinariae'. This mockery is even more effective because the connotations of cookery are obvious; since the comedies of Plautus, the cook has traditionally been at the bottom of the servant hierarchy; he is in constant contact with raw material and flesh, is uneducated and speaks like a peasant. The kitchen, in the eyes of the stylisticians, is a place where language goes off the rails, and where the mind is at the mercy of the stomach's whims and forgets the principles of philology. Among the cooking pots, as at table, discourse goes astray, escapes from academic constraints and is contaminated by popular jargon. Kitchen talk threatens to lead to literary lawlessness, with nature reasserting itself in the preserve of culture. It is to defend the unchangeable Latin of the classics against the *barbarolexis* of the uneducated that pedagogues scornfully brandish the symbol of the cook ruining correct speech.

But the norm of scholars is not shared by writers. What the former condemn and try to correct, the latter find amusing, and try to exploit its comic potential. Dog or kitchen Latin and the

---

[2] See P. Lehmann, 'Mittelalter und Küchenlatein', and R. Pfeiffer, 'Küchenlatein'.

mixture of languages provide humorous possibilities which literature profits from. Certain satirists, for example, have the same aim as the purists, attacking the semi-learned, the uneducated monks or the retarded scholars who speak a bastardized form of Latin jargon. But once those being attacked are allowed to speak, the pamphlet becomes comic: the *satyrica mordacitas* turns into *satyra ludens* and the ill-bred person, a great one for joking and mixing words together, discovers his literary credentials. We shall see in this chapter what innovative powers Latin can have once it is freed from rules and becomes a cook's utensil.

Moreover, the Humanists, at least when they are not being serious, recognize that they are both judge and accused. They too speak a rather dubious form of Latin, they too (as Luther shows) mix up elements in an unconventional way. A vast self-mocking corpus of literature displays the playful bilingualism of the learned and increases the incongruity of a dead language served up in a hundred different ways. The Germans especially resorted to this tradition of the academic joke – and continued to practise it until quite recently. They enjoyed parodying scholastic language and gave special prominence to dog Latin, with drinking songs turned into classical verse ('Cum bibo vinum, loquitur mea lingua latinum'),[3] burlesque travesties of academic manners, and the learned professions turned into figures of fun. These were so many literary games, like the *Carmina Burana*, in which the Latin-speaking elite gently mocked itself, giving a sort of literary dignity to the *barbarolexis* at the same time.

The grafting of one language on to another, mixtures and shifts between them, burlesque effects and neological games all took up much space in the Renaissance, but I cannot explore this in any depth here. Such elements were also linked to a variety of themes, but, as we have just seen, there is a special relationship between the areas of food and of linguistic experimentation; the tendency noted elsewhere is confirmed. The next few pages deal with just one or two examples of this association.

---

[3] 'When I drink wine, my tongue speaks Latin' (quoted by G. Hess, *Deutsch-Lateinische Narrenzunft. Studien zum Verhältnis von Volkssprache und Latinität in der satirischen Literatur des 16. Jahrhunderts*, p. 241). Hess's study provides a mass of documents and analyses of bilingualism in sixteenth-century Germany and the literary exploitation of this.

Rabelais follows a tradition which was well established in the Middle Ages by presenting churchmen who cultivate their stomachs and talk about it in bad Latin. Their discourse is usually bilingual, and all it takes to create the incongruity which leads to laughter is for the relationship between the two languages on the one hand and the subject matter on the other to be upset. This is what happens when Latin is used to discuss fine food. Master Janotus de Bragmardo may be a good theologian, but he is a pitiful orator and a deplorable philologist. Above all he is a greedy pig. He pleads as much for the sausages and breeches he has been promised as for the bells of Notre-Dame. As if by chance, physiological imagination and linguistic fantasy are well matched. He mixes languages: ' "Ho, by God, *Domine*, a pair of breeches is a good thing, *et vir sapiens non abhorrebit eam*" ' ('And a wise man will not dislike them' – *Gargantua*, p. 77).[4] When he talks about food, he naturally expresses himself in dog Latin: ' "Nos faciemus bonum cherubin. Ego occidi unum porcum et ego habet bono vino" ' ('We will make good cheer-ubim. I have killed a pig and I has good wino' – ibid., p. 77). Some of the titles of books in the Saint-Victor library combine witticisms and good food: '*De brodiorum usu et honestate chopinandi*', '*De differentiis soupparum*', '*De croquendis lardonibus libri tres*', '*De modo faciendi boudinos*' ('The use of Soups and the Propriety of Hobnobbing', 'On the Varieties of soups', 'On Bacon-eating – three volumes', 'On the Art of Making puddings' – *Pantagruel*, pp. 187–8).

The confusion of languages is not necessarily satirical, and still less blasphemous. Monks themselves enjoyed the generally accepted privilege of parodying the words of the liturgy or other passages of scripture for their entertainment. Here too the transfer of the sacred into the realm of the culinary and the degeneration of proper Latin into schoolboy jargon often go hand in hand. Friar John, who is cast in the mould of the greedy and lewd monk of medieval tradition, often lurks in the kitchen and brings with him phrases from the liturgy, including some humorous metatheses: for example his ' "*Venite apotemus*" ' (*Gargantua*, p. 129), which transfers the *Venite adoremus* of the mass into the domain of food and drink ('Come and adore', 'Come, let us take liquor'). The

---

[4] This is a reference to Ecclesiastes 38: 4.

following comic inversion also nudges religious language into the register of auditory and gustatory sensations: ' "*Brevis oratio penetrat celos, longa potatio evacuat cyphos*" ' ('A short prayer pierces heaven, a long drink clears out the hump', ibid.). Shifts of this kind abound; ecclesiastical Latin is so well known that it lends itself to infinite manipulation and penetrates even the most unexpected areas, combining highly incongruous fields. Whereas the purists defend a fixed corpus, the ill-bred, through their love of words, transform and reactivate a form of Latin that continues to develop. John, Janotus and their like are perhaps wrong linguistically, but they are right verbally. Their greed certainly has something to do with this.

This 'stomach philology', in Rabelais, is merely a diluted version of the vast tradition of farce which existed on the periphery of scholastic and conventual life in the Middle Ages. Following a parodistic impulse which the authorities tolerated even in the classroom and the cathedral square, ceremonies and liturgical texts were given a burlesque version; a parallel literature which reduces official institutions to the level of instinct and demystifies the seriousness of high ideas by giving them a resonance on the level of the body. The themes of food and conviviality play a major role in this as if they, like popular celebrations, enjoy special permission to defy censure and to subvert institutional discourse.[5] In a similar clowning way, clerks laugh at received wisdom and at their own greed and tarnish the fine Latin of their masters.

The famous *Cena Cypriani*, which was copied and reworked throughout the Middle Ages, uses the scenario of the banquet to turn the scriptures upside down: many characters from the Old and New Testaments, grotesquely accompanied by their traditional attributes, come and plonk themselves down at a wedding feast. Nothing is spared, not even the holiest sacraments, in the extraordinary fantasy of this grandiose celebration. For example, after the revels, it is time for games: while Martha does the housework and Pilate fetches something to wash his hands in, David plays the harp, Herodias dances, Judas kisses everyone and the Pharaoh falls into the water. A Saturnalian breeze blows over

---

[5] See Bakhtin, *Rabelais and his World*, chapter 4 and P. Lehmann, *Die Parodie im Mittelalter*.

the peaceful words of the catechism; the freedom of the table
authorizes the most daring distortions and brings characters,
words and holy symbols to life through laughter.

The grafting of festive and Bacchic motifs on to sacred texts can
take many forms, but the comic effect it produces remains the
same. Everything goes: the language of the liturgy is travestied, as
in the *Messe de Bacchus*:

> Introibo ad altare Bacchi
> Ad eum qui laetificat cor hominis
> (Quoted by Lehmann, *Die Parodie*
> *im Mittelalter*, p. 233)[6]

Words from the Eucharist are used to celebrate food, the
Evangelical pericopes are rewritten to the glory of drinkers, we
find greedy prayers, gastronomical hagiographies, and so on.
Doubtless given at the feast of fools, all sorts of parodistic sermons
invite people to orgies and praise drinking bouts and sex. One of
these, dating from the end of the fifteenth century, tells of the
escapades of Saint Ham and Saint Chitterling up until the time of
their martyrdom when they are salted, hung, boiled or roasted, cut
into slices and finally eaten (*Sermon joyeux de Saint Jambon et de
Sainte Andouille*, in *Quatre sermons joyeux*). Another is explicitly
aimed at an audience of diners and inevitably drifts into dog Latin:

> Et vos omnes qui soupatis,
> Prio vos quod escoutatis
> Ouvrant grandos horeillibus!
> (*Sermon d'un cardier de mouton*, lines 10–12, ibid.)[7]

The clergy are naturally involved in this great reversal: the Curia is
seated around a table in grotesque poses and in caricatural
portraits; in the Goliard tradition, the menus, debauchery and
natural functions of a particular greedy and lewd abbot are
parodied. And each time we find the same Latin, the same verbal

---

[6] 'I shall enter unto the altar of Bacchus, he who makes the heart of man
rejoice'.

[7] 'And all you who are having supper,/I ask you to listen to me/Opening wide
your ears.'

rhythms and the same *topoi* from religious life subtly shifted to
sing the glory of the gut, as if the mouth wanted to reclaim the
signifying power of the word and apply it to its own domain, that
of taste and sensuous pleasure.

According to a code which Bakhtin has studied, the authorities
(whether of the Church or not) knowingly open the door to cooks
and kitchen Latin. But they can be hoist by their own petard, and
institutionalized parody can turn to satire. The opportunity was
too good for the Protestants to miss. Their pamphleteers proclaimed
the indignity of a clergy which seemed able to parade its gluttony
and mortgage its Latin with impunity. The comic effects are
virtually the same, but the motive and the tone have changed. In
the hands of those who denounced Latin as a means of mystification,
barbarolexis is no longer innocent: it adds fuel to the controversy.
In this way the Lutherans published parodistic masses as the case
for the prosecution, and the Calvinists exploited traditional
linguistic debasement for their own ends in order to turn it against
its authors and use it as an anti-papist weapon.

I shall take the *Satyres chrestiennes de la cuisine papale* as an
example of this kind of polemic set against a background of
culinary insults. This was one of a series of pamphlets exchanged
around 1560 between Geneva and Paris. It is anonymous, but was
probably written in whole or in part by Théodore de Bèze. The
diatribe is 2926 lines long and leaves no stone unturned, but it is
organized around the metaphor of food. The pope is lampooned as
a great expert on food, the Curia is compared to a vast kitchen and,
by extension, the Roman Catholic Church, with its dignitaries,
monks and nuns, is seen as a school of gluttony and bawdiness.
The influence of Rabelais's satire on the Papimania and the
Gastrolaters (*The Fourth Book*, chs. 48–54 and 58–60) is discernible. Whether they are concocting poisonous dishes (reflecting
the scandals of the papacy) or filling their paunch to the extent of
practising theophagy, Catholics are seen as obeying no other law
than that of the belly.

Such invective would be merely banal were it not for the fact
that the satire (faithful to its Latin origin as a pot-pourri)[8] also
cooks up some linguistic concoctions, thus participating in the

[8] See chapter 6, Satire and its cooking.

exceptional verbal fecundity of the symposiac tradition. The comic force of the pamphlet lies above all in the inventiveness and plasticity of its style. Although the papists' blow-outs are revolting, the text is there to be savoured like a meal: 'Feast Happily on this text. Drink, eat' (*Satyres chrestiennes*, p. 5). Latin and foreign languages are not used; only the French language is having a good time, but it is French in all its glory. Verbal fantasy, the creation of neologisms and 'an astonishingly rich, abundant and flavoursome vocabulary which is varied, full of images and vivid' (Y. Giraud, 'Le Comique engagé des *Satyres chrestiennes de la cuisine papale*', p. 64)[9] derive stunning effects from a language which is still malleable, coming up with terms such as *trupelu, tartevelé, flamusse, fanfarisme, saturion, desgombrer, balatron, haligorne, passeligour, paradouze*, etc. Again, we are not far removed from Rabelais and his lexical shenanigans. In an even more characteristic way, the text uses all possible forms of wordplay: homonyms with their ambiguities (*penser/panse*), paranomasia (*bordeliers/cordeliers; vesse/messe*), comic Freudian slips ('A ces veaux pères confesseurs') and ambiguous rhymes (*Platina/plat il n'a*), and many other phonic procedures all of which reveal a sensual attraction to the sound qualities of words. To this is added a dense network of intertextual references – the satire is full of Humanist erudition, which is pointed to by marginal notes. This should suffice to show that language with its inventions and shifts, and literature with its allusions and transformations, occupy centre stage in this Protestant satire. Perhaps it was not only the Catholics who were greedy.

Before grammarians intervened in the next century, Renaissance French had sufficient freedom to respond to the stimulus of the theme of food. But this phenomenon is circumscribed: outside the Rabelaisian tradition attempts at bilingualism and linguistic mixtures are rare – even dialects are almost totally banished from official literature. Centralizing tendencies and demands for a uniform language are already noticeable. In such conditions, dog Latin, linguistic pot-pourris and gibberish did not flourish in the written language. After Rabelais, it is not until Molière that we find another significant demonstration of their comic qualities, in the

---

[9] The following examples are taken from this article.

famous final interlude in *Le Malade imaginaire* with the medical
profession's improvised Latin stuffed with French words – one of
the rare monuments to interlinguistic ridiculousness, taking its
place on the periphery of French classical literature.

In less homogeneous socio-political circumstances, other cultures
and languages are more flexible and more disposed to this kind of
experiment. Later we will see what strange bedfellows Italian and
Latin make. German too is sometimes mixed with Latin, as I have
said, often grafting this cross-breeding on to the themes of
drinking and eating. *Trinkliteratur* has a Humanist side, and
alongside its popular sequences and scatalogical motifs mingle
some academic formulae – classical Latin enlivened by incongruous
juxtaposition, or dog Latin sanctioned by the atmosphere of
gaiety. The evocation of unbridled pleasure in a language which
itself is free of constraints produces a powerful feeling of freedom.
This is further enhanced by the text's exploitation of venerable
classical references. These tendencies produce, for example, the
following collage of German origin, an extraordinary mosaic of
pieces of different languages, literary fragments, different levels of
style, a virtually unlimited polyphony celebrating the joys of the
blow-out:

> Nunc est bibendum, nunc pede libero pulsanda tellus etc. So gehen
> wir secundum psalmographum de virtute in virtutem, von einer zech
> in die andern, ut scribitur in Taberna Culis rusticorum (im land zu
> Sachsen) cap. ubique, in antiquo pariete cum albis carbonibus:
>
> > *Sauff dich vol and leg dich nider,*
> > *steh früe uff and full dich wider;*
> > *so vortreibt ein full die ander,*
> > *das schreibt der gutt frumm priester Arslexander . . .*
>
> Haec enim, socii, haec, inquam, est illa magna navis, das grosse schiff
> der preiten geselschafft, die do schiffen und segeln mit halben wind
> versus Narragoniam, in Schlauraffenland, do die heusser mit
> bratwürsten gezeunet und mit honig bekleibt und mit fladen gedeckt
> seyn. De qua felici patria dictum est: Dabo vobis terram fluentem lac
> et mel, da uns die grebaten tauben in die meuler fligen. (F. Zarncke,
> *Die deutschen Universitäten im Mittelalter*, p. 121)[10]

---

[10] 'Now we must drink, now we must stamp the earth unrestrainedly [Horace,
Odes, I, 37, line 1], etc. So, in the words of the psalmist, we move from one virtue

Horace, the psalmist, the promised land: the tabernacle (rather roughly treated), Saxony and the Land of Cockaigne; on the one hand Latin and the academic practice of the erudite quotation, on the other broad drinking-house jokes and the voice of the guts; all of this runs the gamut of the genres and verges on delirium. The melting pot of satire here produces one of its richest dishes. Rarely have *barbarolexis*, the practice of mixing up languages, parody and free association attained such a high level of fantasy without being reduced to the out and out absurdity of random discourse.

Another German example, this time on a bigger scale, deserves mention here: namely *Die Geschichtklitterung* (1575), Johann Fischart's adaptation of *Gargantua*. This is one of the most dazzling texts ever written because of its linguistic originality, and one of the richest in its combination of food and words, but it is virtually unknown in France and does not have the recognition it deserves in Germany. Its difficulty no doubt has much to do with this: the exuberance of Rabelais, aided by the plasticity of a language capable of all kinds of acrobatics, inspires unbelievable caprices in his German interpreter. Because of its various expansions, the *Geschichtklitterung* is three times as long as *Gargantua*: the Rabelaisian *copia* burst through all the floodgates. The theme of food is the prime beneficiary; with their monstrous bodies and grotesque anatomies, the giant and his companions are bottomless pits which no feast can ever fill. The few lines in Rabelais about Grandgousier's larder ('a good store of . . . hams, plenty of smoked ox-tongues, an abundance of chitterlings' – *Gargantua*, p. 46) expand in Fischart's prolific writing to fill about thirty pages

---

to another [Psalms 83: 8], from one drinking bout to another, as it is written in Tavernacul of the peasants (in the land of Saxony), in the chapter called "everywhere", on an ancient screen, with white coal:

> Get completely drunk and lie down on the floor,
> Get up early and fill up again;
> One feast leads to another,
> As the good, pious priest, Arslixander, wrote . . .

Here, my companions, here it is, I say, the big ship, the big ship of good people, who sail, filling their sails with a small breeze, towards the land of madmen, the Land of Cockaigne, where the houses are surrounded by roasting sausages, coated with honey and covered with cakes. Of this happy land it is said: I shall bring you unto a land flowing with milk and honey [Exodus 3: 8], where pigeons fly ready-roasted into your mouth.' Quoted by Hess, *Deutsch-Lateinische Narrenzunft*, pp. 193–4.

(*Geschichtklitterung*, chs. 3 and 4). But I will not attempt to compare the two books in detail, limiting myself to a brief enquiry connected with the theme of this book.

A critic wrote of Fischart that he uses 'a gigantic vocabulary, perhaps the most extensive and certainly the most whimsical that a German writer has ever had at his disposal' (H. Sommerhalder, *Johann Fischarts Werk. Eine Einführung*, p. 59). But it is not sufficient just to record the size of his lexicon, which takes its material from all areas of language and from all kinds of jargon. With a virtuosity and boldness which leave Rabelais and French far behind, Fischart endlessly coins new words; he does not work within a closed vocabulary, but rather, through creating new words and hybrids and by lexical transformation, seems capable of indefinitely enlarging his repertoire. All kinds of combinations – previously unknown additions of prefixes and suffixes, metatheses, polyglot contaminations and wild derivations – seem possible. Moreover they produce some of their finest mutations when language both toys with words and evokes the pleasure of eating. An example (from the prologue) is the following invocation to boozy poets, a modulation *ad absurdum* on the Latin roots *po-* (to drink), *pot-* (to be able), *pet-* (to search), and the Greek *poi* (to do, and poetry):

> O ihr Potulente Poeten, potirt der pott and bütten, unnd potionirt euch potantlich mit potitioniren, compotiren unnd expotiren, dann potiren und appotiren kompt von petiren und appetiren, unnd pringt potate poesei, dieweil potantes sind potentes. Unnd Potentaten sind Potantes. (*Geschichtklitterung*, p. 29)

Such verbal delirium cannot be translated; it can only just be understood. Language here reaches one of its limits, where links in the poetic chain and the call of the paronym govern the discourse. The distortions and transformations of words, the dynamic of musical variation and the semantic telescoping they provoke require our attention. Absurd configurations of grammar give rise to grotesque creations, a collage of syllables from which disturbing and fantastic figures emerge, like the 'Fressschnaufige Maulprocker, Collatzbäuch, Gargurguliander: Grosprockschlindige Zipfler und Schmärrotzer' (ibid., p. 19). Fischart is not telling a story but giving us sounds, rhythms and comic morphology and syntax to savour. This is all the more true in passages where the verbal dance produces no intelligible meaning and indeed becomes just sound: 'Kurant zum vich, virlam enten, ku klee ass, kräh sand ass, mistelinum gabelinum, treib den Son auss dem stalino hinab das Stiglinum, speckorum Kelberdantzen' (p. 204).[11]

The rules of communication seem not to apply; language has slipped its moorings and shifted the phonatory act into the realm of sensory pleasure. Words are worth their weight in sound, they are seen as so many articulated vibrations. Rabelais's message has been received: while the German *Gargantua* hustles the original, it restores, or even enhances, the affinity between reverie about food and verbal creativity.

Language in celebration shows the way: 'Sed oportet nos fortfahren, Quia non habemus multum der zeit' ('But we must continue as we haven't much time' – *Facetia facetiarum*).[12]

Folengo and the ars macaronica

Dog Latin, like a poor schoolboy translation, superimposes Latin words and endings on to the structures of the mother tongue. It is a superficial Latinization of the vulgar tongue which translates word for word without managing to imitate Latin syntax. It is usually associated with satire in that it denounces ignorance; as we have seen, it is the comic side of Humanism, the ridiculous culture of badly educated people.

'Macaronic' Latin on the other hand produces an educated concoction based on an obviously impeccable knowledge of the ancient language. The rhythm of the phrase, the morphology and even the neologisms and barbarisms used betray their origins in classical philology. Instead of the vulgar tongue absorbing Latin, here Latin imposes its own structure. It is emancipated and vulgarized without losing its identity. If there are errors, if it offends grammar or vocabulary, it does it as a joke; it is designed to show unambiguously that it is in control of the operation. The

[11] Quoted as an example of *'philologischer Unsinn'* ('philological nonsense') by Hess, ibid., p. 238.
[12] Quoted by Hess, ibid., p. 242.

following line is an example: 'Tres parat exiguam propter fabricare fritaiam' ('He prepares three of them to make a small omelette' – Folengo, *Baldus*, II, line 180, in *Opere*).[13] The character takes three eggs to make a little omelette, and the author makes three mistakes in writing a little sentence. *Propter* followed by the infinitive is a solecism; *fabricare* exists in Latin, but its use here is inappropriate; *fritaia* is a borrowing from Italian. However, the elegance of the construction, the arrangement of the words and the strict hexameter bear the marks of a connoisseur.

Kitchen Latin and macaronic Latin may be produced according to different recipes, but their effects are similar. Whether the result of ignorance or academic jokes, they attack the classical model, infuse it with foreign material and give rise to ridiculous linguistic juxtapositions which revitalize the dulled perception of language. The two operations are governed by an impulse to the burlesque, by the challenge to the noble paradigm and by triviality of purpose. When he invokes, for example, 'merdipotens o Iuppiter' (ibid., XX, line 641), the macaronic poet is introducing a vulgar and incorrect adjective into an elegant and correct phrase, thus giving new life to the worn formula of invocation. It only takes one incongruous departure from the model to give the following line (which in other respects is strictly Virgilian) a comic appearance: 'Quo fugis? unde venis? quis te facit ire galoppum?' ('Where are you fleeing to? Where do you come from? Who is making you gallop?' – III, line 382).[14]

Another characteristic of macaronic Latin should be emphasized: apart from its faulty Latinity, dog Latin, as we have seen in several examples, often alternates with sequences in the vulgar tongue, creating a juxtaposition or a mosaic of heterogeneous systems which do not mesh. On the other hand, the *ars macaronica* integrates foreign elements, it proceeds by hybridization and produces a more or less uniform mixture. Suddenly, Latin is no longer atrophied, it is reshaped, regenerated and transformed into a new language through contact with abstruse but organic material. The means of achieving this naturalization are varied. A word may be used which is found in both Latin and the vulgar language but

---

[13] The quotations from *Baldus* are from C. Cordié's edition. The line quoted here is given as an example by U. E. Paoli, *Il Latino maccheronico*, p. 17.

[14] A parody of Virgil, *Aeneid*, X, 670; quoted by Paoli, ibid., p. 65.

has different meanings, the ancient form being retained but with the new sense: for example *toti* (like the French *tous*) is used instead of *omnes* to mean 'all'. Or terms may be created which are not authentic, but which sound plausible: for example *suspiramentum* for 'sigh', *fluctivagare* for 'meandering on the sea', *pigritatim* for 'slowly' and *sibi cagare* for 'to shit oneself'. Or a word may be borrowed from the modern language, have a Latin ending tacked on to it and be incorporated into a classical structure or even into a classical cadence. Such a grafting of one language on to another is possible using German: 'Nos binas Sprachas in Wortum einbringimus unum' ('We introduce two languages in a single word' – quoted by Paoli, *Il Latino maccheronico*, p. 54); but it is Italian which, because of its closeness to Latin, offers the most successful combinations, and it is in this particular overlap that macaronic language works best. Latin is Italianized, Italian is Latinized, and the symbiosis is so close that it is difficult to see where one ends and the other begins. We can see this in the work of Folengo, the great macaronic master, who throws into his melting pot not only classical Latin but also vulgar and Humanist Latin and literary Italian (contemporary Tuscan), not to mention several northern Italian dialects such as Mantuan, Paduan, Brescian and Bergamasque, as well as popular and peasant vocabulary, specialist terms and so on.[15]

Macaronics spread throughout Europe in the Renaissance. It is found of course in Fischart, who calls it *Nudelverse*; the Germans generally were not slow to meddle with academic language or to mock the classics, and they provide many other examples.[16] The most important of the sporadic French attempts[17] are related to religious controversies and take their place alongside the *Satyres*

[15] On Folengo's macaronics, see Paoli, ibid., E. Bonora, *Le Maccheronee di Teofilo Folengo*, and the studies by L. Goggi Carotti, 'La Rielaborazione degli episodi della Domus Phantasiae e della Zucca (*Baldus*, XXV)', E. Paratore, 'Il Maccheroneo folenghiano', and C. Segre, 'La Tradizione macaronica da Folengo a Gadda (e oltre)'.

[16] See especially the anonymous poem *Floia* (1593), an example of *Flohliteratur* (flea literature) in F. W. Genthe, *Geschichte der Macaronischen Poesie und Sammlung ihrer vorzüglichsten Denkmale*. On macaronic poetry in France, Germany, England and Italy, see Genthe, and O. Delepierre, *Macaronéana, ou Mélanges de littérature macaronique*.

[17] Macaronics was more developed in Provence than it was in the north. See F. Garavini and L. Lazzerini (eds), *Maccaronee Provenzali*.

chrestiennes de la cuisine papale. I shall not dwell on these texts: they do not exploit the alimentary metaphor and their literary quality is very limited. For reasons of linguistic affinity, it is Italy, as I have said, which is the adoptive country of the *ars macaronica.* The Italian experiment started around the beginning of the *Quattrocento* and was confined to the area around Padua and its monasteries and university; in a milieu of bilingual academics, with considerable tensions between Latin and the vulgar language and between Tuscan and local dialects, sensitivity towards and a taste for philological jokes came together to create a composite and extravagant language to contrast with the purism of Ciceronian Humanism. The local Benedictine monks, who loved learned pranks and enjoyed the freedom which charactrized Italy before the Council of Trent, played an important role in this.[18]

Teofilo Folengo came from this milieu and wrote several macaronic poems in the early decades of the sixteenth century.[19] But it is his *Baldus* which is most relevant here, a neglected masterpiece containing twenty-five books and about 15,000 lines, and one of the most outstanding products of the affinity between feasts and words.[20] Without Folengo, Rabelais would not have been what he was.[21]

Baldus, a descendant of Renaud of Montauban, the grandson of Charlemagne, is one of those heroes who parodistically perpetuate the tradition of the medieval epic into the Renaissance. Accompanied by various companions like Fracasse the giant, Cingar the joker and Boccalo the clown, he has innumerable adventures and rises to all kinds of challenges. When still a child, he displays his bravery in the familiar milieu of Mantua, complete with local colour. He becomes a knight errant, travels over land and sea, achieves many feats of prowess, comes up against monsters and miracles, finally descending into Hell, rubbing shoulders with devils and ending up in a pumpkin, at which point the unfinished story ends. Epic *topoi*

---

[18] See G. Billanovich, *Tra don Teofilo Folengo e Merlin Cocaio.*

[19] See especially (in Luzio's edition) *Zanitonella*, a parody of the bucolic love song, and *Moscheidos*, an epic parody on the war between flies and ants.

[20] Various versions of the text existed between 1517 and 1552. The editions used here give the definitive version (published posthumously in 1552 and known as the Vigaso Cocaio edition).

[21] See 'My country is a pumpkin', below.

and fantastic devices abound: Folengo alludes to a mass of semi-heroic, semi-fabulous tales, like Pulci's *Morgante* and Ariosto's *Orlando furioso*. But the charm of the poem lies elsewhere – in its language, its clowning and its supreme lack of reverence for serious tradition. Interlinguistic and intertextual humour constantly broaden the reader's horizon, combining academic pleasure at recognizing the references with amusing travesty of the old masters. The *Aeneid* bears the brunt of this, saturating the narrative with epic commonplaces and highly characteristic stylistic, rhetorical and prosodic forms.

One comic device Folengo shares with other writers lies in seating the characters at table and diverting their appetite for glory towards more nourishing pleasures. Food is a focus in *Baldus*. Meals and snacks set the tone, occurring throughout the narrative and especially in the early books. This procedure is common, but it gains significance by a subtle shift: contrary to usual practice (illustrated for example by Rabelais), food is seen less in terms of a finished product than as something in the process of being made. It is as much a question of cooking here as of consumption: the setting is the wings of the banquet. If there is abundance, if there is a glut of food at the feasts, it is because skilful cooks have transformed raw material into cleverly balanced dishes.

Right from the start the narrator puts his poem under the wing of the nourishing Muses and describes the luxuriant landscape (rivers of soups and sauces, boat-like tarts, mounds of pâtés) where they welcome him. The model of the Land of Cockaigne is obvious, but there is a significant difference. Instead of pigeons flying ready roasted into the mouths of the diners, gastronomic pleasure is hard won, and food only releases its true savour if prepared according to complex recipes. The nymphs are busy,

> grating the cheese with pierced graters: some work at shaping succulent gnocchi [*teneros gnoccos*] . . . Others knead the mixture, filling fifty basins with fat fritters and pancakes [*pampardis grassisque lasagnis*], and others, seeing the frying pan getting too hot, pull it from the embers and blow on it . . . In short, everyone is striving to finish her gallimaufrey [*menestram*], so that you will see a thousand smoking chimneys and a thousand cauldrons attached to them, hanging from chains. (Folengo, *Baldus*, I, lines 47–61, in *Opere*)

A little later we have the same scenario. The king of France is giving a feast to celebrate the end of a tournament. But the episode opens around the ovens, with copious detail on how the dishes are made (ibid., I, lines 392–430). The chef is a learned man, well versed in the 'study of the mouth' (*studium golae*) and the 'bible of the palate' (*bibia palati*) (I, line 489). The narrative is above all concerned with the agents of transformation: the fires and smoke, the utensils, the bevy of butchers and cooks:

> There was one who was fricasseeing poultry livers with bacon: another sprinkling ginger and pepper on to the fricassees: another making a yellow sauce for the waterfowl . . . Others are taking out of the oven potted pâtés on which they put Venetian cinnamon: another takes boiled capons out of the pan, puts them on to a big dish and then sprinkles sugared rosewater over them. (I. lines 414–29)

Spices are used lavishly, sauces and soups are adroitly seasoned. They favour the most complicated dishes: slowly cooked stews and roasts, and pasta, of course, cooked with real Italian skill. The raw is constantly being converted into the cooked through chemical operations which make natural produce into works of art.

The vividness of the vocabulary, enhanced in the original by the mixture of languages, suggests an analogy between the cooking, transformation and amalgamation of food and of the various ingredients of macaronic Latin. The alimentary and culinary motifs act as a *mise en abyme*, reflecting the way in which the text operates on words. The shift from consumption to production and the emphasis on the mixing of raw material draw attention to the writer and his verbal concoctions. The association of food with linguistic experimentation recurs, focusing here on mobile manipulation, for the most remarkable feature of the *ars macaronica* is its extraordinary flexibility. Folengo freely adapts and combines familiar semes and morphemes, creating an inexhaustible series of neologisms. He mixes forms, concocts words and creates a kind of language which is original yet intelligible: *asinaliter*, asininely; *transgluttere*, to devour; *trippifer*, with a big paunch; *mangiamentum*, food; etc. But he does more than just enrich his own language with new terms. He rejects the principle that a given signified must correspond to a fixed form. His hybrid creations are never

automatic and give rise to an infinite variety of possible combinations. A root can undergo many transformations without an
apparent change in meaning: *furcifuga* or *fugiforca*, *ventramine* or
ventronem or *ventralia*, *macaronea* or *macaronesca* or
macaronica, etc.[22] It is as if Latin was continuing to evolve and to
produce original means of expression. The poet produces a living
language out of a dead one and an expanding vocabulary out of a
supposedly closed lexicon. The plasticity of the lexical apparatus,
the new mixture of ingredients and the cross-fertilizations thus take
the language to its limit. Macaronic Latin is constantly changing, and
is made up as it goes along; it is a language which is not really a
language, continuously developing, immediate, provisional and
spontaneous, like speech.

While he's about it, Folengo sometimes abandons the realm of
intelligible language to produce pure sound. An example is the
following onomatopoeia evoking the sound of paving stones under
the hooves of a donkey: 'Tichi tich et tichi toch resonat per mille
lapillos' (XX, line 800); or devils gibberish:

> Papa Satan, o papa Satan, beth, gimel, aleppe,
> Cra cra, tif taf noc, sgne flut, canatauta, riogna.
> (Ibid., XXIV, lines 639–40)

It is not surprising that Folengo adds marginal notes here and there
to explain his pidgin, but these too are sometimes comic, providing
another way of mimicking academic institutions. But here the cook
is not uneducated: the macaronic concoction may adapt recipes
and defy customs, but it maintains an affinity with familiar forms
and is readable. It is unusually successful in transforming language
while respecting its spirit, liberating words but preserving communication.

Muses with greasy hands

Folengo explains the origin and meaning of the term 'macaronic' in
the following way:

---

[22] These examples are quoted by Paratore, 'Il Maccheroneo folenghiano'.

This *ars poetica* is called macaronic after macaroni, which is a thick
and unrefined rustic dish made of a mixture of flour, cheese and
butter. For this reason, macaronic verse should only contain that
which is coarse and crude, along with vulgar words. (Quoted in
Luzio's edition, *Le Maccheronee*, vol. II, p. 284)[23]

The reference to food is obvious (except that Folengo's macaroni is
more like gnocchi), and the connotations of crudeness and rusticity
are clearly emphasized. The word does not only denote a variety of
pasta but also a stupid, thick and clumsy man: a noodle. However
learned and cunning it is, macaronic speech aims to take language
back to its organic relationship with the tongue and aims to be seen
as an oral pleasure. It is cooked up like a nourishing local dish, as I
have said. This transfer of the verbal into the sphere of food and
this fantasm, which we have already seen in Rabelais, of the word
as matter and fodder are confirmed by another of Folengo's
farcical etymologies. Cingar the joker parodies the Gospels ('Man
shall not live by bread alone, but by every word [*verbum*] that
proceedeth out of the mouth of God' – Matthew 4: 4) when he
says:

> Man shall not live by bread alone, but by beef [*bovis*] and fatty lamb
> [*vervecis*]. That is what the Gospel means when it says that we
> should live by words [*verbo*]. (Quoted in the introduction to
> *Histoire maccaronique*, p. xvii)[24]

The burlesque etymology recognizes in the two syllables of *verbo*
the words for beef and lamb. This charade is emblematic: we can
live on words, but only if they are edible!

The two fundamental traditions of feeding on the divine word or
on the body of Christ, and tasting ambrosia or the nectar of the
gods, exploit food metaphors extensively. But it is the spiritual side
which is conventionally emphasized, the reference to food and the
role of the body being largely glossed over. The burlesque poet

---

[23] 'Ars ista poëtica nuncupatur ars macaronica a macaronibus derivata, qui
macarones sunt quoddam pulmentum farina, caseo, botiro compaginatum,
grossum, rude et rusticanum; ideo macaronices nil nisi grassedinem, ruditatem et
vocabulazzos debet in se continere.'

[24] The French translation, *Histoire maccaronique de Merlin Coccaie, prototype
de Rabelais*.

breathes new life into these pallid analogies, putting back inspiration, creation and work into everyday experience. This is the meaning of the invocation of the culinary Muses at the beginning of *Baldus*, parodying the traditional call to Apollo's daughters, for 'all this Parnassian crap can do nothing for my paunch' (*Baldus*, I, lines 11–12 in *Opere*). The metaphor of the nourishing Muses is taken at face value, the Nymphs are 'fat' and swim in gravy (ibid., I, line 17), they have big stomachs and vulgar names:

> May the Muses and the learned pot-bellied sisters, Hairy-face, Glutton, Fatty, Fat-face, Piss-head and Flat-foot, come and macaronically fatten their nursling and give me five or eight pans of pap! (Ibid., I, lines 13–16)

The invocation to these clever housewives recurs from time to time, at the end or the beginning of a book, putting the activity of the macaronic poet back into its proper context of the steam of the oven and the taste of stews. For writing does not only involve the mind, it also mobilizes the body, awakening instinct and titillating the palate. Once more we see how ambiguous the language of the stomach is: it rejects the dominance of literary tradition in order to assert its own spontaneity and its connection with basic desires, but its aims only make sense in relation to the learned institutions to which it refers. The image of the kitchen, the meeting point of art and nature, of pleasure and the law, encapsulates this ambiguity perfectly.

During the narrative, the original myth of the 'fat poet' (XXII, line 8) reiterates the theme of the initial invocation. Near Mantua, the Mincio separates two rival cities: Pietola, proud of being the birthplace of Virgil; and Cipada, with neither poet nor renown. Cipada therefore sends an ambassador to Apollo: but he has already bestowed all his gifts, Homer and Virgil having exhausted all his resources. So there must be a change of register: ' "You'd better go among the kitchen scullions",' Apollo says, ' "and find the bright and shining Realm of fritters and pancakes [*regna lasagnarum*]" ' (XXII, lines 82–3). It is there, in the land 'where the people tie up their vines with sausages, and where trees everywhere have puddings and tarts as fruits' (XXII, lines 98–9) that Cipada will find its poet. According to Apollo, 'No one yet excels in this new art' (XXII, line 90). Letting the stomach speak is the way to get out of the impasse and to avoid the routine – but this is only done with the authority of a god and the inevitable reminder of Virgil: one cannot get out of repetition.

As an author and as a character, Folengo adopts the pseudonym of Merlin Cocaie. Merlin, it is explained in *Baldus*, because a blackbird (*merla*) came to feed the infant-poet (XXII, lines 116–17); and the recollection of Merlin the wizard is not unconnected with this choice. The name of Cocaie is not commented on, but suggests several associations which reinforce the theme of food. First, there is the homonym with the Mantuan *cocai* (or the macaronic *coconus*), a cork or bung.[25] By paronymic attraction, it could also imply the cook (*coquus*) or someone from Cockaigne (*Cuccagna*), not to mention that *cocochia*, in Folengo's language, is a synonym of *zucca*, a pumpkin. Whatever the case, these allusions have something in common: the myths of origin of the poet and his inspiration, and the latent meanings of the pseudonym all contribute to mark food as the closest approximation to the literary process.

To open a poem with praise of good food, and then to reiterate this theme throughout, is of course to reveal an aim which is burlesque and to give an easily identifiable horizon of expectation to the book. As in Rabelais's prologues,[26] food functions as a generic indicator. By making the poet swim in the kitchen-grease and by substituting pasta for ambrosia, the text clearly places itself in the most vulgar register. Taking for granted the traditional hierarchy of values and, *inter alia*, the absolute supremacy of Virgil, it reduces the sublime to the level of material impulse. Parody subverts an ethic and an aesthetic, or at least claims to, and if eventually its threat is not realized (the sublime remaining the point of reference and the base wallowing in its inferiority, for therein lies its charm), the system will have been tested and both poles given a new tension. Folengo replaces the *topoi* of epic grandeur with the buffoonery of Baldus and his companions, in the realistic and moderate setting of Mantuan peasantry. He prefers a

[25] See C. Cordié, 'Ancora Cocaio'.
[26] See chapter 5, 'Our after-dinner entertainments', and The marrow bone.

comic fairy tale which dispels fear to the serious and threatening representation of Hell in his reference to Dante. A single line can evoke the solemn formulae of fear and, in an abrupt shift, ridicule them, for example: 'Terra tremat baratrumque metu sibi cagat adossum' ('The earth trembles and the abyss shits itself' – I, line 4); or 'Fit rumor, strepitatque ingens per nubila tuf tof' ('There is a noise and an enormous tuf tof reverberates through the clouds' – (IX, line 531).

Folengo even makes the hell that he demystifies a symbol of his own work. He explores zones thought to be forbidden to poetry and enjoys transgressing the fine rules of classicism, occupying an area which reeks of sulphur but which in the end is not so frightening. Hell and the kitchen are homologous: they give writing a troubled, strange, but fertile location. A fable 'en abyme' illustrates this idea. A Roman innkeeper who used to feed Church dignitaries is allowed after his death to open a hostelry at the Gates of Paradise in order to maintain his clientele. But business is bad. The prelates and other rich people are not in Heaven, and the blessed are without money and eat lenten fare. No one asks for his 'boiled capons with saffron soup and puddings with bottles of various sweet and strong wine' (XXIII, lines 330–1). The hotelier knows what he must do: he takes his business to Hell, where gastronomy flourishes among the *bons viveurs*. The implication is that the Heaven of literature is not a happy place, and that elevated and edifying genres go stale. Hell is more fun, and more suitable for the art of cooking and poetry. Consorting with the impure, the coarse or the aberrant, and subverting the laws of elegance, Folengo discovers an inexhaustible field of expression. He is certainly no Romantic and the charms of satanism and the flowers of evil are not his cup of tea. His universe is not derived from ideology but from a grotesque vision which liberates the resources of the ugly and the base without radically challenging the established order. His Hell is not a place of metaphysical revolt, but rather the upside-down and innocent world of the carnival, a place of freedom and imagination. The fact remains that, from the steam of kitchen to the marvels of the underworld, Merlin Cocaie, as a poet and clown, is in favour of the unusual and the extravagant. He is in cahoots with the little devils of legend – Rabelais attributes to him a fictional *De patria diabolorum* in his imaginary library.[27] After all, Cocaie himself roams around Hell with Baldus's troupe and, because of all the fibs he has told, finally ends up in a pumpkin. This is a macaronic journey which it is worth examining in more detail.

'My country is a pumpkin'[28]

Is Folengo provocative, satirical or diabolical? Or fantastic and playful? It is worth trying to resolve this question: it also concerns Rabelais, and allows us to evaluate the moral dimension of the alimentary theme.

Cooking and Muses with greasy hands are not so one-dimensionally vulgar or polemical as they seem. Baldus's parents, a knight and his princess, arrive one day in a peasant's cottage and lend a hand in preparing the pasta for a rustic meal (Folengo, *Baldus*, II, lines 191–275). This perhaps debases them, as comic scenes do in an epic, but their country meal has all the charms of an idyll and is as good as any banquet. The spirit of the celebration and the collective participation in physical pleasures wipe out any shame. In the euphoria of conviviality, it is no longer a question of humbling oneself or the next man. The table is not an exclusive place; it welcomes diverse people and makes harmony out of discord. We are still at the beginning of the narrative (as with the feasts which open *Pantagruel*, ch. 1, and *Gargantua*, chs. 4–6), and already the usual hierarchy is lacking.

The situation in Folengo (as in general in Rabelais) is more complex and subtle.[29] The theme of food does more than provocatively reveal what classical orthodoxy leaves unsaid: it is more than a simple foil which conforms to received hierarchies and is subordinated to a parodistic aim. Rather than reinforcing the fixed and vertical dualism of the material and the spiritual, of the vulgar and the sublime, it challenges it. The device it uses is not antithesis, but ambivalence; the antithetic structure on which the burlesque is normally based is replaced by an integrated axiological

---

[27] See *Pantagruel*, chapter 7 and *The Third Book*, chapter 11.

[28] 'Zucca mihi patria est' (Folengo, *Baldus*, XXV, line 649, in *Opere*)

[29] See especially Bakhtin, *Rabelais and his World* and, less centrally, M. Jeanneret, ' "Ma patrie est une citrouille": thèmes alimentaires dans Rabelais et Folengo'.

and literary order – a discursive mode which goes beyond its satirical relevance to set out a programme which reconciles oppositions. Instead of simply inverting the sublime and the base, Folengo stresses their interdependence and interaction. Virgil, Aristotle and serious tradition are neither celebrated nor disqualified, but rather absorbed into folklore and revitalized by contact with popular themes. Conversely, the role of the body, far from being glorified or disparaged or seen as a machine of war, reveals more subtle and unforeseen dimensions which are ordinarily reserved for more abstract themes. *Baldus* substitutes a unitary and dynamic system for the hierarchical and static disjunction of opposite poles. What is therefore at play, beyond the burlesque, is the search for a more all-embracing and generous vision, the quest for a totalizing wisdom, free from stratification, classification and other exclusions. Therein perhaps lies the source of the serenity and well-being which Folengo communicates to his readers.

Among Baldus's companions, the role of cook is played by an admirable clown called Boccalo, a practical joker and magician who also transcends the categories of sublime and base through his versatility and absolute lack of inhibition. An anti-hero and a comic fat man, he is better at spicing sauces than using a sword. He cannot be criticized, for he entertains more than he scandalizes, he dodges official censure and he discredits the morality of right-thinking people. He is like macaronic language itself, which is also spicy, extravagant and so picturesque and amusing in the way it invents its jargon and so independent of systems that it upsets the norm and breaks down the mechanisms of judgement, thus provoking a powerful feeling of release.

This comic, playful and capricious tone dominates the main part of the poem (as it does so many parts of Rabelais). The paradigm of satire, like that of allegory and other didactic devices, is present throughout the discourse as a possibility, but one which is rarely actualized: the preposterous and the gratuitous win the day. Adventures proliferate and the bizarre appears without having to justify itself. In its view of the world, as in its language, *Baldus* represents the triumph of the imagination. The whole narrative could be read in this way, but here I shall just examine two key passages, the beginning and the end of the text, which will bring us back into the realm of food once more.

The first words of the book set the tone: 'I had the fantastic fantasy of writing' (ibid., I, line 1). The *mens phantastica* however has an unfortunate reputation in classical medicine; it verges on madness. But the poet is telling of a place where normative categories are suspended, and imagination, entertainment and arbitrariness are the order of the day. The polemic function of laughter is immediately defused. The invocation to the fat Muses and the rest of the narrative are marked as irrational, presented as a game and dedicated to pleasure. As in Rabelais's prologues, the initial placing of the book within the realm of food is there less to shock than to create the convivial atmosphere of friendship, trust and freedom in which literary invention can permit itself the greatest eccentricities.

The final episode brings this operation to its logical conclusion. The last person the friends meet on their journey to Hell is a clown, 'completely mad, as he was riding a long stick like little children do' (XXV, lines 582–3); he sports all the symptoms of lunacy – jumping, ringing his little bells and, 'giving his hand to Baldus, starting to dance' (XXV, line 592). Our hero accepts this invitation to dance, and does more than this: 'this madman . . . often falls down: Baldus helps him up, and indeed thinks of nothing else than helping the clown up again and again' (XXV, lines 597–9). This solicitousness is symbolic. The protagonist himself is a product of the imagination, and he shows allegiance to it by letting himself be drawn into a world of incongruity, of innocence and of digression. This is not all: the madman dances the friends along their last journey. He leads them to a vast pumpkin which once 'was edible and could have provided a good meal [*menestra*] for everyone' (XXV, lines 604–5), but which is now hollow, light and full of air. The clown goes in to it with the friends behind him: this will be the last time we see them, as they are absorbed for ever in the supreme inanity of the pumpkin. They merge with what they have always loved (food), and with what they have always been (vain and futile creations of the imagination).

The descent into Hell, which is full of allusions to Virgil and Dante and of heroic paradigms, thus ends in gentle madness and the absolute frivolity of the characters. This discordance might seem polemical: but in fact it is consistent with the bizarre and gratuitous nature of a fiction which sees itself as pure fantasy; this, the virtuosity of the cooks and the malice of the clowns and the devils are all outside moral or rational norms, moving the centre of gravity towards other values – those of the carnival or those of spiritual freedom, which are two complementary expressions of a world turned upside down. The forms of satire and parody could have won the day, in which case the stomach would have only been a symbolic challenge, a banal instrument of derision. In fact, it liberates a radically different voice speaking a language which itself is aberrant, declaring laws null and void and suspending logic. The entry into the pumpkin brings to its culmination the imaginative impulse of a story which is won over by a child-like spirit and the joy of entertainment. Macaronic Latin is therefore no longer a shameful or derisive reflection of the classical norm, it is one of the indications of rightful freedom gained over rules. Similarly, cooking is neither disgusting nor subversive. It represents the liberty of people released from inhibition and curious about the world in all its aspects. When words and food are being celebrated like this, the usual conventions – the moral norm and aesthetic hierarchy – seem petty. For something else is in play, and on a different scale.

Montaigne was to write one of his finest essays (III, 9) in defence of vanity, asserting the plenitude of emptiness in contrast to received ideas. The same paradox inspires Folengo's discourse on macaronics and on the status of the fiction. The final pages of the narrative present a fundamental reflection on the inanity of literature, which is as futile as it is attractive, as beneficial and ephemeral as the bouquet of a good wine.

So the characters disappear into the pumpkin. At a loose end, the narrator soon joins them, since

> it is the home of poets, bards and astrologers, who invent, make up, sing, foretell and interpret several dreams for each person and from whose lips pour forth fresh madness and vanity. (Ibid., XXV, lines 608–10)

The hollow space of the pumpkin is the symbolic location of the futile word, the meeting place of chatterboxes, storytellers and imposters, held captive by their dizzying insubstantiality. Obeying the law which says that a vacuum attracts a vacuum (XXV, line 626), it is the natural home of poets – Homer and Virgil are already there – and it is here, taken in hand by an army of tooth-drawers, that they pay the price of their lies until the end of time. For Merlin Cocaie, fantasizer and master joker, it is the logical conclusion of his journey: the pumpkin is his country (XXV, line 649); 'I will have to lose as many teeth as I have put lies into this big book' (XXV, lines 649–50). This is a striking epilogue, as the poet, like the creatures of his imagination, disappears with them into oblivion, and the fiction – *flatus vocis* – is absorbed with its author back into its own nullity. This is the final flourish of the imagination and the epic fizzles out: the conquest of hell is deferred – perhaps it will be achieved by someone else.

Slightly earlier in the last book, another reflexive fable illustrates the lightness and insubstantiality of literary games. While the friends travel from one surprising miracle to the next, and just as they are telling each other about 'the follies invented by poets' (XXV, lines 419–20), they suddenly become befuddled: it is as if they had gone mad; they are deceived by mirages and unable to communicate. Overcome by the void that surrounds them, they become exceedingly light and start to float weightlessly. Without knowing it, they have entered the land of Fantasy – 'Undique phantasmae volitant':

> You can hear the fantasies flying around endlessly, dizzy spirits, dreams, thoughts provoked with no reason, anxiety which is harmful to the head, imaginary worries, the different kinds of image produced by the mind. It is a madhouse. (Ibid., XXV, lines 479–83)

This unstable and ethereal world is the home ground of philosophers and grammarians in which dialectical arguments, misleading categorizations and the sophistries of scholasticism fly around like winged chimera. The concepts and methodologies of logicians and pedantic subdivisions are so many ridiculous games and vain forms which only exist in the imagination of their authors. Beleaguered by these fantasms and punch-drunk from all these ideas and words, the travellers attempt to grasp them, but they are volatile substances and slip away and hover. One of the friends, however, manages to eat some abstractions: he 'received from Paul of Venice and Peter of Spain a thousand deceits, which he swallowed in a trice, as easily as if they had been candied coriander' (XXV, lines 522–4). So they become contaminated by the delirium of the academics, whose theories are dreams and whose speeches are hot air.

There is much in common between the volatile words of Folengo and the thawed words of Rabelais (*The Fourth Book*, chs. 55–6) – in particular their ambivalence. The overt meaning of both phenomena is malevolent (the sounds of war in *The Fourth Book* and the futility of scholasticism in *Baldus*), and yet both sets of friends are amused by them and delight in consuming them. But why should it be a scandal that the ideas of the erudite are only worth their weight in air? They are simply part of universal folly, just one more extravagance which Folengo adds to the catalogue of incongruity in his poem. Pedants have their jargon, their academic Latin and their abstruse conventions: they too are language-mad, delirious philologists neither more nor less fantastical in their verbal acrobatics than the macaronic poet himself. Although Merlin Cocaie feigns indignation (as Rabelais does with his jabberers), his laughter is well intentioned: he, like them, is a putter-together of words and a creator of fables, perhaps the only difference being that he does not take himself seriously.

So here is a poem which reveals the mechanics of its own fiction and the strangeness of its language, and ends by proclaiming that the greatest vanity (in both senses of the word) is to play with words and indulge the whims of one's imagination – not to mention the self-sufficiency of a narrative which reflects with satisfaction on itself. The book deploys its finest artifice, and then destroys itself, an 'aboli bibelot d'inanité sonore'.

One thing remains. A fine word is as good as a fine meal. Books cooked macaronically are no doubt futile, but they do fill one's mouth with tasty words. If Folengo chooses to examine the poetic affinities between greed and logophilia, if he sets himself up as a gastronomic writer, why should we try to dissociate what he has assimilated and to separate, against his will, the dual operations of the tongue? Verbal jubilation, making fables, savouring food and being attentive to one's body are all futile, but pleasurable. In the eyes of eternity, neither a good stew nor a good tale is significant. But Folengo's Humanism made no mistake: he who plays the Angel ends up playing the goat.

9

'The centre of all books'[1]

'Monarch of ecumenical symposia'[2]

For many years Béroalde de Verville's *Le Moyen de parvenir*[3] was thought to be a collection of nonsense, a scatological compilation of unreadable logorrhoea. But the elements which decency frowned upon – its obscenity, verbal delirium and rhapsodic character – are precisely those which have now begun its rehabilitation.[4] *Le Moyen* is a neglected masterpiece, and forms a very appropriate conclusion to our series of banquets. It brings the potential of the genre to a culmination and takes the subversion of narrative and linguistic structures to extremes rarely achieved in

---

[1] Béroalde de Verville, *Le Moyen de parvenir. Oeuvre contenant la raison de tout ce qui a esté, est, et sera: avec demonstrations certaines et necessaires, selon la rencontre des effects de Vertu*, chapter 12, *Vidimus*. Quotations are from the oldest known edition, republished under the editorship of H. Moreau and A. Tournon.

[2] Ibid., chapter 44, *Benediction*.

[3] *Le Moyen* appeared anonymously, with neither date nor place of publication. Its attribution to Béroalde is no longer disputed, and its probable date is around 1610. On Béroalde, poet, novelist, translator and polymath, who was first a Protestant, then a Catholic and became a canon in Tours, see V.-L. Saulnier's biography and bibliography 'Etude sur Béroalde de Verville. Introduction à la lecture du *Moyen de parvenir*'.

[4] See especially I. Zinguer, *Structures narratives du 'Moyen de parvenir' de Béroalde de Verville*; A. Tournon, 'La composition facétieuse du *Moyen de parvenir*'; and 'Hors Texte' at the start of the transcription of *Le Moyen* (see note 1); B. Bowen, 'Béroalde de Verville and the Self-destructing Book', and *Words and the Man in French Renaissance Literature*; and M. Renaud's excellent *Pour une lecture du 'Moyen de parvenir' de Béroalde de Verville*.

French literature, in a double climax confirming the disruptive and innovative forces at work in the symposiac device.

There is a banquet-like setting for the interminable chatter which, interspersed with laughter and libation, extends over the 617 pages of the original edition. A 'fellow', who is also called 'Sir' (*Le Moyen*, ch. 1, *Question I*) has invited a jovial and licentious crowd: 'He was the cup-bearer and we drank good fresh, cool wine' (ibid.). A mysterious 'lady' (ibid., ch. 4, *Axiom*), who is as evanescent as the other diners, presides over the feast. Around the table secretaries note down the conversation, of which the book is supposed to be a transcription. Abundance and variety, earthy realism and plain speaking are the order of the day. The code of propriety and the supremacy of ideas are suspended: emancipation is the rule. There are also various hints throughout the narrative that it belongs to the convivial genre: Rabelais is mentioned several times as a model and his participation in the meal is a precondition (ch. 6, *Proposition*); 'Plutarch was at the end of the table writing his *Moralia*' (ch. 10, *Circumcision*): not far away from him sit Plato and Socrates, the two archetypal figures of the symposiac tradition, privileged among the mass of diners as the first to be named (ch. 3, *Paraphrase* and ch. 6, *Proposition*). It is true that the banquet, which has never been a homogeneous genre, is even less so in a text as cavalier as Béroalde's, and other paradigms also come into play: dialogue, of course, and more precisely the variation introduced by Lucian, namely dialogue between dead figures (although the ancients rub shoulders with the living and their identity, as we shall see, is problematic); and collections of short stories, tales within tales and all-night conversations also provide models. But the eccentric Menippean satire has also left its mark on *Le Moyen de parvenir*, which resists from the outset any kind of classification and is an irreducible text which challenges common sense.

This 'symposium and philosophical supper' (ch. 11, *Last Pause*) is really only a symposium by dint of parodic inversion. The search for truth, the accumulation of knowledge and all traces of seriousness are banished. The Platonic prototype is in fact only there to highlight the derisive and subversive aim of the text. If Socrates's friends celebrated the spiritual powers of Eros, love is only present in *Le Moyen* in terms of carnality and sex. The myth of the hermaphrodite is rewritten, but in a smutty register.[5] Socrates himself, carried away by the celebrations, wears a clown's mask.[6] He allows himself to be confused with a boilerman of the same name (ch. 99, *Histoire*), he tries to act, he is called a fool and he causes hilarity:

> Everyone from the Angels to the snakes, except the stones and pebbles which thereby fizzled out, started laughing so loudly that the mule of St Eustache the priest had the squitters out of pure joy and his life slipped away out of his fundament. (Ibid., ch. 45, *Text*)

Affinities with *Le Moyen* are to be found not in Plato but rather in other banquets which also mock the classical model. *Le Moyen* echoes to the same liberating laughter as the comic narratives of Petronius[7] and Rabelais, as the ridiculous feast of the *Cena Cypriani*[8] and other farcical and loquacious revels of the popular tradition. But in Béroalde the inexhaustible verbosity of the guests, the infinite profusion of anecdotes and the expansiveness of the dialogue also recall, through their scale, the encyclopaedic banquets of late antiquity.[9] The content is different but the proliferation remains, confirming the association between the theme of food and unfettered discourse, between the *copia rerum* and the *copia verborum*, which are here in unparalleled virtuosity. It is true that Béroalde shares a taste for summation and miscellany with many of his contemporaries: he himself was the author of serious compilations,[10] he may have read Bouchet's *Les Sérées*,[11] and *Le Moyen* is in a way one more in the long line of enormous *aides-mémoire* and

---

[5] 'When Jupiter had cut the hermaphrodite in two, he ordered Mercury to sew both of their stomachs up . . . He sewed up the man with a thread that was too long, so that at the end a bit was left over; he sewed up the woman with a thread that was too short, so that there was not enough and a slit was left' (chapter 43, *Annotation*).

[6] He also appears like this in Xenophon's *Symposium*: see chapter 6, Philosophy at meal time.

[7] *Pace* Saulnier, 'Etude sur Béroalde de Verville', and others, Béroalde could have been aware of extracts from the *Satyricon*, but not the *Cena Trimalchionis*, which was only discovered around 1650.

[8] See chapter 8, Dog Latin, cooks' talk and gibberish.

[9] See chapter 6, Greedy grammarians.

[10] *Le Cabinet de Mercure* (1596) and *Le Palais des curieux* (1612).

[11] See chapter 7, Guillaume Bouchet: stuffings.

erudite anthologies which proliferated at the end of the sixteenth century. We should not be surprised by the volubility of the diners, considering that Montaigne still enjoys great credit with his 'stream of chatter' and the invasive 'stuffing' of his *Essays*. The differences between them are considerable, it is true, but they share the chatter, the zigzag movements and the mania for collecting.

Le Moyen is not so much an 'anti-banquet' as an 'archi-banquet'. It is a caricature of the range of works I have examined, exacerbating their tendencies and exhausting their potential without breaking with their tradition. It is a whirlwind, an orgy, and I shall try to show in what ways it is the wild apotheosis of a form which is dedicated to experiment and excess.

Other authors had used the abundance and disjointedness of table talk in support of an encyclopaedic programme. But Béroalde presents variations on a single theme. His is certainly the most extensive collection of lewd stories ever put together in France. It is less an anthology (for it has good and bad parts) than a compilation of smutty anecdotes, a vast store of spicy stories and an inexhaustible series of comic variations on sex and the grotesque body. It has two kinds of comedy: one derives from humorous situations and is contained in funny stories (i.e., it is found in the content); the other derives from verbal incongruity and calls on the salacious resources of language. The humour varies from detailed stories – genre scenes which La Fontaine, Diderot perhaps and Balzac later imitated – to neat puns, from ambiguities to riddles. The situations – eating, drinking, sleeping, laughing – are more stereotyped, as is the range of characters among which one finds, unsurprisingly, the stock figures of farce: women of easy virtue, smart Alecs, naïve young dolls who are easily seduced, pimps, cuckolds, bawdy monks and lively nuns, important people confounded by beggars, etc.; characters whose sole function is to amuse, according to a typology which goes back into the mists of time.

For Béroalde is a compiler of diverse material rather than an inventor of it. We have already seen throughout this book that the virtuosity of convivial discourse depends less on the novelty of what is said than on the quality of the way of saying it. *Le Moyen* gets its jokes from various sources. Some come from books such as the collections of tales and funny stories (for example Boccaccio,

Poggio, Des periers, Du Fail and the *Cent Nouvelles nouvelles*)
which proliferated in the sixteenth century following the invention
of printing. Others come from folklore and the oral tradition
through other means which are more difficult to identify: jokes
passed on by word of mouth, overheard in inns, at fairs or at
festivals. Béroalde read, listened and noted a great deal and wanted
above all to inject new energy into old stories, timeless stories
whose origins were lost. Like Bouchet's *Les Sérées* (but with
special emphasis on oral material), *Le Moyen* serves as a record of
the collective memory.

The disjointed structure of table talk allows an infinite number
of discontinuous elements to be thrown together. Béroalde does
not try to classify his material or give it a direction. Like several
other banquets, his has the dislocated character of the miscellany,
and, like satire, it has recourse to the alimentary metaphor to
describe this 'piecemeal' nature (ibid., ch. 10, *Circumcision*). The
narrator says that he has mixed things together 'without distinction,
gloss or commentary, just as when you are at table . . . you eat food
taken from this or that dish'. He compares the narratee to a person
who mixes 'in his bowl bread, meat, broth; soup, wine, sweet and
dessert' saying that in any case it all ends up 'mixed together in the
stomach'. Reading the text produces a similar mixture: the narrator
says 'this should be mixed together in your brain' (ibid.), and this
is just what happens: the conversation is confused and fragmented
and has no order or progression; it is served up in portions, built
up haphazardly and gets lost so often that one of the guests
becomes impatient:

> You are only passing through, so why don't you finish your story
> without beating about the bush so much? I can see Plato getting
> angry because there was more order in his works. (Ibid., ch. 61,
> *Ridicule*)

For his part, the author is simply reproducing – or rather
provoking – the disjointedness of the conversation. The narrative
markers he leaves here and there are deceptive: far from indicating
a structure, they only show the absence of one. The division of the
text into 111 chapters is utterly futile: dialogue and anecdotes often

spill over from one to the next, as if the prolific talk of the drinkers cannot bear the slightest pause. The titles of the chapters, like that of the book, are also demonstrably absurd. One expects them to set out a programme and to facilitate synthesis, but they never correspond to their content and operate, as we will see, on a different level. Some of the titles do more than just illustrate, through their inappropriateness, the text's lack of control: they actually contribute to it. Towards the beginning, chapter 11 is called *Last Pause* and starts with the words: 'Now, let us start to conclude'. A little later, chapter 13 is called *Conclusion*, whereas the last chapter (111) is called *Argument*. *Le Moyen* is a book with no beginning or end, and it makes strenuous attempts to undermine the unreflecting assumptions of linear reading. It claims it can be read in any order: 'Whether you begin here or there does not matter . . . It's all one, wherever you read it from' (ch. 10, *Circumcision*). Since the content is selected according to the principle of analogy, the syntax of the narration is a trap and Béroalde takes pleasure in exaggerating this dysfunction.

The chaos through which the reader has to make his own way is also a necessarily unfinished corpus, a work in progress which the public is invited not only to arrange as it wishes but also to complete. If the reader finds any gaps, says the narrator, he should fill them in. Reading, like cooking, involves balancing the ingredients: 'this is what my grandmother does; if her soup is brought to her too hot, she will cool it; if it is too salty, she will add water; if it . . . ' (ch. 99, *Story*). *Le Moyen* presents itself as a book still to be written or a site to be built on. The bigger it gets, the more gaps appear: 'Others can collect what I have left out' (ch. 111, *Argument*).

It is a text which rejects autonomy and closure in order to set itself up as a collective undertaking, genuinely belonging to everyone. It contains anonymous and diffuse material for which no one authorial subject takes responsibility. No internal, structural or psychological necessity determines its limits. It offers itself as a free space into which any message can be written, and it is in this sense that its oft-repeated claim of totality should be understood. My book, says the narrator, contains every secret; like alchemy or the cabbala, it attains a state of absolute and perfect completeness:

> It contains everything that anyone knows, has known and will
> know, or should know and understand; it embraces the *bona fide*
> mysteries of all the sciences. (Ibid., ch. 12, *Vidimus*)

The discrepancy between such hyperbole and the book's actual
narrowness of perspective (man as a sexual being) doubtless
contains a large dose of irony. A hint of a confession is also
discernible: this work is not a personal or self-sufficient product,
but rather a crossroads where many voices and material from
various sources come together, where there is a bit of everything,
without rhyme or reason.

The book's claims to uniqueness and centrality are part of the
same idea. 'THIS BOOK IS THE CENTRE OF ALL BOOKS'
(ch. 12, *Vidimus*), it proclaims: it contains the substance of all
other books ever written. There is no point in buying or reading
any other books or hanging around in libraries. *Le Moyen* is the
melting pot *par excellence*, an impersonal focus where everything is
potentially present. Other books are 'extracts from this one, and if
everyone had put back into it what they had taken out, there
would only be one book left in the world' (ch. 91, *Doctrine*).
Because it deals with material which belongs to all ages and all
countries, *Le Moyen* also claims to be timeless:

> It always has been and will be for ever known as and called the Book
> by those who understand fine literature because of its excellence and
> its worth. (Ibid., ch. 12, *Vidimus*)

The elements it includes are so public and universal – eternal
truisms – that the book does not only recapitulate past works but
also anticipates those to come: 'Everything that is said everywhere
else comes from here' (ch. 44, *Benediction*). It is the turntable, the
central point, where everything converges and where everything
begins again. The freedom of the banquet allows the narrator of *Le
Moyen* to proclaim in all its enormity what innumerable faceless
compilations and imitations could have said:

> Receive therefore this present, this past, this future . . . and you will
> find great benefit, given that all books that have ever been written or
> will be written by men or women . . . are signs or marks or
> paraphrases or predictions of this one . . . which is the final and

intelligible culmination of all of them; and so all books are and will
be mere interpretations of the secrets contained herein. (Ibid., ch. 13,
Conclusion)

It follows logically that the spatio-temporal co-ordinates of the
banquet in *Le Moyen* remain indeterminate. A too clearly
circumscribed or defined setting would have compromised the
totalizing impulse. The temporal axis remains vague: the date of
the event is not clearly stated, and the fact that the guests come
from many centuries (ranging from Ancient Greece to the
contemporary period) confuses the matter further. The duration of
the feast is no less unreal: like the subject of the conversation, it is
virtually infinite. The comparison between the banquet and a
library is significant – words, like books, are immune to the
passing of time, which seems to stand still. The location too
remains abstract, stripped of local detail. Just as each of the tales
told has a precise setting, so the meeting place of the guests, the site
of the narration, is undifferentiated. It is like an empty frame, an
anonymous place where messages arrive from all quarters before
being sent on elsewhere. It is a genuinely literary, rather than
mimetic, space, a transitional place where units of narrative are
temporarily grouped, a store of commonplaces open to anyone.
The book's subversive impulse puts this to good use: the content
of the narrative, instead of being organized into a network of
realistic references, is randomly arranged and laid bare.

In an even more obvious way, the characters give the same
impression of unreality and disintegration. Not only do they come
from all ages, they form a never-ending series. There are about 350
to 400 of them, appearing and disappearing like so many ephemeral
and chimerical extras. Their names are given – they are great
figures from history or the world of letters – but this is belied by
their speeches, which almost without exception do not correspond
to the characters as we know them. The dialogue is an apparent
concession to realism but in fact only underlines the impersonal
nature of the exchange. Anyone could tell the stories that are told in
Le Moyen. Demosthenes, Erasmus and Caesar are interchangeable,
and the distribution of speeches is quite random. The guests are
present, but their discourse does not belong to them and their
identities are hollow. They are totally without psychological,

ideological or historical consistency and have no recognizable style, for they are mere echoes, anonymous mouthpieces relating stories heard elsewhere. Their names are inappropriate, arbitrary or must give way to indefinite terms which will do just as well, such as Thingy, Someone, Anyone and The Mortal. Moreover the distribution of speeches is incomplete: many speeches are unattributed. Faceless voices are heard, as if it were of little importance in the end who is speaking about what.

The figure of the author receives similar treatment, being broken down and stripped of privileges. The authorial depositary is absorbed in the uncertainty of the fiction and withdraws from his role as guarantor, renouncing ownership of his work. What he recognizes at the end – 'I think this book eludes all of us' (ch. 111, *Argument*) – he could have said all along, in each of his manifestations. The writer himself was elusive in his relationship with the public: *Le Moyen* appeared anonymously and Béroalde covered his tracks so well that the problem of authorship was debated until well into the twentieth century – Rabelais and d'Aubigné amongst others were thought to be responsible. It is logical for the person who transcribes what is common property not to sign his book.

The author is similarly evanescent in his role as orchestrator of the narrative. All signs of authority and traces of effective control over the development of the narrative are lacking. The text comments continually on how it is functioning, but less to convince the reader than to unsettle or mystify him. Take this disclaimer, for example, which alleges outside interference as a means of freeing the author from his responsibility:

> This book . . . was once written in fine crossed rhythms, but the person who transcribed it took no heed of this, mixing up bits from here and there and ensuring that it has no obvious rhyme or reason (Ibid., ch. 38, *Arrest*)

When he speaks about himself, the narrator readily adopts a feature of Parisian dialect which acquires new meaning and reveals his unstable status: 'I were here, we said, I were at ease about it, and I certainly were learning a lot from it' (ch. 6, *Proposition*). Is the subject singular or plural? The grammatical confusion says much about the uncertainty of the origin of the utterance.

It is not long, moreover, before the voice of the author disappears completely. It takes up the first few pages, presenting the banquet and the book, but then withdraws to make way for the guests' speeches. Seven-eighths of the text, from chapter 14 onwards, are in direct speech, almost without external interference. As in the theatre, the speeches alternate without apparent control or authority. From now on, the author dons the mask of his characters; he is just another joker engaging in tittle-tattle around the table in jolly company. He has given up his privileged position and pretends to let the story drift along. One of his incarnations has a marvellously appropriate name – L'Autre (The Other), which is almost an anagram of 'auteur' (author). He whose discourse is peopled with voices from elsewhere is, in fact, always somewhere else. As the banquet echoes with timeless and universal motifs, as it opens the floodgates of language, the person who is speaking is definitely the other, or one or the other, everyone and no one.

'You only talk about sex'[12]

'The centre of all books': for a work which certainly gets its material from many sources, but revolves exclusively around two themes, this claim is somewhat presumptuous. Béroalde pays little attention to the usual rule of *varietas* in table talk,[13] and his banquet is not one of those which reflects the eclecticism of conversation about everything and nothing.

As I have said, circumstantially the narrative comes down to very little. The text essentially functions on two other levels: second degree narratives told by the diners, and the gloss on them, which is divided among various figures. A particular theme corresponds to each of these two levels, and it would be futile to look for others.

I have just shown that *Le Moyen* contains much reflexive commentary. The narrative axis is continually interrupted by critical interference and the text repeatedly draws attention to its own functioning. This mixture of genres challenges convention,

---

[12] Béroalde, *Le Moyen*, chapter 41, *Sermon VI*.
[13] See chapter 4, Convivial speech.

but it goes without saying that the narrator disclaims responsibility for this. He is a mere transcriber who 'wrote it all down in one go, mixing together gloss and text without distinguishing them' (Béroalde, *Le Moyen*, ch. 10, *Circumcision*). At the price of ruining any effect of mimetic illusion, the banquet (as it often does elsewhere) reveals the mechanics of communication, from production to reception. It is words which interest Béroalde: their origin, their meaning and their ambiguity; and the means of their transmission, the contract between the author and the reader and the conditions for pleasure. Like his predecessors, Béroalde is a philologist who loves language and literature too much to pretend they happen naturally: he puts them on display and, as with everything else, overdoes it. The stories attract him less for their referential value than as material for research into words or for reflection on discourse. Once again, alimentary activity and sensitivity to wordplay coexist happily.

The book's exaltation – or its complicity with the bookish – is obvious from the choice of the titles for the chapters. They are aberrant yet consistent: with a few exceptions, they refer to the written object – the way the text is organized, literary form and genre and scriptural materiality. I shall just quote here the titles beginning with 'p': *Point, Paraphrase, Proposition, Last Pause, Paragraph, Plumitive, Problem, Parable, Parliament, Passage, Part, Production, Parenthesis, Palinody*. This pedantic terminology parodies the subdivisions of the scholastic treatise, the ossification of fixed frameworks, the language of grammarians and jurists. At the same time it exploits the incongruous disjunction between the seriousness of the technical titles and the triviality of the comic content. The effect is all the more ridiculous since this bookish ostentation also conflicts with the pretence of orality and improvisation inherent in the book. Two extremes are opposed: the representation of textuality and the pursuit of the natural, the celebration and the destruction of the literary. I shall return to this paradox.[14]

When the dialogue is not turning back on itself, it is concentrating on licentious anecdotes. This second monolithic theme explores the body below the belt in all its postures and functions. There is

---

[14] See my Conclusion.

an enormous contrast between the anatomy of the book and the physiology of sex, the sophisticated display of textuality and traditionally non-written material. For Béroalde's public, the subversive effect of *Le Moyen* did not perhaps lie where we would now think: it was less in its impropriety than in the uncompromising adoption by literature and science of essentially oral material, scarcely bowdlerized. In the Renaissance there was no lack of spicy stories or ribald collections, but their transfer into the field of writing tends to moderate their crudity to some extent. No doubt following the example of Rabelais, Béroalde exploits the contrast between opposing cultural spheres to the full.

The jokes are so many variations on sex and scatology. Often they are just witticisms: 'I wish my pussy were a holy stoop, said a lady, so that everyone would put their fingers in it' (ibid., ch. 68, *Respect*). Sometimes they are riddles: How do you recognize a virgin? Put your left hand over her crack, with your right hand open her arse-hole, and then blow: 'If the air goes through and you can feel it on your left hand, then she is not a virgin' (ch. 22, *Plumitive*). This is the general and rather crude tone of the book. The body's revels contain no trace of feeling or concern. Desire is reduced to its most simple expression and relieves erotic tension as soon as it arises. But although all sublimation is excluded, the code of the dirty story also banishes those forms of pleasure thought to be aberrant: homosexuality, masturbation and sodomy. Debauchery respects the rules (avoiding both the heavenly and the hellish aspects of love), rules which help to limit still further the thematic range of the dialogue.

This is all the more true since the liberation of instinct and the displacement of corporal topography to the nether regions are static and unilateral. Bakhtin has shown that burlesque inversion in Rabelais and in popular comedy is not degrading but rather that its ambivalence emancipates man's true potential.[15] The carnavalesque concentration on the organs which are normally taboo is therefore part of a regenerative and dynamic impulse. It restores nature to its rightful place and works towards the full development of *all* vital energies. *Le Moyen* has the right material to support this ideology: serious characters who talk nonsense and let their instincts get the

---

[15] See Bakhtin, *Rabelais and his World*.

better of them, and a culture and language which tear off the mask of respectability and achieve an integrated grotesque vision, with the potential to revitalize the sublime through the base in the positive and totalizing spirit of the popular festival.

But the process is short-circuited. The reduction of human beings to their basic needs functions in one direction only. It is less a question of recycling pleasure into a global vision than of immobilizing the body in immodest postures and setting this up as an absolute. The typical actor in these stories is fixated on the organs of eating, evacuation and reproduction. The reply to a diner who complains about hearing so much filth is: 'Aren't you delicate! You were born between shit and piss, and you want to give us lessons'. Another guest adds 'I am the fruit of a woman's belly, and the fruit of the belly is shit, therefore I am shit' (ch. 41, *Sermon VI*). A taste for the base and the attraction of degradation both contribute to a deliberately bestial representation of humanity. The world of these dirty old men is in fact full of animals and the affinities between the species are obvious: they have the same driving appetites and the same mechanical lust.

Libidinal compulsion is evident even in a linguistic feature which is frequently heard in the mouths of the guests or of the characters in their stories – the Freudian slip. The sexually repressed haunts the discourse and reveals itself through words whose meaning it diverts from that which was intended. It is literally consciousness that conceals the unsaid: 'concupiscence – oh, I meant to say consciousness' (ch. 100, *Attestation*). Language is liable to go off the rails at any moment: 'I shall talk about endelechia – I nearly said end-licking' (ch. 10, *Circumcision*); or it shamelessly reveals the obverse of righteousness: 'to sing in the latrines with the queer boys . . . I meant to say to sing at the lectern with choirboys' (ch. 45, *Text*). Cultural signs are automatically absorbed into the sphere of instinct: 'amber'/'member', 'discretion'/'excretion', etc.

Apart from the carnavalesque vision, the ideological break-up of the book also affects other systems of thought, which are invoked and then invalidated. Fragments of satire, for example, crop up more or less everywhere: religious polemics, criticism of monks, mockery of professional bodies, etc. But these attacks are sporadic and as flimsy as the speakers themselves. No one seriously defends any lasting conviction. The fragmentation of the dialogue and the whims of a language which is caught up in its own games compromise the scope of the criticism. Laughter could have been used to serve a cause or an idea, but instead it preserves its spontaneity and gratuitousness. As a satirical or didactic theme, alchemy has a special position in the book, but here too the threads seem too loose to convey any consistent message, even a cryptic one. There are fragments of mystery and furtive invitations to discover a hidden meaning, but then the trail goes cold and some joke or other comes along to nip the hunt in the bud.

The title of the book is similarly deceptive. It seems to link the book with the genre of the manual (which was already well known at the time) giving practical advice on acquiring particular skills. But what 'means' (*moyen*) is to be used, and to 'achieve' (*parvenir*) what? The promise of the title is not kept. There are no clearly defined ends or means. The text does not lead to anything other than a contradiction of its apparent programme. The glosses throughout the book offer contradictory explanations which only increase the doubt. Rarely can the reader at the end of a book have less an impression of achieving anything. The most sceptical commentary is perhaps the best: '*Le Moyen de parvenir* is composed of the four elements of deceit with a fifth which is their quintessence' (ch. 34, *Genealogy*).[16] The diners' language does not convey knowledge or doctrine; it enjoys itself and makes itself up as it goes along. It touches on serious problems, short-circuits them and asserts its supreme futility: 'We were no more able to get to the heart of the matter than a knob of butter can get into the crack in a nut tree; we are just wasting time' (ch. 35, *Notice*). Unless of course in a supreme act of mockery the absence of all recognizable markers is supposed to have the sense of signifying nonsense, in an infinite circle . . .

The only firm point is the body's nether regions. The guests do try to get off this subject a few times, but are inexorably brought back to their centre of gravity. To participate in a banquet, all that is needed is something to sit on: 'I'm here, said the narrator when he arrived, and I'll take my place alongside any other man as long as I've got an arse to sit on' (ch. 6, *Proposition*). Such is the

---

[16] See A. Tournon's elegant commentary in 'Paracelse, l'Autre: change et piperie dans *Le Moyen de parvenir* de Béroalde de Verville'.

common ground between the guests: from matters spiritual, their activity has slipped towards other areas. They, and their thoughts, are arse over tip. Their historical position, their personal destiny, their upbringing and their class all become undifferentiated as they unite in basic instinct.

The extent of their degradation can be measured against the model of the banquet as a symbol of totality.[17] The man who combines eating and speaking, according to the Humanist ideal, achieves synthesis of body and soul. He links thought and pleasure, seriousness and laughter, and through the integration of his various faculties attains a certain fulfilment. Such an ideal of equilibrium is swept aside here. One pole has cancelled out the other. The spiritual side is systematically denied or aggressively disparaged. Philosophy, science and history – everything suggested by the names of the famous participants and by the literary theme of the banquet – sinks to the level of the latrine. Béroalde's feast is perhaps not as innocent as it seems.[18] From the jetsam of ideologies, another emerges which is wholly negative – one of derision and rejection. If it is legitimate to look for a coherent vision in *Le Moyen*, then it lies in contempt for and destruction of Humanist values. Nothing remains of the dignity of thought, the supremacy of the book and the search for truth. Undifferentiated bodies and matter impose a regime where the intellect is ousted and banished. The only kingdom is that of satiation, and everything else is dust. For example, one of the principles of Humanism, philology, is swallowed up in the atmosphere of scatology: the metaphor of digestion is taken at face value, and commentators are bersmirched as

> Latinizing people of a sort that chew the cud of what the erudite Ancients have thrown away or shat out, scratching away in the filth and rubbish of Latin and the sinks of eloquence to salvage some rag or other. (Ibid., ch. 2, *Point*)

The classical tradition and the hope of renewal it inspired succumb to ridicule: the religious and moral debates of the Renaissance are desecrated, taken over by the omnipotence of chance and thrown

[17] See chapter 1.
[18] See Renaud, *Pour une lecture*.

into the realm of the grotesque. The accepted nobility of the individual dissolves under the reign of the body. There are further victims of this massacre. The atrophied and negating universe of Béroalde points to a cultural crisis: ribaldry, laughter and cynicism are like levers working against the beliefs of an entire era. The banquet lent Humanism a symbol for its ambitions: in *Le Moyen* the symbol has ruptured and deviated, displaying the decomposition of this philosophy.

'Edible syllables and letters'[19]

The weight of the body does not just drag down all the representatives of the human condition, from sages to wretches. Its attraction is so powerful that it even affects the realm of discourse and of the book. Like most authors of banquets (only more extravagantly), Béroalde extends the theme of the stomach to the literary object. As we shall see, the alimentary metaphor opens up a shared space in which the text, as if contaminated by the festivities it is representing, pretends to penetrate into the sphere of the physical. But this assimilation is not just fictive: it gives the language of *Le Moyen* a material and resonant density like a physical substance. Language and the book are under the thumb of the body, and what they lose in dignity they gain in vigour and colour.

Interference between the various levels of narration encourages this. In theory three distinct levels are superimposed: stories within the story, recounted by the guests; the narration of the banquet; and the narrator's glosses and addresses to the narratee. To each of these levels there corresponds a dialogue, the participants in which usually belong to separate spheres. But the system is not watertight: Béroalde mixes up the distribution of roles and freely intermingles the various levels of narration. The narrator in particular is unstable and readily changes his status. As the fictive authorial figure, he directs and comments on the text as it unfolds. But he also mingles with the mass of guests and chats

---

[19] Béroalde, *Le Moyen*, chapter 75, *Chapter*. The reference is to syllables or letters which are elided.

with them. He frequently addresses other people or, by using the first person plural, allies himself with them, and it is often impossible to tell whether they are his companions at the feast or images of the reader – whether the communication is intra- or extra-diegetic. This ambiguity has the important consequence that the production and reception of the narration (as represented) become confused with the action and behaviour at the banquet. The narrator takes over the genesis of the book, but without stopping enjoying the food, which immediately makes the narratee one of the guests. As in the prologue to *Gargantua*, the reader is absorbed into the world of the fiction and is implicated in the festivities. To read *Le Moyen* is to take part in the conversation of the revellers. The text is composed at table and presents itself as a carbon copy of the meal: the book and the banquet, reading and convivial exchange coincide. Deixis – 'this', 'here', 'now' – confirm the ambiguity: do they refer to the meal or to the narrative? When Béroalde writes, for example, 'if you were to take these words out of here, this banquet would be imperfect' (*Le Moyen*, ch. 76, *Consistory*),[20] does 'here' mean the conversation between the drinkers or the book? Does 'this banquet' mean the event or the text? The questions are otiose, since the tricks of narrative perspective blur the distinctions between the two levels.

The alimentary metaphor is extensively used and is also designed to bring narrative language and the book closer to the activity of the guests. When the text is offered to be 'tasted, savoured and digested' (ibid., ch. 55, *Canon*), we encounter a very familiar image of reading. When Béroalde invites us to drink the contents of his volume 'like a fine glassful of good wine', because 'volumes can be both books and hold wine' (ch. 11, *Last Pause*), he is recalling bottles in the shape of breviaries which were familiar to Rabelais and ecclesiastical satire. Further analogies between the bric-à-brac of the narrative and the traditional pot-pourri of satire, and between literary composition and the culinary measurement of ingredients also reproduce well-known variations on the theme of bibliophagy.[21]

---

[20] Quoted by Bowen, *Words and the Man*, p. 118.
[21] See the examples quoted in 'Monarch of ecumenical symposia', above; cf. the alimentary metaphors analysed in chapter 5, Metaphors of bibliophagy.

But the chaos of *Le Moyen* shifts clichés and pushes them to their logical extreme, contributing to the generally bizarre character of the narrative. Edible words are treated as concrete phenomena, objectified and tangible signs which take their place in the physical solidity of everyday life. The poet's dream comes true: words become substance and can be manipulated like objects, the gap between the thing and its name disappearing. To illustrate this idea (at the cost of revealing its absurdity by treating it over-literally), Béroalde tells a story:

> We began to work our jaws, but there were some who . . . were opposed to any words being wasted, or dropped or lost or getting away; so we set up spiritual barriers and intellectual fences . . . On another occasion when such precautions were not taken some words fell on the ground, and sprouted. (Ibid., ch. 7, *Couplet*)

Béroalde is here acknowledging other authors who had consumed or planted words: he is recalling Rabelais in particular, whose myth of frozen words he continues in his description of scientists in search of 'a glue to freeze words and keep them together' (ch. 2, *Point*).

These images are not meaningless: they symbolize a love affair with language. As we shall see, Béroalde fashions words as resonant matter, exploiting the power of the signifier, whose sounds he listens to and which he manipulates with virtuosity. His anecdote about a man from Geneva who was aware of the dual meaning of words can be read as a reflexive parable: when the man is summoned before the consistory court for beating his wife and is told to use a measure of tolerance, he hits her with a yardstick; on his second appearance he is told to remonstrate with his wife using Holy Scripture, and he beats her with a large edition of the New Testament; finally he is called upon only to use the tongue in punishing her, and he deals with her using a smoked beef tongue (ch. 103, *Palinody*). This final part of the episode says it all: the tongue itself is a material object, one solid body which impacts on another. The pun on 'tongue' ('langue') reveals the power of language, and its concrete reality. Words contain hidden meanings for those who really listen to them and exploit their resources: more than this, they can transform themselves into objects, as the pious injunctions of the consistory court are transformed into blunt instruments.

It is no surprise then that the guests come to table to feast on words as well as food. Their speech has a vibrant resonance, their mouths are full of rare terms that they chew over and savour greedily. The story of a feast of words which was served to travellers in Spain figuratively reflects the whole of the banquet at which it is told:

> They regaled us magnificently, and with words alone. I never saw such a bonny banquet of paraphrases: the words were prepared in all sorts of ways, some were covered like venison pâtés, some were leftovers to be eaten with fresh bread: there was a fricassée of the small words, of edible [elided] syllables and letters in poetry and prose, they certainly made a fine meal out of them. It passed apostrophically into our mouths: the preserves and dessert were reverences; and as titbits we ate passwords and puns. (Ibid., ch. 75, *Chapter*)[22]

This ludicrous scene is all the more extraordinary in that it is made up of linguistic manipulations itself. In a typical move Béroalde takes a traditional metaphor and, as if to test the resistance of words, treats it literally and takes it to its logical conclusion, thereby demolishing it.

He subjects the *topos* of literary imitation as digestion to similar treatment. The image of the reader absorbing his model and transforming it into a new work (which itself will be consumed by other readers) is given a comic (but consistent) twist: speaking of the meal and/or the book, one guest comments:

> I am making a meal of this, then, after I've digested it, I'll make a bolus to be ruminated on, like when I go and shit after a good meal and the pigs eat that up. (Ibid., ch. 55, *Canon*)

Aided and abetted by the licence of the banquet, we were bound to end up with this: the analogy is usually limited to consumption and digestion, but here it is taken to the extreme: the work

---

[22] The same episode occurs in chapter 108, *Reprise*.

becomes excrement and the reader a coprophage. In *Le Moyen* the physiological metaphor for the literary operation extends into a whole series of scatological modulations marking the ultimate reification and the most radical degradation of the book and its discourse. This can be seen if we examine the logic used: eating is a phase in a process which ends in defecation. The interdependence of orality and anality is taken for granted: the mouth is 'the funnel of the arse', because 'the tastiest things are ultimately just made into shit by the teeth' (ch. 41, *Sermon VI*). This is bluntly stated, but irrefutable. The rest of the argument is more unusual and obscene. Eating and excreting are complementary; eating and speaking are also linked; therefore speaking and excreting are analogous. Discourse (especially scientific discourse, which is produced after the laborious assimilation of knowledge) is evacuation. Words are to the mouth what excrement is to the anus: waste, the stinking remains of nutrition or culture: 'So I shat Latin out of my mouth' (ch. 84, *Continuation*); 'Those who printed this are commissars of excrement. This is the crap of my mind' (ch. 91, *Doctrine*). It follows that the book's rightful place is in the latrine: 'Your fine books are used by people . . . to wipe their arses' (ibid.); and that the reader is a dung-gatherer: 'Those who are amused by our follies are like Doctors who examine and analyse the excreta of other people' (ch. 6, *Proposition*). Literature and language, which are usually venerated as vehicles of thought or spiritual arenas, are thus reduced to the lowest level, and received ideas are brutally demystified.

Here Béroalde has something in common with Montaigne, who denigrates his *Essays* and condemns the vanity of an interminable undertaking by using scatological metaphors himself.[23] But Béroalde is doing more than just using an outrageous analogy to shock decent people: he is revealing a dominant aspect of his enterprise. The comparison between the book and a penis (ch. 12, *Vidimus*), for example, may seem gratuitously provocative: but in fact it is complementary to the symposiac metaphor. The former indicates the dominant theme of the narrative (sex), while the latter gives the generic model. Elsewhere, when Béroalde makes one of his characters say 'It would be good to *parler du cul* [talk of sex/arse],

---

[23] *Essais*, III, 9; p. 946, already quoted in chapter 5, Metaphors of bibliophagy.

that would make a fine discourse' (ch. 41, *Sermon VI*), he is commenting on two aspects of his project, combined in the two meanings of 'cul'. First, 'parler du cul' can mean speaking *through* the arse, challenging the well-worn *topos* of reading as digestion, and attacking the monolithic prestige of official culture through the physiological affinities between expression and excretion. But it also means talking about 'cul', and as such defines *Le Moyen*'s special place in literary tradition. For the sexual and the scatalogical ('cul' as sex and 'cul' as arse) are not just used to provoke humour or scandal. They give Béroalde's language a rich injection of words and images which are usually taboo. Language imagined as physicality and matter has formidable powers – as I shall show.

'I've never seen people talk so much'[24]

As a collection of jokes (which are not always funny and are often indigestible), *Le Moyen* would not deserve rehabilitation. It is the language used that makes the difference. Just as what is said is simple and static, so the way of saying it is dynamic, stunning and seductive. Verbal invention makes up for the trivial anecdotes; the frenetic dialogue which is never at rest is energetic and challenging, and without it the book would be unreadable. The true humour of the book lies less in the vulgar behaviour of the foul-mouthed guests than in the language, which is astonishingly mobile and innovative. *Le Moyen* is not concerned with narrative illusion and is fragmented into a mass of small sub-plots, with neither beginning nor end. It displays its own mode of production, constantly drawing attention to its devices and style. It is a literary work primarily because it exploits the creativity of forms and language.

The fiction of the meal and the illusion of orality legitimize the linguistic fantasy. The conversation has no rules: the exuberant speeches are not restricted either by the code of manners or by the constraints of communication. The festive discourse is the opposite of social conversation and is free from forms and prescriptions, shaking up automatic responses and revitalizing ready-made

---

[24] Béroalde, *Le Moyen*, chapter 105, *Memory*.

formulae such as maxims, commonplaces and proverbs. At each level of the dialogue, whether within the stories being told or between the guests, there is an astonishing corpus of linguistic liberties and discoveries which guarantee the liveliness of the exchange. Within the stories, the characters deal in ambiguities and dubious metaphors, speak in jargon or dialect, exclaim and question each other. The more ludicrous the subject, the more amusing the expression:

> Where have you come from? said he. From the oven, said she. What were you doing there? said he. A tart, said she. Is it good? said he. Try it, said she. Is it hot? said he. Blow on it, said she. Where? said he. On my arse, said she. Whore! said he. Cuckold! said she. Ha! Ha! said he. Ah! Ah! said she. (Béroalde *Le Moyen*, ch. 52, *Part*)

As for the guests, they are rarely as concise. They heckle, tell stories, listen to each other, talk about nothing and let themselves be carried away by the phonic links between words. As with Panurge the talker and Friar John the life and soul of the party, their garrulousness knows no limit. They are faithful to the tradition of the literary banquet, celebrating a feast of words and wallowing in grammar and vocabulary. They are not content just to *say* they are having fun, they *are* having fun, and having fun juggling with sound, as the following (untranslatable) sequence shows:

> Et qui sommes nous? Je sommes ce que je sommes, je joüons. Et que joüonge? Je joüon ce que j'on. Et qu'onge? J'on ce que j'on. On je en jeu? Si je n'i on j'y fon. (Ibid., ch. 45, *Texte*)

Béroalde is one of the last exponents in literary history of the malleability of a language still capable of creativity and experimentation. He gets maximum advantage from the plasticity of the French language before the intervention of the purists and the grammarians of the early decades of the seventeenth century. Norms which were to fix the language, control the lexicon and order syntax could still be evaded. Elements which writers were soon to have to banish from their works, such as triviality, impropriety, provincialism, technical and vulgar terms, *le Moyen* uses to great benefit. All the peculiarities it draws on have left valuable material for linguistic historians and lexicographers.[25] It is not surprising that the location of such an event is a banquet.

The creation and revitalization of forms are even noticeable in the way the dialogue progresses. By imitating the twists and turns of real conversation, moving from one subject to another by association, the author is able to experiment with all kinds of correlations and disjunctions. Occasionally a speaker will arrive at the end of his story; but the smallest trifle will set him off at a tangent, adding a chance remark which leads on to others. Questions and answers, and arguments for or against something, occasionally set off a genuine exchange between two or more guests. But more often there are interruptions, digressions, oblique developments and 'roundabout words' (ch. 110, *Order*) which make communication problematic. Replies do not follow on from each other, and voices intersect without engaging with each other. The entire Renaissance investment in the art of dialogue is reduced to incoherence and cacophony.

'I never saw such desultory conversation' (ch. 23, *Problem*), protests one of the guests. And in fact the disorder of the narrative progression and the fragmentation of dialogue do take on wild proportions – the outpouring of words becomes completely lawless, disjointedness is the rule throughout and the gaps in the narrative widen. Disintegrated and centrifugal units of narrative are telescoped into configurations which are never predictable. The comparison with collections of short stories like Boccaccio's *Decameron* (and books which imitated it), where discussions between the different narrators are reproduced, is significant. On the one hand we have ordered conversations and the polite exchange of abstract ideas: on the other there are anarchic outbursts and capricious chatter. On the one hand analyses in which the speakers defend lucid and coherent theses: in Béroalde snippets and trifles. Béroalde's *bricolage* is similar to that of the *nouveau roman*: it breaks down discourse to reveal its mechanisms, problematizes the transmission of meaning and challenges and stimulates the reader.

---

[25] See L. Sainéan, '*Le Moyen de parvenir, ses deux auteurs et l'origine de l'humour*'.

The guests have acute linguistic awareness: they are happy to let words take over and discuss the power of language. They linger over the terms they use and offer serious or comic definitions or derivations. They note the geographical or social origin of expressions and their connotations; they are interested in the ambiguity of the signifier, as in homonymy and polysemy, and reveal the pitfalls it presents. Above all, they are not satisfied with speculation: they actively exploit verbal material. Their language dusts off everyday speech, and it is worth examining a number of the ways in which this is done.

French classical literature was soon to ban dialects and idiom in the name of the unity of the language and the centralization of power. One language was to serve for everyone, and was designed to paper over social, local and professional differences. As for Béroalde, he welcomes variation and dissonance and records the differences of vocabulary, style and even pronunciation found in normal conversation.[26] In this way the incoherence of the speeches is compounded by heterogeneity of idiom to disturb the dialogue still further. The speakers are too undifferentiated, though, to have individual styles: eccentric voices belonging to everyone and no one circulate and clash.

Here and there foreign languages surface in the great melting pot of table talk: quotations in Greek and Latin, snatches of Italian and Spanish. But the French language of the time, with its regional expressions, itself offers a linguistic variety which gives the conversation colour. We have already seen how Béroalde exploits the unusual Parisian verbal inflexions. He also introduces other dialects, from Norman through Genevois to Savoyard, which are duly commented on, since the guests like collecting lexical curiosities. Someone says the word 'coquebin' (greenhorn):

> Varro. — What, fair lady? What is 'coquebin'?
> Sister Jeanne. — In Tours they call it 'coquebin', in Angers 'jagois', and in Paris the women call it 'brinquenel'. What sort of a person is it? Someone who hasn't seen his wife's cunt. (Ibid., ch. 28, *Fen*)

Idioms from specialist jargon also require explanations. There are samples from the vocabulary of coopers, carters and millers, and

[26] *Le Moyen* is a good illustration of Bakhtin's idea of polyphony (see *Problems of Dostoevsky's Poetics* and *Esthétique et théorie du roman*).

parodies of the lingo used by philosophers and doctors, theologians and lawyers. The guests have a good ear and pick up differences of usage and the meaning of stylistic nuances. Not everyone uses 'lie with'; 'reformists say "live with" and Jews say "sleep with" ' (ch. 56, *Theorem*).

Whether by mixing different languages or delving into everyday speech, the diners like lining up series of terms which are broadly synonymous, in another way of satisfying their philological greed. It is of course the vocabulary of sex and defecation that produces the longest lists. 'Our French language is the most extensive of all, *sic probo* [I shall prove it as follows], it has the most terms for describing copulation' (ch. 46, *Synode*), claims one guest, and he goes on to prove his point in a list not all of the elements of which are, of course, translatable:

> Horses 'saillent' [cover], donkeys 'baudouinent', dogs 'couvrent' [cover], pigs 'souillent', goats are 'boucsies', bulls 'vétillent', rams 'empreignent' [impregnate] sows, stags 'rutent' [rut], fish 'frayent' [spawn], cocks 'cauchent', cats 'margaudent' . . . But what do men do to women? They 'do it'. Do what? They just do it. (Ibid., ch. 47, *Tome*)

However the terminology of human coupling is not as restricted as that. The technical precision often gives way to the art of periphrasis, to euphemism and metaphorical virtuosity (again only partially translatable): *besogner* ('to work hard at'), *travailler* ('to labour'), *fouailler* ('to thrash'), *accrocher* ('to buttonhole'), *bricoler* ('to tinker with'), *bricolfrétiller, frétillnaturer, encrucher, épousseter* ('to give a dusting to'), *envahir* ('to invade'), *historier* ('to touch up'), *verminer, vétiller* ('to niggle at') . . . The abundance of verbal variations relating to the nether regions is also limitless. Such lexical luxuriance makes the discourse unusually vivid, but also makes reading slightly difficult: the glossary of the Royer edition (a storehouse of lexicographical curiosities) is more than fifty pages long.

The euphoria of naming is not only expressed in the piling up of synonyms. Once the theme of the meal comes up, a variety of words crowds forward with the sole aim of imitating in their profusion the opulence of the menu and the flow of table talk. As in Rabelais,[27] the complicity between speech and stomach is expressed through the energy of the verbal performance. What did the guests do at table?

> They spoke, they ate, they drank, they went shh, they were quiet, they were noisy, they protested, they were witty, they laughed, they yawned, they understood, they argued, they spat, they blew their noses, they were astounded, they were dumbfounded, they admired, they sneered, they recounted, they heard, they got confused, they were enlightened, they debated, they agreed, they drank to each other, they got drunk together, they made remarks, they fidgeted, they put their elbows on the table, they shouted quietly, they were quiet loudly, they joked, they murmured, they got advice, they started again, they were happy, they passed the time, they doubted, they feared, they got wiser, they became, they succeeded. (Ibid., ch. 11, *Last Pause*)

Once again language is having a field day and the narrative of the banquet is getting carried away. But the diners' logophilia can be satisfied by other ways than mere quantity; it leads them to dwell on details, to listen to the resonance of a term and to discover unexpected meanings hidden beneath sounds and abscured by automatic everyday usage. A vast horizon for puns is thereby created. The examples offered by Béroalde often seem flat and laboured, but they do bear witness to the extraordinary linguistic activity generated around the table. The duplicity of words can come from the way in which a single sign can contain two or more meanings – ambiguity or diaphora, which usually exploits the confusion between the literal and the figurative meaning. A client is advised to grease the palm of her lawyer, and she rubs lard on to his hands (ch. 18, *Atlas*). Consultants prescribe an 'aperitif concoction' for Cardinal du Bellay, and Rabelais, his doctor (who is not mentioned here by chance), has some keys boiled up, since they are able to open (*aperire* – ch. 12, *Vidimus*). Such is the speakers' taste for double meanings, which they examine and set out, even at the expense of losing the thread of what they are saying.

Imaginative etymologies also uncover hidden meanings within a

---

[27] See chapter 4, A mouth full of words.

signifier, giving words unknown values and helping to undermine the obvious ones. Aretino explains (in Italian) that the whore (*putana*) is aptly named because 'gli putte la tana' ('she smells like a tannery' – ch. 58, *Stanza*). A Latin verb, taken from a psalm (Psalms 55: 2) is broken down in an unexpected way; as a prioress teaches a nun a canon, she

> taught her about the word *conculcavit*: now, my dear, sing it well, hold that 'con' [cunt] firmly: con. Then 'cul', lift that 'cu', 'cu' [arse], then the 'cas' [pussy], hold that 'cas', then the 'vit' [prick], hold on to that 'vit' for a long time. (Ibid., ch. 109, *Archive*)

Sometimes all that is needed is for one of these syllables with lewd connotations (like *con*, *cu*, *ca*, or *vit*) to surface in a word (and this happens quite often) for a trivial meaning to be detected and for the word to shift into the burlesque register.

But the king of wordplay is the pun – a variation on homonymy or paronymy. The diners' mouths are full of them, and they tirelessly look for phonetic similarities to produce incongruous connections. Some of their discoveries are perhaps satirical: 'parabole' ('parable') produces 'faribole' ('nonsense' – ch. 104, *Satire*), and 'Souisse' ('Swiss') seems to be similar to 'sottise' ('stupidity' – ch. 46, *Synod*). But most of the puns are gratuitously playful, producing comic concatenations whose incongruity is often ridiculous and which are again dictated by the omnipresence of sex (recalling the Freudian slips referred to above). 'Grace' and 'garce' ('whore') are interchangeable, since 'one just has to transpose two letters' (ch. 17, *Journal*); 'fortification' implies 'fornication' (ch. 64, *Emblem*) and 'bienvenu' ('welcome') implies 'bien ventru' ('big-bellied' – ch. 32, *Minute*). A lady, instead of saying 'à votre avis' ('in your opinion'), says 'en vos trois vits ('in your three pricks') to which her interlocutor makes the logical reply 'à vostracons' ('to your cunts', cf. 'à votre compte', 'for your part' – ch. 55, *Canon*). The many riddles derive from the same technique:

> What is the difference between women and priests, both of whom wear long robes . . . ? Priests put their 'amicts' [amices] over their heads, and women put their 'amis' [boyfriends] between their legs. (Ibid., ch. 110, *Order*)

It is a well-known fact that puns are rarely funny, and Béroalde's are no exception. But I am less concerned with evaluating them than with stressing their frequency and role. I do not wish to look for cratylic elements in them, nor lend them a depth which they do not in fact possess: the guests play with words merely through love of language, listening and savouring rather than reflecting. A pun, however pointless and clumsy, can suffice to make the conversation go off at a tangent, thus operating as a motive force behind the dialogue. When a diner talks about Greece, up comes the homonym 'grease', changing the subject immediately (ch. 48, *Allegation*). Once conversation reaches this sort of level, infiltrated by the accidents of language, it gives up any semblance of coherent communication. It escapes from the realm of ideas and organizes itself around the creative power of verbal forms.

The discourse therefore bounds along under the impulse of the exuberance of language. There is a complete contrast between the stories that are told and the character of the surrounding narrative. In the anecdotes, rudimentary figures act like so many sexual automata, inhabiting a narrow world dominated by compulsion and repetition. Thematically, *Le Moyen* contains a reductive and pessimistic philosophy, with a cynical outlook which sees culture and morality as no more than a series of vulgar actions which bring everything down to the same level and are in the end very tedious. The vitality of the text lies elsewhere, in the verbal performance of the narrators. The ideological perspective may be a dead end, but the production of the discourse is dynamic and seductive. Language defies systematization, defining the only space in which the individual can express his freedom and creativity. Wordplay does operate within narrow semantic limits, proving nothing beyond its own virtuosity: but it occupies centre stage and offers the reader the euphoric spectacle of boundless energy. The diners in *Le Moyen* have empty heads, but full mouths (and other active organs). Such is to be our last banquet, marking the end of a long evolution.

Conclusion

Imitatio/mimesis

Writing and Nature

The banquets we have read have an ambiguous relationship with literature. They make no secret of their artificiality, but claim to be part of everyday life; they draw attention to the process of writing (through intertextual *bricolage*, the autonomy of the signifier, and so on), while simulating symbiosis with the natural world (the body, speech and food). These simultaneous but apparently contradictory tendencies are all the more noteworthy because they relate to a paradox which is found in various forms in many sixteenth-century works and which, I believe, is one of their most important features. In this chapter, I shall attempt to place the banquet in a wider context and put forward some general ideas on the status which Renaissance literature, in a constant impulse of reflection, assigns to itself.

One thing Rabelais, Montaigne and a good number of poets among their contemporaries have in common is that they make use of existing written material and make no secret of it. Their discourse does not only transmit a message, it also reveals the bare facts of its genesis. The referential dimension is combined with a reflexive element. The texts represent their relationship with pre-existing models, the tensions of works which try to gain independence while knowing they are caught in a cycle of repetition, and the scissors and paste transition from reading to writing, from imitation to difference. As well as the process of their creation, they also freely dramatize the idiosyncrasies and power of language, they comment on their own structure and they set a programme for their own reception. Such literature reveals itself for what it is – work on words, a montage made from all sorts of components.

And yet this same literature, in its preoccupation with reflection, also provides an inverted image of itself. In contrast to the mirage of reflexivity and autonomy, it can also have a transitive relationship with the physical or psychical universe it claims to reproduce. It is wary of literarity and rejects the circularity of a discourse which, once disengaged from the resistance of objects, risks becoming a closed system. Reacting to the danger that the text will turn in on itself, it seeks to put down roots in tangible reality in order to underpin the work with an external guarantee. If art tends towards autonomy of function, it simultaneously asserts an organic link with the world: a dialogue and an exchange of material goods with the public, the fusion of speech and action, the involvement of the book in the heart of experience. The prologue to *Gargantua* starts by invoking the learned model of Plato's *Symposium*, but ends with a celebration from which literary mediation seems absent. A sonnet by Ronsard presents itself as a spontaneous outburst of emotion, but at the same time it displays its debt to Petrarch and to mythology. This conflict of references is universal, this crisis of identity general.

These two opposing facets of the work of art correspond to the two traditional aspects of imitation. On the one hand there is the inevitable recourse to the heritage of culturally acceptable texts, the complex relationship between submission and transgression in respect of the old masters, the operation of rewriting which legitimizes all classical literature: *imitatio*. On the other hand there is the subordination of art to nature, *mimesis*; few authors do not claim to practise this. Without venturing here into the enormous theoretical and historical problems associated with this concept, I would propose the following definition: *mimesis* uses strategies designed to imitate, in and through the text, realistic effects; it does not reproduce the world, but creates a new one out of words and stories which is realistic enough for the imagination to go along with it, to attribute life-like qualities to it and to recognize in it a universe which is coextensive with the world of actual experience. Now, these two kinds of imitation seem incompatible. They would normally give rise to two different kinds of aesthetic: art as a reflection of the world, and art as an autonomous mechanism. I would like however to stress the fact that they are interdependent, and to show that the Renaissance, far from dissociating them, exploits the potential of both (whether in banquets or elsewhere).

The debate between *imitatio* and *mimesis* is all the more pertinent in so far as it coincided with a historical problem, and occupied centre stage in the search for a new poetics. In the way it was perceived by the Humanists and in the way it actually worked, medieval literature (with the exception of the novel) existed in isolation. Both poetry and scientific activity developed as separate systems in which writing generated writing and texts interacted with texts, like robots gaining momentum from their own movements. Discourse was endogenous, its interest deriving from the virtuosity of its combinations and the subtlety of its intertextual and autotextual network, without having to reckon with external events or creative subjectivity. The bookish regime of *imitatio* reached its peak towards the end of the Middle Ages. The Humanists denounced the way in which literature turned back on itself as one of the aberrations of scholasticism.

The Renaissance indeed attempted to break the circle. It was not that sixteenth-century man could dissociate himself from tradition: fidelity to classical models remained an article of faith. But it was precisely in this fidelity that their originality was based. The reason for subordinating oneself to Greek and Latin models was in fact that classical writers knew better than anyone how to reproduce the world and to speak to men in a language which touched them. Their words are objects, their poems reflect the sensuality of forms and their prose faithfully reflects thought and experience. Reading the Ancients does not mean shutting oneself away in a library, it is a preparation for the better understanding of the present. So *imitatio* is no longer an end in itself; it becomes the means and justification of *mimesis*. Recognition of the past is no longer a matter of closed writing: it is the basis of an ideology which is that of openness to the world. It even gives art a new ambition: by imitating classical models, it will remember how to rival nature and will regain lost authenticity. The book will be freed from itself and actualized, and will acquire an external necessity. 'I shall make art natural just as they make nature artificial', says Montaigne (*Essais*,

III, 5; p. 874). The text which is *inter*posed and conceals the real
world in the name of its internal rules is baleful: the only legitimate
text is one which *trans*mits and mediates life, one which adapts to
circumstances and is at one with the solidity of reality and the
intensity of creative thought. The not inconsiderable aim of the
mimetic impulse was therefore to reinstate what 'Gothic art' had
debased.

For the critic, there is a great temptation to isolate one of the poles
and to ignore the tension between them through which Renaissance
texts seek a difficult balance. Traditional criticism, from Sainte-
Beuve to literary historians and the positivist methodology of the
first decades of this century, has celebrated the realistic or
naturalistic qualities of works which were being read for their
documentary value: biographical, psychological or ideological
interpretations acknowledged the authors' wish to be present in
the world and recognized the mimetic power of their discourse.
But this type of criticism neglected the role of montage and
quirkiness, treating as faithful documents texts which also obeyed
literary rules and based their vision on fixed paradigms. The
historical approach was at the expense of the literary.

Modern critics have changed all that. They have invoked the
internal mechanisms of writing and the ability of words or
structures themselves to produce fictive universes, and we have
seen the withdrawal of the referent and the demise of meaning. The
signified has become a product of the signifier and authenticity a
rhetorical trick. The text now expresses nothing except itself. It is
treated as an autotelic system, having no contact with actual
experience. The author is a manipulator of forms, the impersonal
echo of composite voices. It is in these terms that the difference of
literature has been reinstated. Once considered as the circumstantial
use of pre-existing sources in the service of an autonomous
thought, *imitatio* (latterly developed into the notion of intertextuality) has been taken seriously as a way of thinking and writing
governing the work of art.

This modern approach was no doubt necessary, but it may have
gone too far towards the exclusion of sense. The danger is that it
will forget that the Humanists wanted to break the circle of self-
reference and promote an effective discourse about the world. The
modern approach recognizes that language has exceptional creative

powers, but omits to ascribe a purpose to it. Writing is seen to hold up a strangely narrow mirror, which reflects only itself. But the fact is that what modern literature and modern criticism have been trying for a century to undo (representation, the subject–author agency, the book as a manifestation of thought and action) is precisely what the sixteenth century constructed. What we mistrustfully regard as mimetic illusion and the tricks of intentionality and referentiality, the Renaissance enthusiastically championed against the abuses of scholasticism and the deviations of a discourse bound up in form. This is why the pages which follow, like those throughout this book which have illustrated the mimetic power of table talk, are on the side of naturalism in art: they also reflect a desire to restore to the texts the energy and evocative power which structuralism and post-structuralism threaten to gloss over.

To banish either of the two poles is to simplify a literature which is not stable or integrated. But to try to achieve an elegant and definitive synthesis through thesis and antithesis would be to over-systematize that which remains unresolved. Instead I shall attempt in this chapter to pick out a few points where the two axes meet and to show how *imitatio* and *mimesis*, in the areas where they overlap, coexist without cancelling each other out. Renaissance literature (and *inter alia* banquets) do not of course represent the world; but neither can they not represent it. The relevance of banquets perhaps derives from this tension.

Paradoxical metaphors

How can one renaturalize discourse? How can one give it that quality which would make it another object, that energy which would make it part of real life? One solution lies in referring to the work of art through metaphors or reflexive themes taken from nature, which therefore help transport the book into the biological or human field. These analogies used for mimetic ends are however themselves products of *imitatio*, literary fictions largely sanctioned by tradition. They point towards both kinds of imitation and demonstrate their curious complicity. I shall examine some of them here.

One series of metaphors is familiar to us: measuring out the ingredients of a text as of a dish, tasting or eating knowledge, incorporating or digesting old books. A whole network of alimentary metaphors[1] helps to transpose the literary process, from conception to reception, into the sphere of gastronomic pleasure. The banquet scene, which gives words the flavour of foods and learned discussion the vividness of table talk, does just this.

Discourse can give the illusion of accompanying a meal because it also has the qualities of speech. The association is common: the text is a thing to be heard; more than just reproducing a conversation, it claims to enter into a dialogue itself, as if the literary exchange were a physical act, or a slice of life – the meeting of two speakers. To follow the logic of the metaphor, it seems as if the message escapes artifice by appropriating the qualities of the oral, so that the reader is supposed to be able to hear the author speaking as if he were present in voice, gesture and accent. 'I speak to the paper in the same way that I speak to anyone I meet' (*Essais*, III, 1; p. 790), says Montaigne – 'The speech that I love is a simple and natural speech, the same on paper as on a man's lips' (*Essays*, I, 26; p. 79). Moreover Montaigne praises conversation as the foremost means of communication, seeing in it a model for his *Essays*: his is a book in which one voice resounds, a document which bears witness to and reproduces a presence and suggests others. Rabelais no doubt shares the same ideal: there are many indications in his books of the attraction that oral exchange and its paradigmatic value held for him. The merry banter around the giants' table, the resounding verbal challenges of the narrator and the power of the mouth and of the tongue, which can contain worlds or create them, all show that speech has a special role. The same could be said of Renaissance poets who celebrate the immediacy of direct speech in the way they set up their utterances (addressing the second person and simulating dialogue) and in their representation of love. In the great works of the French Renaissance as in the banquets, it is as if writing wanted to escape from itself by using as a *mise en abyme* the model of spontaneous speech through which reading strives to assume the qualities of sensory experience.

But these images are paradoxical – one more paradox with which

[1] See chapter 5, Metaphors of bibliophagy.

Renaissance writers enjoyed playing, as a way of subverting one-dimensional truths and revealing the ambiguous nature of things.[2] They postulate the possibility of exchange or continuity between the book and referential reality. The subject or the thing is actually present, undiminished, in the act of saying. These metaphors are more than innocent approximations: they are to be taken at face value. Something of nature is supposed to be actually present at the heart of the writing. And yet these images are *topoi* hallowed by tradition, and cannot not be seen as products of culture, well-worn stylistic effects whose mimetic power is debatable. The desire to fill the gap between words and things is itself a product of verbal strategy. Thus we come up against two interpretations which are incompatible and yet, individually, compelling.

This contradiction is at work for example in these lines of Ronsard;

> . . . I am like a bee
> Which gathers sometimes from the scarlet flower,
> Sometimes from the yellow: drifting from meadow to meadow,
> Flying to the place which appeals to it most,
> Piling up much food for winter:
> In the same way, running and leafing through my books,
> I accumulate, sift and choose the most beautiful,
> Which I sometimes make into one picture with a hundred colours,
> Sometimes into another: and, master of my painting,
> Without forcing myself, I imitate Nature.
>
> (*Hylas*, lines 417–26)[3]

There is a strange osmosis here: the poet is dealing with a question of literary theory, the progress from reading to writing according to the principle of *varietas*, but he uses two analogies (the bee and painting) which seem to use nature to give the operation legitimacy. To gather material from books is like gathering pollen from flowers or reproducing a landscape. *Imitatio* is not only a technical device, it is a hungry walk through a library which is like

---

[2] On paradox in the Renaissance, see R. L. Colie, *Paradoxia Epidemica. The Renaissance Tradition of Paradox.*

[3] In *Oeuvres complètes*, vol. XV, p. 252. See also *Responce aux injures* . . . , lines 873–92, ibid., vol. XI, pp. 160–1.

a garden. The act of rewriting, which is signified to us by a commonplace, none the less claims for itself the privilege of spontaneity. Reading does not exclude nature; it restores and stimulates it. It is as if the two fields were indistinguishable.

The metaphoric transfer of the text into the realm of plant life has many variants in Pléiade poetry which I shall not describe exhaustively here. In a famous passage in *The Defence and Illustration*, Du Bellay describes the development of languages as being like the process of grafting and the bearing of fruit (I, 3), Latin being enriched by the remains of Greek and French germinating from seeds sown by both classical languages. Ronsard uses the same analogy of grafting (*enter*) to describe the interweaving of the Petrarchan intertext into his own work (*Ode à J. Du Bellay*, line 68).[4] Writing is arborescent: the vital sap is passed on from one author to another: tropes which both acknowledge and challenge the autonomy of literature. The poem puts itself forward as the work of a craftsman and a spontaneous outpouring; the product of nature but also of learning. This vision of the text as a plant or vegetation is not limited to the figures of *imitatio*. The 'flowers of rhetoric', the 'garlands' and other poetic bouquets are part of the same paradox, catachreses which are often stale, of course, but which are sometimes given a new impetus and recall the forgotten referent. Several of the most elaborate of Ronsard's sonnets use the image of the plant as a reflexive metaphor. The poem is compared to a pine tree, to ivy or to a floral tribute,[5] gaining biological qualities but through a stylistic device which as such undercuts the metaphor. 'A symbol involves absence and presence', as Pascal said (*Pascal's Pensées*, p. 248, fragment 265).

Other analogies – which are at work particularly in Montaigne – are just as ambiguous. As a mirror of the self, the work for example is presented in terms of a body, and much of the reflexive dimension of the *Essays* is expressed in physiological terms: 'I put my whole self on show, a SKELETOS in which, at a glance, the veins, muscles and tendons appear, all in their correct place' (*Essais*, II, 6; p. 379). Words are supposed to function as organs and the text is supposed to imitate the composition of living tissue.

[4] Ibid., vol. I, p. 112.
[5] See *Sonnets pour Hélène* II, sonnet 8; ibid., vol. XVII, p. 253; *Les Amours diverses*, sonnet 47; ibid., p. 327; *Sur la mort de Marie*, sonnet 3; ibid., p. 125.

The *Essays* 'present me to your memory in my natural state', because they are organized into a 'solid body' (*Essais*, II, 37; p. 783) and come alive like flesh and blood. But it is not as simple as that. To physicalize his work Montaigne uses the model of classical poetry whose power of *representation* he praises:

> It depicts something more loving than love itself. Venus is not as beautiful naked, alive and panting, as she is here in Virgil. (*Essais*, III, 5; p. 849)

For the language of classical poets

> is brim full of natural and sustained energy; they are all epigrams, not just the tail, but the head, the stomach and the feet. (*Essais*, III, 5; p. 873)

The accomplished text does not only name the body, it takes possession of it, substitutes itself for it and is indistinguishable from it. Successful writing is that which through an astonishing transfer of substance evokes a physical presence and is tangible. However, the fact remains that such a text does not renounce its textuality, and that this writing makes no secret of being a product of art and *imitatio*. When Montaigne stresses the energy of his style and boasts that his language is physical, substantial and fecund, he does not claim to achieve it through the magic of *mimesis*, but rather invokes the example of his favourite prose writers: Plutarch, Epicurus, Seneca and Tacitus. It is through imitating their muscular and dense style that he succeeds in revitalizing bland words and in reproducing in his sentences the movements of the body. He promotes the naturalization of art (*Essais*, III, 5; p. 874) while recognizing that it is art which produces the effect of nature. Banquets have provided ample proof of this. The illusion of immediacy is dependent on repetition; the text and what is beyond it are inextricably linked.

The analogy with walking and travelling, which Montaigne develops particularly in the essay 'On Vanity', contains the same tension. Any reality – interior or exterior, human or inanimate – is carried along by the flow of time. Mimetic style therefore seeks to reflect, in its rhythm, the universal state of flux. Metaphors of walking abound to describe the pace of the discourse: 'I would have everyone see my natural and ordinary pace' (*Essays*, II, 10; p. 160); 'I give myself up to change, indiscreetly and tumultuously. My style and my mind wander about in the same way' (*Essais*, III, 9; p. 994); 'My pen must travel in the same way as my feet' (*Essais*, III, 9; p. 991). Since the unstable self is realized through union with the passage of time, the mirror of the text will be in endless gestation. Montaigne says that he does not write to make time stand still, but to reproduce a succession of ephemeral and discontinuous moments. He has good reason to stress the meandering way in which he creates the *Essays*: 'Sometimes I reflect, and sometimes I compose and dictate my reflections, walking up and down, as at present' (*Essays*, III, 3; p. 262). Here too the metaphor is to be taken seriously. It is not enough to say that the work describes itself in terms of movement or compares itself to a journey; it actually intends to be this. The ductile and uneven progression of the texts contributes to this and the essay 'On Vanity' demonstrates it. It postulates at the very beginning that to write is to set out on a journey: 'Who cannot see that I have taken a road along which I shall continue, without stopping and without working, as long as there is ink and paper in the world?' (*Essais*, III, 9; p. 945): at the end of his journey it has reached Rome, like Montaigne himself after he had set out for Italy. Most importantly, between departure and arrival, the essay combines the motifs of writing and of travel so closely that the two processes appear interdependent.

And yet the aporia is obvious. The mimetic metaphor, whether it be vegetable or physiological, kinetic or alimentary, aims to write life into the structure of the book. It tries to remove the book from the supplementarity of the *lexis* and put it into the domain of *praxis*, so that literary activity becomes an everyday activity like any other. But to say this is immediately to undermine it. The reflexive figure may suggest that the literary is natural, but it also attracts attention to itself and to its content as specifically textual products. The book exists, and is not life. The illusions of presence will always be substitutes, effects of fiction, which the mediation of a metaphor or an intertextual resonance will always cause to be differed and separated from their object. The idea of integration founders on an inverse movement: a ludic combination, a dance of signs which generate self-referential systems. *Mimesis* cannot escape from *imitatio*: the illusion of reality is just a trick of art.

This is a vicious circle that no one-sided theory can break. Structuralism had the merit of restoring autonomy to the text and signification to forms. Post-structuralism rightly problematized unicity of meaning and the stability of the referent. No writing illustrates these principles better than that of the sixteenth century. But the danger is that this neutralizes the mimetic power of the discourse and in attempting to restore the literarity of literature neglects its representative value. Modernity was wrong to ignore the power of the imagination. The sophistication of contemporary readings has emptied works of their presence and powers of illusion. But what appears false and hollow to analysis can seem real to the imagination. Naturalizing metaphors, banquet scenes and mimetic strategies may be illusory, but they work; they captivate the reader, they display and seem to contain the very qualities they represent. To believe in images and the fiction is no doubt erroneous, but responds to the incorrigible desire to produce or to reproduce the real world. The pleasure of reading lies not only in deconstructing the mechanics of the text, it also lies in one's right to be deceived: the power of literature is perhaps that it can requisition what is outside it. We have shown that the close relation of feasts and words, underpinned by the sound of language and the reader's libidinous contribution, ends up by seeming quite obvious. This is the realm of *mimesis*. It is always encroached upon by its opposite, always caught in an intrinsic and insoluble paradox, and yet it is still strangely effective, because of the cognitive force of the imagination.

Naturalizing the narrative?

Until now the mimetic aim has been seen as a theoretical postulation implicit in the work and animated by the imagination. But what of the actual functioning of the texts? What role do the two imitations play in style? Does the revelation of the secrets of fabrication preclude the referential dimension, or do the words after all reflect something of the world? I shall approach these questions by taking the familiar example of Rabelais, some of

whose major themes will provide evidence which is also applicable
to other narrative compositions and to some varieties of dialogue,
thus taking us back to the banquet, our starting point.

One of Primaticcio's pictures, *Apelles painting Alexander and
Campaspe*,[6] is structured in two parts. In the foreground on the
right is the painter in front of his canvas. Facing him, in the
background in the centre, is the subject of his painting, a couple
embracing. There is nothing exceptional about this, but it is a good
illustration of the way in which a narrative like Rabelais's operates.
Just as the artist mediates between the spectator and the central
object of the work, the narrative act shares part of the scene with
the story itself. Production is represented, the effect of *mimesis*
admits its subordination to artistic technique, without the sensuality
of the couple or the vividness of the Pantagruelists being in the
least diminished.

In Rabelais's work, there is a clear mixture of heterogeneous
material which seems to be thrown together piecemeal, without
any concern for uniformity. *Imitatio*, given free rein, produces a
disparate discourse, what Montaigne calls a 'hotch-potch' or 'badly
assembled marquetry'. Thus bits of all kinds of language rub
shoulders: classical and modern languages, popular speech and
academic idiom, ecclesiastical, legal and medical jargon, and
provincial expressions and barbarisms. Erudite references are
juxtaposed with fragments of farce, snippets of spoken language
and extracts from the wisdom of nations. Different styles too are
mixed up into all kinds of cocktails, from the most refined to the
most trivial, from the serious to the comic. There are also clashes
of genre: narrative finds itself next to satire, the didactic turns into
the grotesque, popular entertainment interacts with Humanist
learning. Far from integrating and therefore concealing the
diversity of voices he assembles, the author seems to display the
whole gamut of possible means of expression. He parades his
resources and exhibits the process of production as well as the
finished product.

In this great medley of centrifugal elements, the function of the
author seems to be suspended. The normal process of selection,

---

[6] Reproduced as an engraving by Master L. D., in Henri Zerner, *L'Ecole de
Fontainebleau: gravures*, Plate L. D., 51.

ordering and prioritizing the material seems to be lacking. Extracts and gobbets from all sources reverberate throughout the text, but these seem too varied and disjointed for them to be under the control of the subject of the utterance. This chaotic process of creation has implications for the reading of the text. The former is like making a mosaic, and the latter follows an uneven path, often disturbed by the way in which fragments interfere with each other within the story itself and upset its continuity. There is no absence of plot, but at each stage of the narrative an alternative emerges: which way will the story go? What system is it derived from? Since there is no narrative axis strong enough to integrate all the fragments, the reader cannot resist going off at a tangent. Led astray, a sign can part company with the apparent context and attach itself to other underlying structures, such as intertextual echoes, cultural resonances or the classical heritage, which redetermines its value. The non-problematic linear progression of reading is replaced by a vertical decoding of erudite references. Memory and learning take over, and the pleasure of participation gives way to the pleasure of discovery. The signifieds then no longer innocently transmit their message: they are seen as vehicles, and acquire the opacity of signifiers. The narrative displays its own workings; normally confined to the wings, *imitatio* occupies centre stage and thus encroaches on *mimesis*.

The banquets have accustomed us to the kind of discourse which is free from the logic of the story. Narration sacrifices effects of continuity in favour of the exploration of what is underneath or alongside the text. Moreover, this conflict between two kinds of reading does not only arise from the dialogue with other systems; it can function within any given work. For example the structural similarity between *Pantagruel* and *Gargantua* (two biographical sequences) invites a vertical decoding which can isolate relevant parallels between comparable passages. The composition of *The Third* and *Fourth Books*, which each in their own way contain equivalent episodes (consultations, visits to islands), leads to the same hesitation: should we read an episode as an integral part of the internal progression of the story, or should we take it out of its context and replace it in the virtual network of all the other episodes which are similar to it? Whether because of their repetitive structure or because of their intertextual tangents, the narratives do lend themselves to a paradigmatic decoding. By multiplying variations on given themes, they show writing in its laboratory, revealing what stimulates invention, demystifying fables and challenging naïve readings. This would seem to be enough to destroy realism and natural effects.

But this is not the case. The preceding analysis is a true but partial view. Here too truth has two sides to it. Although in Rabelais the narrative is frequently interrupted, a story, with characters, a setting and action does emerge after all. More or less consistent psychological portraits, fateful moments and components of the plot come to life and support the framework of the narrative with varying degrees of success. Groups of characters, sequences of events and the logic of the plot all bind the text together and enable it to simulate reality and encourage participation. Verisimilitude, in so far as it puts together what could happen, is not totally absent. Of course the book does not reproduce the world as it is, but through the quality of the story it invents it creates the conditions for the suspension of disbelief.

Other factors also contribute to the reinforcement of the referential foundation of the narratives. Sometimes, for example, the text in a given sequence stabilizes around an ideology, even if it soon adopts another. And the carnavalesque perspective, whose coherence Bakhtin has demonstrated,[7] or the principles of evangelical morality, or the values defended by satire also contribute to holding the fragments together. My purpose is not to identify Rabelais's philosophy, but rather to point out that a personal vision does occasionally emerge out of the great admixture of ideas and voices. There is a double anchoring effect: a subject who is responsible for the text seems to give the discourse purpose and to mark it as a personal reflection; and at the same time the book is full of references to contemporary events and so can take its place in the world around it. A work which is so full of thoughts and personal commitment cannot be reduced to an interplay of forms; it intervenes in the here and now and is a part of the sphere of beings and objects. .

Rabelais's narratives, like most of our banquets, are also coextensive with experience through the setting in which they

[7] See Bakhtin, *Rabelais and his World.*

place their characters. The strange and the marvellous in these stories do not exclude familiar landscapes. The Chinon countryside and the Parisian chronicle, popular customs and ecclesiastical habits all provide a framework in which the reader feels at home. The convivial atmosphere and the society of friends also tend to root the event in the real world. The circumstances of daily life, a decor which is concrete are precisely identified or described: these realist elements do not only derive from books. They go beyond literary references, breaking the circle of specularity and – no matter whether true or false – add to the mimetic success of the narrative.

What Bakhtin called 'polyphony'[8] can also serve as an example of this and lead us back into familiar territory. The discourse of the narrator, like the conversation of the characters, has a variety of inflexions: the licence of popular speech, the elegance of academic language, the liberties taken in oral communication, the constraints of writing, the jargon of the town square, echoes of parody and so on, all lead the reader to feel s/he is being plunged into the disorderly flux of everyday verbal exchange. To reduce this linguistic and stylistic hotch-potch to the level of simple intertextual manipulation would be to stultify it. For we are dealing with something more than a meaningless combination of words and forms. This expansive and composite language seems to be part of the creativity of nature. It is not enough to acknowledge that the action and characters reflect the chaotic burgeoning of life: speech itself is heterogeneous and prolific and seems to imitate the energy of living beings. Other genres and other eras, in the name of a homogeneous culture, strove to make their discourse harmonious, sublimating centrifugal forces and accepting the constraints of an artificial purity. *Varietas* and *copia*, in Rabelais as in table talk, are on the contrary on the side of the profuse spontaneity of ever-changing life. The Renaissance was more sensitive to the dynamics of a *natura naturans* than to the order of a *natura naturata*, and there is no doubt that linguistic diversity was part of this ethos. Polyphony arises from a profound realism and is related to a mimetic strategy as much as to the technique of *imitatio*.

---

[8] See Bakhtin, *Problems of Dostoevsky's Poetics* and *Esthétique et théorie du roman*.

Sacrificing either of the two poles would therefore amount to mutilating a coherent system. The example of Rabelais, following that of the reflexive metaphors, provides a wider context for and a confirmation of the dual postulation we have seen in the narration of banquets. Once we adopt a wider perspective it is clear that these two kinds of imitation are by no means mutually exclusive, nor, conversely, mutually indistinguishable: each in fact implies the other.

Imitatio needs *mimesis* – and the stronger the *imitatio*, the greater this dependence is likely to be. For if the collage of commonplaces, the interplay of quotations and parody were left to their own devices, it would be mere formal acrobatics. A threshold of readability and suspension of disbelief must be attained, without which the text, in spite of its virtuosity, would not come to life. The more *bricolage* and the more visible and composite its texture seems, the more material is needed to bind it together so that it does not descend to the level of a compilation or an academic exercise. The tricks of *mimesis* – plot, setting, dialogue, etc. – make all the difference. They bring life and motivation to material which would otherwise just be repetition. This is the sole function of the symposiac setting for philosophical debates or encyclopaedic collections.

Conversely, *mimesis* needs *imitatio*.[9] Words, as I have already said, do not reproduce a mirror image of reality. At most they can create, through scriptural effects, the verbal equivalent of a particular object. Aristotle's definition is still valid: language does not describe the true, it produces the probable; this is the price of engaging the imagination. It names and actualizes the thing, giving it a configuration and a form which is not its own. Even at this level language is not functioning in a vacuum, but necessarily refers to paradigms which have already been tried and tested. A realistic effect cannot be improvised. It copies, modifies and improves pre-existing discourse. Mimetic writing does not spring from experience; it is articulated on earlier models and is the product of rewriting. There is another reason for the dependence of *mimesis* on *imitatio*: the raw object taken from the world of phenomena has no meaning as such; the text gives it meaning. This process of semantization

[9] See L. Jenny, 'Poétique et représentation'.

does not only depend on internal associations, but is also based on a corpus of conventions and traditions, in a kind of intertextuality perpetuating a cultural or literary memory which determines the value of signs and their relationships and connotations. Without a dimension of meaning being established or conveyed in the writing, the mimetic figure would be a hollow image. Representation cannot fail to be a retrospective act of re-presentation. The naturalization of the narrative occurs through reading the classics and recycling ancient models. Just as *mimesis* must give the illusion of life to *imitatio*, so *imitatio* must give *mimesis* form and meaning. This reciprocal relationship can result in the balance and harmonization of the two poles: this will be the seventeenth century's 'naturel', with its compromise between nature and culture. Integration has not yet been achieved in the sixteenth century, the literature of which clearly reveals the interplay of forces which, although interdependent, have lost nothing of their individual vigour.

Writing in action

This complicity of opposites can also be detected in the perspective of the author. How do the two kinds of imitation occur in the genesis of a new work? How much of the task is repetition and how much creativity? In what guise does 'nature' intervene in the search for an individual voice? These questions are at the heart of Montaigne's *Essays*, which I shall use here as an example.[10]

One thing is obvious: Montaigne's discourse is full of learned references. The text reveals an enormous knowledge of books; an inexhaustible library provides the major part of the material. It is not important whether Montaigne's borrowings are acknowledged or not, whether they take the form of quotations, allusions or summaries, or whether their ideas are praised or criticized. We may merely observe that through his extensive and obvious use of erudite material, Montaigne demonstrates (and explores all the consequences of) the practice of *imitatio*.

[10] For more details, see R. Regosin, *The Matter of my Book. Montaigne's 'Essais' as the Book of the Self.*

He says he has 'a nature which apes and imitates' (*Essais*, III, 5; p. 875). Although he puts forward all sorts of criticisms of the bibliomania of intellectuals and pedagogues, he himself is an avid reader and someone for whom writing is a direct extension of reading. Like all literate people of his time, he is imbued with classical culture: his thoughts intermingle with those of other authors, and his self-knowledge and the organization of his life are mediated by the classics. In places, the *Essays* are like the compilations which were in fashion at the time. The earliest essays, and the original versions of books I and II (which are almost like anthologies or gnomic collections), have the same encyclopaedic aim as many of our banquets. They are not very different from Plutarch and Bouchet: there is the same erudition, the same curiosity and the same eclecticism. Montaigne too is a collector: a taste for quotation, the random mixture of themes and the scissors and paste approach give his discourse the character of *copia* and *varietas* which we know so well.

Although it is impossible not to repeat the masters, it is equally impossible to repeat them. Their authority is incontrovertible, but it is also oppressive and alienating. The subject risks being stripped of his identity under the weight of a tradition which he anonymously reproduces. When Montaigne ironically describes parrot-like pedants who reproduce discourse which is not theirs, he has himself in mind, threatened by the proliferation of impersonal knowledge in which individuality is broken down. Infiltrated by other people's books, the self becomes submerged: if it does not incorporate, appropriate, and transform pre-existing truths, it sinks into the undifferentiated mass of copyists, covering pages which signify nothing of one's individual existence. He speaks with voices which are not his own: 'Some part of my reading sticks to this paper, but to myself little or nothing sticks' (*Essays*, I, 26; p. 50). Fragmentary utterances abound and coalesce into more or less coherent wholes, without it being possible to unravel who is responsible for which part. So writing simply combines endless cycles of unmotivated material:

> I go around scrounging here and there snippets from books which I
> like, not to keep them, as I have no where to store them, but to put

them into this book where, to tell the truth, they are no more mine than they were where I found them. (*Essais*, I, 25; p. 136)

Without a stable subject or a referent to govern the development of the discourse, the book records a profusion of fragments which there is no real justification for controlling. *Imitatio* runs the risk of free-wheeling without ever exhausting the supply of common-places, examples and quotations which are ever ready in the library of memory.

Montaigne compares this activity, which is self-generating and disengaged from reality, to the absurd and constantly repeated action of the Danaides (*Essays*, I, 26; p. 50). It is possible to accumulate discourse, to refer to documents and to introduce commentaries *ad infinitum*. This tendency towards endogenous multiplication is all the more dizzying since it functions on two levels. The intertextual echoes are accompanied by mirror effects of autotextuality in which the utterance turns back on itself and takes itself as its object. Not only is there 'more trouble in interpreting interpretations than interpreting the things themselves, and . . . more books on books than on any other subject. We do nothing but write comments on each other': but through a perverse and narcissistic inversion 'my theme turns upon itself' (*Essays*, III, 13; p. 349). In each case writing becomes redundant: whether it be repetition or introversion, it is circular. Montaigne is a contemporary of Béroalde de Verville and is like him aware of the crisis of Humanism. The *Essays*, more discreetly than *Le Moyen de parvenir* but based on the same experience, take stock (rather teratologically) of the abuse of *imitatio*.

The difference is that Montaigne not only makes the diagnosis but also seeks the cure. His attitude towards books is complex: reading can alienate, but it can also help in the process of self-mastery and self-knowledge. As soon as he recognizes the danger he corrects himself:

To take in so many strange, strong and great minds, it is necessary . . . for one's own to strain, to be constrained and diminished to make place for others . . . But this is not the case, for our mind expands as it is filled, and, set against the examples of olden times, it is seen, on the contrary, that there are men quite competent in the handling of public affairs . . . who have also been very learned. (*Essais*, I, 25; p. 134)

Culture forms part of the education of the individual if it leads to self-knowledge instead of being passively absorbed. Books are beneficial when they do not terrorize but rather lead the reader to use his judgement and to criticize the message of their authors according to personal principles. Correct use of knowledge, for Montaigne, therefore lies less in the acquisition of information (the cramming of minds that are already full) than in the use of discernment (the perceptiveness of well-formed minds). The subject who filters the opinions of others in order to form his own thoughts escapes from the dangers of slavish imitation. He gains his independence by diverting books from their normal function – the conservation of knowledge while respecting intellectual property – in order to see himself through them:

> I turn over the pages of books; I do not study them. What I retain from them is something that I no longer recognize as another's. All the profit that my mind has made has been from the arguments and ideas that it has imbibed from them. The author, the place, the words, and other facts I immediately forget. (*Essays*, II, 17; p. 212)

An able reader naturalizes and assimilates the good things written by others to form his own personality. It is in this context that Montaigne logically uses the metaphors of ingestion and digestion.[11]

The activity of the writer is governed by the same premises. It is legitimate to include the evidence of other authors in one's own discourse provided that it forms part of the representation of the subject and contributes to determining its identity. Dialogue with other books is therefore no longer an end in itself, an academic and centrifugal exercise, but rather a means of introspection: 'I only quote others to make myself more explicit' (*Essays*, I, 26; p. 52). Montaigne creates a stable physionomy as he writes, learning to be himself in the company of the Ancients, through the fusion of, or the distance between, his discourse and that of others. Moreover, the evolution of his use of quotation and reference is well known:

---

[11] See chapter 5, Metaphors of bibliophagy.

documents which at the beginning he found interesting in themselves as items in a collection are soon absorbed into the analysis of the self and used as landmarks pointing the way to self-knowledge. Montaigne is a latent compiler, but he controls *imitatio* and subordinates it to a function within his own intellectual life. It is not without reason that he stresses his lack of memory: to remember is to preserve things without differentiation. The independence of the self, on the other hand, implies choice, neglect or distortion. It gives to the critical activity of judgement what it takes away from the over-anonymous faculty of memory.

Having assimilated books and transported them into his personal sphere, Montaigne can now claim to be talking about himself and give an accurate self-portrait. He emphasizes this: 'I present myself standing and lying down, front and back, facing left and right, and in all my natural attitudes' (*Essays*, III, 8; p. 311). In a stunning volte-face, a text which could have been a vast collection of archives now aims to reproduce nature: 'it is not my actions that I write about, it is my very self and essence' (*Essais*, II, 6; p. 379). *Imitatio* has allowed itself to be converted into *mimesis*. The enormous amount of borrowed knowledge in the *Essays* does not stop them showing life as it is: 'I want to appear in my simple, natural, and everyday dress, without strain or artifice; for it is myself that I portray. My imperfections may be read to the life, and my natural form will be here' ('To the reader', *Essays*, p. 23). The osmosis between man and portrait is so intimate that the exchange even operates in both directions: he puts into the book the most exact image of himself, without omission or coquetry, and in return the book which reflects him helps him to understand himself better:

> Describing myself for others, I have portrayed myself in brighter colours than I originally had. In the same way that I have made my book my book has made me; it is a book consubstantial with its author, having its own function as a part of my life: not with a function and aim derived and foreign, like other books. (*Essais*, II, 18; p. 665)

Faced with the threat of dispersal through other books, the author gains substance in his own eyes by entrusting his portrait to another book, an exceptional book, which is identical with its object. Writing becomes a vital function, the organic and necessary expression of the individual.

However important it may be, however, the mimetic project does not exclude the centrifugal movement of borrowed cultural remnants. The *Essays* achieve unity around a coherent representation of the self, but they also remain a composite, rhapsodic and open work. The diastolic and the systolic coexist: natural effects and the *bricolage* of the texts are found side by side, for better or for worse. As in Rabelais and the banquets, the rejection and the display of literarity confront each other without resolving their differences.

A change has nevertheless occurred. With Montaigne, the object of *mimesis* has been displaced from the external world to the subject of the utterance. Whereas Rabelais and the symposiac tradition had turned towards the physical world, the animation of the table and the profusion of convivial talk, in Montaigne realistic effects are used to underpin a project of introspection. Vitality in the work thus derives from the movement of thought and the accuracy of psychological insight. Discourse no longer tries to rival physical nature: it aims to represent individual nature. More precisely, it is interested less in the permanent qualities of the self – its essence – than in its activity. The *Essays* do not give a fixed portrait of their author, but capture him in the very process of thinking and writing. Montaigne's *mimesis* is turned inwards, but is intensely dynamic, trying to reproduce the mobility of his mood and the never-ending search for the self in books, words and experience. This is not a being but a doing, or better still a being in the making, existing because it acts, perceives itself and reveals itself as creative energy. The real object of the book is its own genesis. The *I* of the *Essays* is not an extrinisic and objectifiable agency: it is indissociable from the discourse it produces, and can only be understood on this level. *Mimesis* is describing less a spectacle than a movement, the movement which is producing the *mimesis*.

This tendency in Montaigne could be said to be characteristic of the sixteenth century as a whole, where the literary text expresses the creative impulse which gives rise to it at least as much as it expresses the outside world. Rabelais, Ronsard and others provide further evidence of this; it is perhaps what is represented that seems alive in their works, but it is also or above all the act of representation itself. Discourse is less important in terms of its content than in terms of a linguistic performance which bursts forth. It is a force in search of a form, an energy which art has not yet fixed. The kind of nature which the Renaissance text seeks to imitate is not an essence but a potential, *natura naturans*, which is realized in the emergence of a voice and in the battle between the subject and words. The field in which *mimesis* operates is therefore above all the act of utterance, an intermediary space between man and discourse, a creative gesture through which the living is expressed and remains perceptible at the heart of the book. Proliferation, the composite and the discontinuous are not the negative opposite of order. They externalize, in the chaotic movement of forms, the work of artistic genesis. The dynamic structure of the open and unstable work of Rabelais, Ronsard or Montaigne represents the very activity of the writer and its power of renewal. As the etymology suggests, the word *author* contains the *actor*, who is manifested through his *action*. Furthermore, poetry, faithful to its Greek meaning, is perceived as doing. The Renaissance text is not a finished monument, but an event taking place. Herein lies some of its mimetic effectiveness.

The dramatization of *imitatio* contributes to this *mimesis* of production. The author who shows himself at work has not yet assimilated or camouflaged his dialogue with the masters. We grasp the discourse through which he is trying to find himeslf at the moment when it is acquiring its own individuality under the impulse of earlier models. This is memory transforming itself into creative effort, *imitatio* progressing into *mimesis*. Writing in the sixteenth century can thus be seen as a transfer of energy. It bears witness to the imperceptible shift in which the power of already formulated speech passes into speech which is in the process of formation, a shift in which admiration for classical works becomes the enthusiasm which inspires the new work.[12]

The two kinds of imitation now become indistinguishable. Art stimulates the emergence of nature and erudition liberates self-expression. The author allows himself to be surprised in the very

---

[12] A. Py, *Imitation et Renaissance dans la poésie de Ronsard*, shows clearly the interaction between nature and art and repetition and renewal in Ronsard's work.

act of transforming his sources. The writer is filtered through writing and through the writer is filtered the reader, who comes up against examples he respects – but which he also seeks to transcend. For the authority of the masters can be experienced as a challenge, a cause of rivalry. Fascination then leads to emulation and the activity of the writer, in his difficult conquest of difference, is all the more noticeable in its aim of equalling or surpassing his betters. *Imitatio* is more than a simple process of fabrication and actualization, it is a struggle to free oneself from the 'anxiety of influence',[13] it is where a new voice attempts to come to the fore, while still preoccupied with freeing itself from oppressive tradition. Like a statue half-freed from a block of stone and captured as it bursts out to freedom, the author is shown engaged in the work through which he frees himself from commonplaces and tries to find his own voice from a collective heritage. The work arises out of a conflict between the past and the present, it seeks a balance between the ascendancy of books and the urgent need for individual involvement: so far from concealing this conflict, it draws attention to it.

But all of this stage management will soon be pushed back into the wings in the characteristic evolution from the sixteenth to the seventeenth century. The author whose emergence had been in the foreground gradually acquire autonomy and, at the same time, removes from the work all traces of its construction. He continues to recall classical models, but the fusion between the voice of others and that of the self becomes closer and closer. A single subject will be the guarantor of the discourse from now on, and it will not point up either its dependence on earlier models or the mechanics of production. It integrates its source and combines them into a homogeneous tone and vision. The rule of monody follows that of polyphony, the demand for order and cohesion takes over from motley compilations, and the law of the natural and the principle of propriety contrast with the complaisant representation of the self. Texts from French Classicism overcome (or repress) the turbulence of earlier eras. The text is smooth and harmonious, controlled by a supreme self which transcends the ups and downs

[13] See H. Bloom, *The Anxiety of Influence. A Theory of Poetry*. On the problems of reading in the sixteenth century, see also T. Cave, 'The Mimesis of Reading in the Renaissance'.

of literary creation and presents its work as an autonomous system.

From this perspective we can see more clearly the position of the banquets and what they reveal at the intersection of several axes which govern sixteenth-century literature. Banquets demonstrate the resources and the difficulties of *imitatio*: an inexhaustible parade of intertextual resonances, the temptation of collection and endogenous reproduction, parodistic rewriting, wordplay and a forum for verbal creations . . . They give full rein to polyphonic miscellany; throughout the works themes and tones vary, burlesque is juxtaposed with serious passages, generic paradigms overlap and the uninhibited performance of the guests gives the dialogue a digressive and composite nature, as if there were no unifying agency to control its progress. Liberated by the euphoria of the table, the fable unfolds with extraordinary virtuosity. For symposiac discourse fits the occasion. It is an element in physiological pleasure, rivalling oral satisfaction and appropriating the savour and substance of the food. Realistic effects, phonetic experimentation and the contamination of words by foods all contribute to the imaginative transfer of the text into the natural world, into the realm of matter and sensual perception. The desire for *mimesis* is bound up in the nature of *imitatio*.

Once the sovereign author and the monodic text take over, the literary banquet has run its course. Verbal exuberance, acrobatic textual combination and the paradoxical interplay of nature and art belong to a time of crisis to which classical simplicity would soon bring order. The feast of words and the interdependence of speech and food will have produced their finest passages. We may even come to regret their passing. For is it not in this ambiguous area where words become things and where things are seen to be words, that the turbid pleasure – and the indistinguishable identity – of literature lies?

Bibliography

~~~~~~~~~~~

Sources

Anthologie grecque, ed. F. Jacobs (2 vols, Paris, Hachette, 1863).

Apicius, *De re culinaria libri decem*, followed by B. Platinae Cremonensis, *De tuenda valetudine*, and Pauli Aeginetae, *De facultatibus alimentorum tractatus*, ed. Albanus Torinus (Basle, 1541).

—— *The Roman Cookery Book*, tr. B. Flower and E. Rosenbaum (London, Harrap, 1958).

Apuleius, *Metamorphoses*, tr. J. A. Hanson (2 vols, London and Cambridge, Mass., Loeb Classical Library, 1989).

Artus, T., *Description de l'Isle des Hermaphrodites* (1605) (Cologne, H. Demen, 1724).

Athenaeus, *The Deipnosophists*, tr. C. B. Gulick (7 vols, London and Cambridge, Mass., Loeb Classical Library, 1927–41).

Aulus Gellius, *Attic Nights*, tr. J. C. Rolfe (London and Cambridge, Mass., Loeb Classical Library, 1960).

Belon, P., *L'Histoire de la nature des oyseaux, avec leurs descriptions et naïfs portraicts retirez du naturel* (Paris, G. Cavellat, 1555).

Béroalde de Verville, F., *Le Moyen de parvenir. Oeuvre contenant la raison de tout ce qui a esté, est, et sera: avec demonstrations certaines et necessaires, selon la rencontre des effects de Vertu*, n.d., facsimile and transcription by H. Moreau and A. Tournon (2 vols, Marseilles, J. Laffitte, 1984).

—— *Le Moyen de parvenir*, ed. C. Royer (1896) (2 vols, Geneva, Slatkine Reprints, 1970).

Boaistuau, P., *Le Théâtre du monde* (1558), ed. M. Simonin (Geneva, Droz, 1981).

Boccaccio, *Decameron*, tr. J. Payne (Berkeley, University of California Press, 1982).

Bodin, J., *Discours sur les causes de l'extreme cherté qui est aujourd'huy en France, et sur les moyens d'y remedier* (1574), in *Archives curieuses de l'histoire de France depuis Louis XI jusqu'à Louis XVIII*, ed. L. Cimber and F. Danjou, first series (Paris, Beauvais, 1835), vol. VI, pp. 425–57.

Bouchet, G., *Les Sérées* (1584–98) (6 vols, Paris, Lemerre, 1873–82).

Bruno, G., *La Cena de le ceneri* (1584), ed. G. Aquilecchia (Turin, Einaudi, 1955).

——*The Ash Wednesday Supper*, tr. E. A. Gosselin and L. S. Lerner (Hamden, Connecticut, Archon Books, 1977).

Bruyerinus Campegius, J., *De re cibaria libri XXII* (Lyon, S. Honorat, 1560).

Bulengerus, J. C. (Boulenger), *De conviviis libri quatuor* (Lyon, L. Prost, 1627).

Casaubon, I., *De satyrica Graecorum poesi, et Romanorum satira libri duo* (Paris, Drouart, 1605).

Casteau, L. de, *Ouverture de cuisine* (Liège, 1604).

Castiglione, B., *The Book of the Courtier* (1528), tr. G. Bull (Harmondsworth, Penguin, 1976).

Cena Cypriani, in *Monumenta Germaniae historica*, series *Poetae Latini Aevi Carolini*, vol. IV, 2, ed. K. Strecker (Berlin, Weidmann, 1923) pp. 857–900.

Cervio, V., *Il Trinciante* (Venice, F. Tramezini, 1581).

Ciacconius Toletanus, P. (P. Chacon), *De triclinio, sive de modo convivandi apud priscos Romanos et de conviviorum apparatu* (Heidelberg, 1590).

Cicero, *Cato Maior: De senectute*, tr. W. A. Falconer (London and Cambridge, Mass., Loeb Classical Library, 1964).

——*De oratore*, tr. E. W. Sutton, (2 vols, London and Cambridge, Mass., Loeb Classical Library, 1967–8).

——*Letters to his Friends*, tr. W. G. Williams (3 vols, London and Cambridge, Mass., Loeb Classical Library, 1965).

Cornarius, I., *De conviviorum veterum Graecorum et hoc tempore Germanorum ritibus, moribus ac sermonibus* (Basle, I. Oporinus, 1548).

Dante, *The Banquet (Convivio)*, tr. C. Ryan (Stanford, Anma Libri, 1989).

Della Casa, G., *Galateo* (1558), tr. R. S. Pine-Coffin (Harmondsworth, Penguin, 1958).

Dialogue des festins (Paris, D. du Pré, 1579).

Le Disciple de Pantagruel (Les Navigations de Panurge) (1538), ed. G. Demerson and C. Lauvergnat-Gagnière (Paris, Nizet, 1982).

Du Bellay, J., *The Defence and Illustration of the French Language*, tr. G. M. Turquet (London, Dent, 1939).

—— *L'Olive*, ed. E. Caldarini (Geneva, Droz, 1974).

—— *Les Regrets*, in *Oeuvres poétiques*, ed. H. Chamard, vol. II (Paris, Didier, 1961).

Du Verdier, A., *Les diverses Leçons* (adapted by P. Messie), (Lyon, T. Soubron, 1592).

Eobanus, H., *Bonae valetudinis conservandae praecepta* (Paris, S. Colines, 1533).

Erasmus, *Adagiorum chiliades quatuor* (Paris, M. Sonnius, 1571).

—— *Le Banquet poétique*, ed. and tr. V.-L. Saulnier (Melun, Librairie d'Argences, 1948).

—— *Cinq Banquets*, ed. and tr. J. Chomarat and D. Ménager (Paris, Vrin, 1981).

—— *La Civilité puérile*, ed. and tr. A. Bonneau (1877), with an introduction by P. Ariès (Paris, Ramsay, 1977).

—— *De civilitate morum puerilium*, tr. B. McGregor, in *Collected Works* (Toronto University Press, 1974–), vol. XXIX (1985).

—— *Colloquies*, tr. C. R. Thompson (Chicago University Press, 1975).

—— *Colloquia*, in *Opera omnia*, ed. J. H. Waszink et al. (Amsterdam, North Holland Publishing Company, 1969–), vol. I, 3 (1972).

—— *Dialogus Ciceronianus*, ibid., vol. I, 2 (1971).

—— *Lingua*, ibid., vol. IV, 1 (1974).

Ficino, M., *De sufficientia, fine, forma, materia, modo, condimento, authoritate convivii*, in *Opera omnia* (2 vols, Basle, Officina Henricpetrina, 1576), vol. I, pp. 739–40.

—— *De triplici vita*, in ibid., I, pp. 495–509 (in this edition the treatise is entitled *De studiosorum sanitate tuenda, sive eorum qui literis operam navant, bona valetudine conservanda*).

—— *Appendix commentariorum, in Timaeum Platonis*, in *Opera et quae hac tenus extitere, et quae in lucem nunc primum prodiere . . .* (2 vols, Basle, Henricus Petrus, 1561).

—— *Commentarium in Convivium Platonis. De amore*, in *Commentaire sur le Banquet de Platon*, tr. R. Marcel (Paris, Belles Lettres, 1956).

Fiera, B., *Coena. De herbarum virtutibus, et ea Medica Artis parte, quae in victus ratione consistit* (Strasburg, C. Aegenolphus, 1530).

Filelfo, F., *Conviviorum libri duo* (Paris, H. Fabri, 1520).

Fioravanti, L., *Miroir universel des arts et sciences*, tr. G. Chappuys (Paris, P. Cavellat, 1586).

Fischart, J., *Geschichtklitterung (Gargantua)*, ed. U. Nyssen (Darmstadt, Wissenschaftliche Buchgesellschaft, 1977).

Folengo, T., *Opere*. Appendix: *I Maccheronici Prefolenghiani*, ed. C. Cordié (Milan and Naples, R. Ricciardi, 1977).

—— *Le Maccheronee*, ed. A. Luzio (2 vols, Bari, Scrittori d'Italia, 1911).

—— *Histoire maccaronique de Merlin Coccaie, prototype de Rabelais* (anonymous translation of 1606), ed. P. L. Jacob (Paris, A. Delahays, 1859).

Galen, *De alimentorum facultatibus libri III* (Lyon, G. Roville, 1555).

Grazzini, A. F., *Le Cene* (c.1560), ed. R. Bruscagli (Rome, Salerno, 1976).

Guazzo, S., *La civil Conversazione* (Brescia, Bozzola, 1574).

Homer, *The Iliad*, tr. A. T. Murray (2 vols, London and Cambridge, Mass., Loeb Classical Library, 1978).

—— *The Odyssey*, tr. A. T. Murray (2 vols, London and New York, Loeb Classical Library, 1966).

Horace, *The Odes and Epodes*, tr. C. E. Bennett (London and Cambridge, Mass., Loeb Classical Library, 1968).

—— *Satires, Epistles and Ars Poetica*, tr. H. R. Fairclough (London and Cambridge, Mass., Loeb Classical Library, 1955).

Huarte, J., *L'Examen des esprits pour les sciences* (1575), tr. F. Savinien d'Alquie (Amsterdam, Jean de Ravestein, 1672).

Isidore of Seville, *Etymologiarum sive Originum libri XX*, ed. W. M. Lindsay (2 vols, Oxford, Clarendon, 1911).

Julian, Emperor, *The Works*, tr. W. C. Wright (3 vols, London and Cambridge, Mass., Loeb Classical Library, 1949).

Juvenal and Persius, *Satires*, tr. G. G. Ramsey (London and Cambridge, Mass., Loeb Classical Library, 1969).

La Chesnaye, N. de, *La Nef de santé avec le gouvernail du corps humain et la condannacion des bancquetz à la louenge de la diepte et sobriété* (Paris, A. Vérard, 1507).

La Varenne, F. P. de, *Le Cuisinier françois enseignant la maniere de bien apprester et assaisonner toutes sortes de viandes grasses et maigres, legumes, patisseries, et autres mets qui se servent tant sur les tables des grands que des particuliers* (Paris, P. David, 1651).

Lemaire de Belges, J., *Les Illustrations de Gaule et singularitez de Troye*, in *Oeuvres*, ed. J. Stecher (Louvain, J. Lefever, 1882–5), vols I and II.

Le Roy, L., *Le Sympose de Platon . . . traduit de grec en françois, avec trois livres de commentaires . . .* (1558) (Paris, A. L'Angelier, 1581).

Lipsius, J., *Antiquarum lectionum commentarius*, in *Opera omnia* (Antwerp, B. Moretus), vol. I (1637).

Le Livre fort excellent de cuysine tres-utille et proffitable contenant en soy la maniere dhabiller toutes viandes. Avec la maniere de servir es Bacquetz et festins (Lyon, O. Arnoullet, 1542).

Livy, [Ab urbe condita], tr. B. O. Foster (14 vols, London and Cambridge, Mass., Loeb Classical Library, 1967–8).

Lucian, *The Carousal or the Lapiths*, in *The Works*, tr. A. M. Harmon (8 vols, London and Cambridge, Mass., Loeb Classical Library, 1961), vol. I.

—— *Lexiphanes*, in ibid., vol. V.

Luther, M., *Tischreden*, (6 vols, 1912–21), in *D. Martin Luthers Werke* (Weimar, H. Böhlau, 1883–).

Macrobius, *Saturnalia*, tr. P. V. Davies (New York, Columbia University Press, 1969).

Maffeius Volaterranus, R., *Commentariorum urbanorum . . . octo et triginta libri* (Basle, Froben, 1559).

Marot, C., *Oeuvres diverses*, ed. C. A. Mayer (London, Athlone Press, 1966).

Le Ménagier de Paris, traité de morale et d'économie domestique composé vers 1393, par un bourgeois parisien, ed. J. Pichon (Geneva, Slatkine Reprints n.d.).

Mensa philosophica, in *The Science of Dining. A medieval treatise on the hygiene of the table and the laws of health (ascribed to Michael Scott)*, tr. A. S. Way (London, Macmillan, 1936).

Messisbugo, C. di, *Banchetti, compositioni di vivande et apparecchio generale* (1549), ed. F. Bandini (Venice, N. Pozza, 1960).

Méthode d'Olympe, *Le Banquet*, tr. H. Musurillo and V.-H. Debidour (Paris, Cerf, 1963).

Montaigne, M. de, *Les Essais*, ed. P. Villey (Lausanne, Guilde du Livre, 1965).

Montaigne, M. de, *Les Essais*, ed. P. Villey (3 vols, Lausanne, Guilde du Livre, 1965).

—— *Essays*, tr. J. M. Cohen (Harmondsworth, Penguin, 1963).

—— *Journal de voyage*, ed. F. Garavini (Paris, Gallimard, 1983).

More, T., *Utopia*, tr. P. Tumer (Harmondsworth, Penguin, 1967).

Ovid, *Fasti*, tr. J. G. Frazer (London and Cambridge, Mass., Loeb Classical Library, 1989).

—— *The Metamorphoses*, tr. F. J. Miller (2 vols, London and Cambridge, Mass., Loeb Classical Library, 1984).

Pascal, B., *Pensées*, tr. M. Turnell (London, Harvill Press, 1962).

Paulus Aegineta: see under Apicius.

Persius: see under Juvenal.

Petrarch, *De remediis utriusque fortunae libri II* (1366) (Cremona, Bernardini, 1492).

Petronio, A. T., *De victu Romanorum* (Rome, In aed. Populi Romani, 1581).

Petronius, *Satyricon*, tr. M. Heseltine (London and Cambridge, Mass., Loeb Classical Library, 1969).

Pidoux, P., *La Fleur de toute cuysine, contenant la maniere d'habiller toutes viandes tant chair que poisson* (Paris, A. Lotrian, 1543).

Platina, B. S., *De honesta voluptate et valetudine* (1474) (Cologne, E. Cervicornus, 1529). See also under Apicius.

—— *Platine en françoys tresutile et necessaire pour le corps humain qui traicte de honneste volupté et de toutes viandes et choses que l'omme menge, quelles vertus ont, et en quoy nuysent et prouffitent au corps humain, et comment se doyvent apprester . . .* (Lyon, F. Fradin, 1505).

Plato, *The Symposium*, tr. W. Hamilton (Harmondsworth, Penguin, 1975).

—— See also under Le Roy.

—— *Le Banquet*, tr. L. Robin (Paris, Belles Lettres, 1929).

—— *Gorgias*, tr. W. R. M. Lamb (London and Cambridge, Mass., Loeb Classical Library, 1967).

—— *Laws*, tr. R. G. Bury (2 vols, London and Cambridge, Mass., Loeb Classical Library, 1967).

—— *Phaedrus*, tr. H. N. Flower (London and Cambridge, Mass., Loeb Classical Library, 1966).

—— *The Republic*, tr. P. Shorey (2 vols, London and Cambridge, Mass., Loeb Classical Library, 1963).

—— *Timaeus*, tr. R. G. Bury (London and Cambridge, Mass., Loeb Classical Library, 1966).

Plutarch, *Moralia* (16 vols, London and Cambridge, Mass., Loeb Classical Library, 1969).

—— *The Dinner of the Seven Wise Men*, tr. F. C. Babbitt, in ibid., vol. II.

—— *Table Talk* (*Symposiaka*), tr. P. A. Clement, in ibid., vols VIII and IX.

Poggio Bracciolini, G. F., *Historiae conviviales* (Strasburg, Knoblouch, 1511).

Pontano, G., *Aegidius*, in G. Toffanin, *Giovanni Pontano fra l'uomo e la natura* (Bologna, Zanichelli, 1938).

—— *De conviventia*, in *Opera omnia soluta oratione composita* (Venice, Alde, 1518), vol. I, 141r.–145v.

—— *De sermone*, ed. S. Lupi and A. Risicato (Lugano, Thesaurus Mundi, 1954).

Puteanus, E., *Reliquiae convivii prisci, tum ritus alii* (Milan, P. Malatesta, 1598).

—— *Comus, ou Banquet dissolu des Cimmériens, songe où par une infinité de belles feintes . . . les moeurs dépravées de ce siècle . . . sont . . .*

décrites, reprises et condamnées . . . , tr. N. Pelloquin (Paris, N. La Caille, 1613).

Quatre sermons joyeux, ed. J. Koopmans (Geneva, Droz, 1984).

Quintilian, *Institutio oratoria*, tr. H. E. Butler (4 vols, London and Cambridge, Mass., Loeb Classical Library, 1969).

Rabelais, F., *Oeuvres complètes*, ed. J. Boulenger (Paris, Pléiade, 1959).

—— *The Histories of Gargantua and Pantagruel*, tr. J. M. Cohen (Harmondsworth, Penguin, 1983).

Regimen sanitatis Salerni, tr. T. Paynell (London, T. Creede, 1597).

Rhodiginus, L. C. (L. C. Ricchieri), *Lectionum antiquarum libri triginta* (1550) (Frankfurt, C. Gerlach, 1666).

Ricciardus, A., *Commentaria symbolica* (Venice, F. de Francischis, 1576).

Romoli, D., *La singolare Dottrina dell'ufficio dello scalco* (Venice, M. Tramezino, 1560).

Ronsard, P. de, *Oeuvres complètes*, ed. P. Laumonier (20 vols, Paris, Didier, 1914–75).

Saint-Victor, H. de, *De institutione novitiorum*, in *Opera* (Paris, H. Stephanus, 1506).

La Satyre ménippée ou la Vertu du Catholicon (1594), ed. C. Read (Paris, Flammarion, n.d.).

Satyres chrestiennes de la cuisine papale (Geneva, Conrad Badius, 1560).

Scappi, B., *Opera* (Venice, F. Tramezino, 1570).

Scott, M.: see under *Mensa philosophica*.

Seneca, *Ad Lucilium: Epistulae Morales*, tr. R. M. Gummere (3 vols, London and Cambridge, Mass., Loeb Classical Library, 1967).

—— *Apocolocyntosis*, tr. W. H. D. Rouse (London and Cambridge, Mass., Loeb Classical Library, 1969).

Shakespeare, W., *Macbeth*, ed. K. Muir (London, Methuen, 1965).

—— *The Life of Timon of Athens*, ed. J. C. Maxwell (Cambridge University Press, 1957).

Stephanus, C. (Estienne), *De nutrimentis libri III* (Paris, R. Estienne, 1550).

Stuckius, J. G., *Antiquitatum convivialium libri III* . . . (Zurich, J. Wolphius, 1597).

Suetonius, *The Lives of the Caesars*, tr. J. C. Rolfe (2 vols, London and Cambridge, Mass., Loeb Classical Library, 1970).

Sulpitius Verulanus, J., *Doctrina mensae* (or *Carmen iuvenile de moribus puerorum praecipue in mensa servandis*) (c.1480) tr. H. Thomas (Oxford University Press, 1949).

Tabouret des Accords, E., *Les Bigarrures*, ed. F. Goyet (2 vols, Geneva, Droz, 1986).

Tahureau, J., *Les Dialogues* (1565), ed. M. Gauna (Geneva, Droz, 1981).

Taillevent, *Le Viandier de Guillaume Tirel, dit Taillevant*, ed. J. Pichon and G. Vicaire, reprint (Luzarches, D. Morcrette, n.d.).

Ursinus, F., *Appendix*, in P. Ciacconius, *De triclinio, sive de modo convivandi apud priscos Romanos et de conviviorum apparatu*.

Valla, L., *Opera* (Basle, H. Petrus, 1540).

Varro, *Satires ménippées*, ed. J.-P. Cèbe (Rome, Coll. de l'Ecole française, 1972).

Virgil, *Aeneid*, tr. H. R. Fairclough (2 vols, London and Cambridge, Mass., Loeb Classical Library, 1967–9).

—— *Eclogues*, tr. H. R. Fairclough (London and Cambridge, Mass., Loeb Classical Library, 1967).

Vivès, J.-L., *Fabula de homine* (1518), in *Opera omnia* (8 vols, Valence, B. Monfort, 1782–90), vol. IV, pp. 1–8.

Willich, J., *Ars magirica, hoc est coquinaria, de cibariis, ferculis, obsoniis, alimentis et potibus diversis parandis, eorumque facultatibus. Liber medicis, philologis, et sanitatis tuendae studiosis omnibus apprime utilis* (Zurich, J. Gessner, 1563).

Xenophon, *The Symposium*, tr. O. J. Todd (London and Cambridge, Mass., Loeb Classical Library, 1961).

—— *Le Banquet*, tr. F. Ollier (Paris, Belles Lettres, 1972).

Critics

Antonioli, R., *Rabelais et la médecine* (Geneva, Droz, 1976).

Bakhtin, M., *Esthétique et théorie du roman*, tr. D. Olivier (Paris, Gallimard, 1978).

—— *Rabelais and his World*, tr. H. Iswolsky (Bloomington, Indiana University Press, 1984).

—— *Problems of Dostoevsky's Poetics*, tr. C. Emerson (Manchester University Press, 1984).

Bardon, H., *Le Festin des dieux. Essai sur l'humanisme dans les arts plastiques* (Paris, Presses universitaires de France, 1960).

Bénouis, M. K., *Le Dialogue philosophique dans la littérature française du XVIᵉ siècle* (Paris and The Hague, Mouton, 1976).

Bierlaire, F., *Erasme et ses Colloques, le livre d'une vie* (Geneva, Droz, 1977).

—— 'Erasmus at School: the *De Civilitate morum puerilium libellus*', in *Essays on the Works of Erasmus*, ed. R. Le DeMolen (New Haven and London, Yale University Press, 1978), pp. 239–51.

—— 'Erasme, la table et les manières de table', in *Pratiques et discours alimentaires à la Renaissance*, Actes du Colloque de Tours, 1979 (Paris, Maisonneuve et Larose, 1982), pp. 147–60.

Billanovich, G., *Tra don Teofilo Folengo e Merlin Cocaio* (Naples, Pironti, 1948).

Bloom, H., *The Anxiety of Influence. A Theory of Poetry* (London, Galaxy Books, 1975).

Bonora, E., *Le Maccheronee di Teofilo Folengo* (Venice, Neri Pozza, 1956).

Bowen, B., 'Béroalde de Verville and the Self-destructing Book', in *Essays in Early French Literature presented to Barbara Craig*, ed. N. J. Lacy and J. C. Nash (York, French Literature Publications, 1982), pp. 163–77.

—— *Words and the Man in French Renaissance Literature* (Lexington, French Forum Publishers, 1983).

Cave, T., 'Ronsard's Bacchic Poetry: from the *Bacchanales* to the *Hymne de l'autonne*', *L'Esprit Créateur*, 10, 2 (1970), pp. 104–16.

—— '*Enargeia*: Erasmus and the Rhetoric of Presence in the XVIth Century', *L'Esprit Créateur*, 16, 4 (1976), pp. 5–19.

—— *The Cornucopian Text. Problems of Writing in the French Renaissance* (Oxford University Press, 1979).

—— 'The Mimesis of Reading in the Renaissance', in *Mimesis. From Mirror to Method, Augustine to Descartes*, ed. J. Lyons and S. G. Nichols Jr (Hanover and London, University Press of New England, 1982), pp. 149–65.

Céard, J., *La Nature et les prodiges. L'insolite au XVIe siècle, en France* (Geneva, Droz, 1977).

Chatelet, N., *Le Corps à corps culinaire* (Paris, Seuil, 1977).

Colie, R. L., *Paradoxia Epidemica. The Renaissance Tradition of Paradox* (Princeton University Press, 1966).

Cordié, C., 'Ancora Cocaio', *Lingua nostra*, 25 (1964), pp. 57–8.

Curtius, E. R., *European Literature and the Latin Middle Ages*, tr. W. Trask (New York, Pantheon Books, Bollingen Series 36, 1953).

Davis, N. Z., 'Beyond the Market: Books as Gifts in Sixteenth-Century France', *Transactions of the Royal Historical Society*, fifth series, 33 (1983), pp. 69–88.

—— *Fiction in the Archives. Pardon Tales and their Tellers in Sixteenth Century France* (Stanford University Press and Cambridge, Polity Press, 1988).

Delbouille, A., *Anacréon et les poèmes anacréontiques. Texte grec avec les traductions et imitations des poètes du XVIe siècle* (1891) (Geneva, Slatkine Reprints, 1970).

Delepierre, O., *Macaronéana, ou Mélanges de littérature macaronique* (Brighton, G. Gancia, 1852).

Derrida, J., 'La Pharmacie de Platon', in *La Dissémination* (Paris, Seuil, 1972), pp. 69–197.

Dickson, C., 'L'Invitation de Montaigne au banquet de la vie: *De l'Expérience*', in *Mélanges sur la littérature de la Renaissance, à la mémoire de V.-L. Saulnier* (Geneva, Droz, 1984), pp. 501–9.

Dubois, C.-G., *L'Imaginaire de la Renaissance* (Paris, Presses universitaires de France, 1985).

Dumézil, G., *Le Festin d'immortalité. Etude de mythologie comparée indo-européenne* (Paris, Musée Guimet, 1924).

Dupont, F., *Le Plaisir et la loi. Du 'Banquet' de Platon au 'Satiricon'* (Paris, Maspero, 1977).

Elias, N., *La Civilisation des mœurs*, tr. P. Kamnitzer (Paris, Calmann-Lévy, 1973).

Faccioli, E., *Arte della cucina. Libri de ricette, testi sopra lo scalco, il trinciante e i vini, dal 14 al 19 secolo* (2 vols, Milan, Il Polifilo, 1966).

Firpo, L., *Gastronomia del Rinascimento* (Turin, Unione Tipografico Editrice Torinese, (UTET), 1974).

Flacelière, R., 'A propos du *Banquet* de Xénophon', *Revue des Etudes grecques*, 74 (1961), pp. 93–118.

Franklin, A., *La Cuisine* (1888) in *La Vie privée d'autrefois*, (Paris, Plon).

—— *Les Repas* (1889), in ibid.

—— *La Civilité, l'étiquette, la mode, le bon ton du XIIIe au XIXe siècle* (2 vols, Paris, Emile-Paul, 1908).

Frye, N., *Anatomy of Criticism* (Princeton University Press, 1971).

Gallardo, M. D., 'Estado actual de los Estudios sobre los Simposios de Platón, Jenofonte y Plutarco', *Cuadernos de filología clásica*, 3 (1972), pp. 127–91.

—— 'Los Simposios de Luciano, Ateneo, Metodio y Juliano', ibid., 4 (1972), pp. 239–96.

Garavini, F., and Lazzerini, L. (eds) *Maccaronee Provenzali* (Milan, Ricciardi, 1984).

Garrisson, J., 'D'où viennent nos manières de table?', *L'Histoire*, 71 (1984), pp. 54–9.

Gente, F. W., *Geschichte der Macaronischen Poesie und Sammlung ihrer vorzüglichsten Denkmale* (Wiesbaden, Sändig, 1836).

Giraud, Y., 'Le Comique engagé des *Satyres chrestiennes de la cuisine papale*', *Studi di Letteratura Francese*, 177 (1983), pp. 52–72.

Glidden, H. H., *The Storyteller as Humanist: The 'Sérées' of Guillaume Bouchet* (Lexington, French Forum Publishers, 1981).

Goggi Carotti, L., 'La Rielaborazione degli episodi della Domus Phantasiae e della Zucca (*Baldus*, XXV)' in *Cultura letteraria e tradizione popolare in Teofilo Folengo*, Atti del Convegno di Mantova (Milan, Feltrinelli, 1979), pp. 186–208.

Greene, T. M., *Rabelais. A Study in Comic Courage* (Englewood Cliffs, N.J., Prentice Hall, 1970).

—— *The Light in Troy. Imitation and Discovery in Renaissance Poetry* (New Haven and London, Yale University Press, 1982).

Haddad, G., *Manger le livre. Rites alimentaires et fonction paternelle* (Paris, Grasset, 1984).

Hess, G., *Deutsch-Lateinische Narrenzunft. Studien zum Verhältnis von Volkssprache und Latinität in der satirischen Literatur des 16. Jahrhunderts* (Munich, C. H. Beck'sche, 1971).

Holban, M., 'Autour de Jean Thenaud et de Frère Jean des Entonneurs', *Etudes rabelaisiennes*, 9 (1971), pp. 49–69.

Hugo, V., *La Légende des siècles* (Paris, Garnier, 1962).

—— *William Shakespeare*, in *Oeuvres complètes*, ed. J. Massin (18 vols, Paris, Club français du livre, 1967–9), vol. XII.

Jeanneret, M., 'Alimentation, digestion, réflexion dans Rabelais', *Studi Francesi*, 81 (1983), pp. 405–16.

—— 'Quand la fable se met à table. Nourriture et structure narrative dans *Le Quart Livre*', *Poétique*, 54 (1983), pp. 163–80.

—— ' "Ma patrie est une citrouille": thèmes alimentaires dans Rabelais et Folengo', *Etudes de lettres*, (1984), pp. 25–44.

—— 'Polyphonie de Rabelais: ambivalence, antithèse et ambiguïté', *Littérature*, 55 (1984), pp. 98–111.

—— 'Gargantua 4–24: l'uniforme et le discontinu', in *Rabelais's Incomparable Book. Essays on his Art*, ed. R. C. La Charité (Lexington, French Forum Publishers, 1986), pp. 84–98.

Jenny, L., 'Poétique et représentation', *Poétique*, 58 (1984), pp. 171–95.

Jolliffe, J. W., 'Satyre: Satura: *satyros*. A Study in Confusion', *Bibliothèque d'Humanisme et Renaissance*, 18 (1956), pp. 84–95.

Jousse, M., *L'Anthropologie du geste. II. La Manducation de la parole* (Paris, Gallimard, 1975).

Knoche, U., *Roman Satire*, tr. E. S. Ramage (Bloomington, Indiana University Press, 1975).

Lange, F., *Manger ou les jeux et les creux du plat* (Paris, Seuil, 1975).

Laumonier, P., 'L'Epitaphe de Rabelais par Ronsard', *Revue des Etudes Rabelaisiennes*, 1 (1903), pp. 205–16.

Leclercq, J., *L'Amour des lettres et le désir de Dieu. Initiation aux auteurs monastiques du moyen âge* (Paris, Cerf, 1957).

Lehman, P., 'Mittelalter und Küchenlatein', in *Erforschung des Mittelalters*, (Stuttgart, A. Hiersmann, 1959), vol. I, pp. 42–62.

—— *Die Parodie im Mittelalter* (Stuttgart, A. Hiersmann, 1963).

Lestringant, F., 'Fortunes de la singularité à la Renaissance. Le genre de l'*Isolario*', *Studi Francesi*, 84 (1984), pp. 415–36.

Löhmann, O., *Die Rahmenerzählung des Decameron, ihre Quellen und Nachwirkungen* (Halle, Max Niemeyer, 1935).

Longhi-Gorni, S., *Lusus, Il Capitolo burlesco nel Cinquecento* (Padua, Antenore, 1983).

McLuhan, M., *The Gutenberg Galaxy, the Making of Typographic Man* (London, Routledge and Kegan Paul, 1962).

Marsh, D., *The Quattrocento Dialogue: Classical Tradition and Humanist Innovation* (Cambridge, Mass., Harvard University Press, 1980).

Martin, J., *Symposion. Die Geschichte einer literarischen Form* (Paderborn, F. Schöningh, 1931).

Murray, O., 'The Greek Symposion in History', *Times Literary Supplement*, 6 November 1981, pp. 1307–8.

—— (ed), *Sympotika. A Symposium on the Symposiun* (Oxford, Clarendon Press, 1990).

Ong, W. J., *Orality and Literacy. The Technologizing of the Word* (London, Methuen, 1982).

Ossola, C., 'L'Homme accompli. La Civilisation des cours comme art de la conversation', *Le Temps de la réflexion*, 4 (1983), pp. 77–89.

Paoli, U. E., *Il Latino maccheronico* (Florence, Le Monnier, 1959).

Paratore, E., 'Il Maccheroneo folenghiano', in *Cultura letteraria e tradizione popolare in Teofilo Folengo*, Atti del Convegno di Mantova (Milan, Feltrinelli, 1979), pp. 37–61.

Pérouse, G.-A., *Les Nouvelles françaises du XVIe siècle, images de la vie du temps* (Geneva, Droz, 1977).

Pfeiffer, R., 'Küchenlatein', *Philologus*, 86 (1931), pp. 455–9.

Pratiques et discours alimentaires à la Renaissance, Actes du colloque de Tours, 1979 (Paris, Maisonneuve et Larose, 1982).

Py, A., *Imitation et Renaissance dans la poésie de Ronsard* (Geneva, Droz, 1984).

Quicherat, L., *Thesaurus poeticus linguae latinae* (Hildesheim, Georg Olms, 1967).

Regosin, R., *The Matter of my Book. Montaigne's 'Essais' as the Book of the Self* (Berkeley and Los Angeles, University of California Press, 1977).

Renaud, M., *Pour une lecture du 'Moyen de parvenir' de Béroalde de Verville* (Faculté des lettres de l'Université de Clermont-Ferrand II, 1984).

Revel, J.-F., *Un Festin en paroles. Histoire littéraire de la sensibilité gastronomique de l'Antiquité à nos jours* (Paris, Pauvert, 1979).

Richter, M., *Giovanni Della Casa in Francia nel secolo XVI* (Rome, Edizioni de Storia e Letteratura, 1966).

Rigolot, F., *Les Langages de Rabelais* (Geneva, Droz, 1972).

Ryan, L. V., 'Erasmi Convivia: the Banquet Colloquies of Erasmus', *Medievalia et Humanistica*, n.s., 8 (1977), pp. 201-15.

Sainéan, L., 'Le Moyen de parvenir, ses deux auteurs et l'origine de l'humour', in *Problèmes littéraires du XVIe siècle* (Paris, De Boccard, 1927), pp. 99-250.

Saulnier, V.-L., 'Etude sur Béroalde de Verville. Introduction à la lecture du Moyen de parvenir', *Bibliothèque d'Humanisme et Renaissance*, 5 (1944), pp. 290-326.

Segre, C., 'La Tradizione macaronica da Folengo a Gadda (e oltre)', in *Cultura letteraria e tradizione popolare in Teofilo Folengo*, Atti del Convegno di Mantova (Milan, Feltrinelli, 1979), pp. 62-74.

Shearman, J., *Mannerism* (Harmondsworth, Penguin, 1967).

Simonin, M., 'Un Conteur tenté par le savoir: Guillaume Bouchet correcteur de sa IIIe sérée', in *La Nouvelle française à la Renaissance*, ed. L. Sozzi (Geneva, Slatkine, 1981), pp. 587-605.

Sommerhalder, H., *Johann Fischarts Werk. Eine Einführung* (Berlin, De Gruyter, 1960).

Starobinski, J., *Montaigne en mouvement* (Paris, Gallimard, 1982).

Stolt, B., *Die Sprachmischung in Lüthers Tischreden. Studien zum Problem der Zweisprachigkeit* (Stockholm, Almquist and Wiskell, 1964).

Strong, R., *Splendour at Court: Renaissance Spectacle and Illusion* (London, Weidenfeld and Nicholson, 1973).

Todorov, T., 'La Notion de littérature', in *Les Genres du discours* (Paris, Seuil, 1978), pp. 13-26.

—— *Mikhaïl Bakhtine, le principe dialogique* (Paris, Seuil, 1981).

Tournon, A., 'La Composition facétieuse du *Moyen de parvenir*' in *Réforme, Humanisme, Renaissance* 7 (1978), pp. 140-6.

—— 'Paracelse, l'Autre: change et piperie dans *Le Moyen de parvenir* de Béroalde de Verville', in *L'Imaginaire du changement en France au XVIe siècle*, ed. C.-G. Dubois (Presses Universitaires de Bordeaux, 1984), pp. 165-86.

Veca, A., *Simposio. Ceremonie e apparati* (Bergamo, Galleria Lorenzelli, 1983).

Vicaire, G., *Bibliographie gastronomique* (Paris, P. Rouquette, 1890).

Wheaton, B. K., *Savouring the Past. The French Kitchen and Table from 1300 to 1789* (London, The Hogarth Press, 1983).

Will, S. F., 'A Note on Ronsard's *Epitafe de François Rabelais*', *Modern Language Notes*, 51 (1936), pp. 455–8.

Yates, F. A., 'The Religious Policy of Giordano Bruno', *Journal of the Warburg and Courtauld Institutes*, 3 (1939–40), pp. 181–207.

—— *Giordano Bruno and the Hermetic Tradition* (London, Routledge and Kegan Paul, 1978).

Zerner, H., *L'École de Fontainebleau: gravures* (Paris, Arts et métiers graphiques, 1969).

Zinguer, I., *Structures narratives du 'Moyen de parvenir' de Béroalde de Verville* (Paris, Nizet, 1979).

Index